PRIMARY TROUBLE:
An Anthology of
Contemporary American Poetry

PRIMARY TROUBLE:

An Anthology of Contemporary American Poetry

edited by
Leonard Schwartz
Joseph Donahue
and **Edward Foster**

Talisman House, Publishers
Jersey City, New Jersey

Published in the United States of America by
Talisman House, Publishers
P.O. Box 3157
Jersey City, New Jersey 07303-3157

Manufactured in the United States of America
Printed on acid-free paper
Cover painting by Gene Blanton

The editors gratefully acknowledge the generous assistance of
Zoë English, Drew Gardner, Mingxia Li, and the staff
at Writers and Anglers in the preparation of this book.

Library of Congress Cataloging-in-Publication Data

Primary trouble :   an anthology of contemporary American poetry /
edited by Leonard Schwartz, Joseph Donahue, and Edward Foster.
    p.   cm.
    "Contributors' book publications" : p.
    ISBN 1-883689-29-5 (acid-free paper). -- ISBN 1-883689-28-7 (pbk.
: acid-free paper)
    1. American poetry--20th century.   I. Schwartz, Leonard, 1963-
. II. Donahue, Joseph, 1954-   .   III. Foster, Edward Halsey.
PS615.P718   1996   95-51249
811'.5408--dc20   CIP

Acknowledgements

Permission to print copyright material is acknowledged gratefully here
and on the following five pages, which are hereby declared to be part of
the copyright page:

Will Alexander, "Psychotropic Squalls," and "Explosive Decibel Journeys" from *The Stratospheric Canticles* (Pantograph Press, 1995). Copyright © 1995 by Will Alexander. Reprinted by permission of the author.

Ivan Argüelles, "Canto the Tenth" from *"That" Goddess* by Ivan Argüelles (Berkeley, CA: Pantograph Press, 1992). Copyright © 1992 by Ivan Argüelles. Reprinted by permission of the author.

Ted Berrigan, "Things To Do in Providence" and "Red Shift" from *So Going Around Cities: New and Selected Poems 1958-1979* by Ted Berrigan (Berkeley, CA: Blue Wind Press, 1980). Copyright

One," "Step Seven" from *The Geographics* by Albert Mobilio (Hard Press, 1995). Copyright © 1995 by Albert Mobilio. Reprinted by permission of the author.

Laura Moriarty, "Rondeaux" from *Rondeaux* by Laura Moriarty (Roof, 1990). Copyright © 1990 by Laura Moriarty. Reprinted by permission of the author.

Sheila Murphy, #13, #22 from *Pure Mental Breath* by Sheila Murphy (Gesture Press, 1994). Copyright © 1994 by Sheila Murphy. Reprinted by permission of the author.

Eileen Myles, "Maxfield Parrish" Copyright © 1995 by Eileen Myles. Reprinted from *Maxfield Parrish: Early and New Poems* with the permission of Black Sparrow Press.

Claire Needell, from "Reaches the Body" from *Not a Balancing Act* by Claire Needell (Burning Deck, 1993). Copyright © 1993 by Claire Needell. Reprinted by permission of the author.

Alice Notley, "Jack Would Speak Through the Imperfect Medium of Alice" from *Selected Poems of Alice Notley* (Talisman House Publishers, 1993). Copyright © 1993 by Alice Notley. Reprinted by permission of the author and Talisman House, Publishers. Passages from *Désamère* from *Close to me & Closer . . . (The Language of Heaven) and Désamère* by Alice Notley (O Books, 1995). Copyright © 1995 by Alice Notley. Reprinted by permission of the author.

Geoffrey O'Brien, "Scroll," "Ornamental Syllable," from *A Book of Maps* by Geoffrey O'Brien (Red Dust, 1989). Copyright © 1989 by Geoffrey O'Brien. Reprinted by permission of the author. "The Prophetic Child," from *The Hudson Mystery* (Red Dust, 1994). Copyright © 1994 by Geoffrey O'Brien. Reprinted by permission of the author.

Michael Palmer, "The Theory of the Flower" from *First Figure* by Michael Palmer (North Point Press, 1984). Copyright © 1984 by Michael Palmer. Reprinted by permission of the author. "Notes for Echo Lake 2" from *Notes for Echo Lake* by Michael Palmer (North Point Press, 1981). Copyright © 1981 by Michael Palmer. Reprinted by permission of the author. "Untitled" ("O you in that little bark") and "Untitled (September '92) from Michael Palmer, *At Passages*. Copyright © 1995 by Michael Palmer. Reprinted by permission of New Directions Publishing Corp.

Simon Pettet, "Annul," "mad lady on the steps asks if my father's on the street," "Rose Garland Sonnet," "Mevlana," "Echo" from *Selected Poems* by Simon Pettet (Talisman House, Publishers, 1995). Copyright © 1995 by Simon Pettet. Reprinted by permission of Talisman House, Publishers.

Stephen Ratcliffe, #40, #43 from *spaces in the light said to be where one / comes from* by Stephen Ratcliffe (Potes & Poets Press, 1992). Copyright © 1992 by Stephen Ratcliffe. Reprinted by permission of the author.

Donald Revell, "Sirius" from *Erasures* © 1992 by Donald Revell, Wesleyan University Press by permission of University Press of New England.

Ed Roberson, chapter III, sections I-VII from "The Aerialist Narratives." Reprinted from *Voices Cast Out To Talk Us In* by Ed Roberson (University of Iowa Press, 1995) by permission of the University of Iowa Press. Copyright © 1995 by Ed Roberson.

Elizabeth Robinson, "The New Language" from *My Name Happens Also* by Elizabeth Robinson (Burning Deck, 1987). Copyright © 1987 by Elizabeth Robinson. Reprinted by permission of the author.

David Rosenberg, chapters 3, 13, 14 of *Job Speaks* from *A Poet's Bible* by David Rosenberg. Copyright © 1991 by David Rosenberg. Reprinted by permission of Hyperion. "Anywhere Out

BY WAY OF PREFACE

WILLIAM BRONK

The Nature of Musical Form

It is hard to believe of the world that there should be
music in it: these certainties against
the all-uncertain, this ordered fairness beneath
the tonelessness, the confusion of random noise.

It is tempting to say of the incomprehensible,
the formlessness, there is only order as we
so order and ordering, make it so; or this,
there is natural order which music apprehends

which apprehension justifies the world;
or even this, these forms are false, not true,
and music irrelevant at least, the world
is stated somewhere else, not there. But no.

How is it? There is a fairness of person too,
which is not a truth of persons or even, we learn,
a truth of that person, particularly.
It is only fairness stating only itself:

as though we could say of music only, it is.

Contents

xvii

Poetics

Introduction

Poetry might be conceived of as both an act of creation and an act that counters social reality as it was read before, both a demiurgical affirmation and negation of all that is written. The struggle to derive from words the sensual textures the body craves from its linguistic landscape, to create regions of thinking and feeling out of those textures, but also the struggle *against* words, against the tyrannies of syntax, the accumulation of enslaved and enslaving meanings, all are constitutive of this poetic life. But any poetry also creates a history, a history that so nearly vanishes at a certain point into its contemporaneous edge that a special effort must be made to illuminate what has happened, as it is happening. When we speak, then, of *Primary Trouble: An Anthology of Contemporary American Poetry*, it is to construct, hopefully from a fresh perspective, a formulation of poetic process as it has been explored by several generations of contemporary American poets for whom these and other phenomena of the word have been the crucial ones.

All of the poets included in this anthology were born after 1933 and began to see their own work emerge substantively into print in America in English in the 1970s, 80s, and 90s. The work presented here comes from writers associated with the "avant-garde" or "anti-academic" segment or "experimental wing" of American poetry, to employ labels that most in the end will find inconclusive. Let us say instead that this anthology draws, for one, from younger generations of poets influenced but unnostalgic about the work represented in Donald Allen's seminal anthology *The New American Poetry: 1945-1960* (1960). Robert Duncan's high mythic imagination, Charles Olson's composition by field, John Ashbery's poetics of ambiguity, and Jack Spicer's aesthetic of impersonality and his absolutely authentic personal voice are among the strongest of these influences, behind which rests a notion of writing as process that reaches back to Pound. Indeed, poets like Anselm Hollo, Robert Kelly, Diane di Prima, and Anne Waldman figured in Allen's second anthology, coedited by George Butterick, *The Postmoderns: The New American Poetry Revised* (1982). The highly original weave of mythic material and compositional technique in the work of poets like Nathaniel Mackey or Peter Cole, to take just two examples, might be seen as indebted to that tradition, although the same sense of a shared poetic *demarche* has never really emerged—for better or for worse—in the generations with which this anthology is concerned. The 1970's, 80's, and 90's have been decades in America in which, to a large

1

degree, poets have advanced without the comforting banner of a poetic movement to wave, without the sense of a shared community to lend solidity to their projects. Perhaps the singular, indeed solitary voice of a poet like William Bronk best anticipates this alienated but engaged poetic labor. In any event, the wealth and variety of poetic languages and mythic vocabularies currently in the process of being created will take time to reach self-consciousness. David Rosenberg's inventions of *The Book of Job* (and *The Book of J*) and Andrew Schelling's invention of an English *Isha Upanishad* strike me as particularly significant in this regard.

Primary Trouble also draws from the New York School and the poets influenced by the various offsprings of that chimerical being. "New York" is here seen moving away from the intense casualness of some of its early practitioners in the direction instead of a richly textured playfulness, indeed towards the invention of a new poetic syntax. Ted Berrigan inaugurates one wing of that magic poetic of nerves, while poets like Alice Notley, Bernadette Mayer, and Eileen Myles carry it forward and then break new ground in their recent work. As for the denser more abstract wing of that "school"—perhaps most associated with Ashbery and Barbara Guest—Anne Lauterbach, David Shapiro, and John Yau remain wells of complicated imagination, in the nourishments of whom the work of a younger writer like Virginia Hooper might begin to be approached.

A third source for this anthology is poets who share some of the formal concerns of, and even may be affiliated in part with, the L=A=N=-G=U=A=G=E project, without on the other hand sharing in that school's agenda for poetic hegemony. The rejection of the bourgeois self at the core of the poem, already prefigured in Rimbaud's "I is an Other" in the "Lettre de Voyant" might be seen as a point at which many (but not all) of these divergent avant-garde poetries coincide—let us say the space in which a brazen surrealism like that of Will Alexander meets up with the epistemological rigor of a poetry such as Aaron Shurin's. Figures like Clark Coolidge and Michael Palmer are seen by some as pivotal to the language movement but also to much other innovation, surrealist and otherwise; poets like Leslie Scalapino, Fanny Howe, Norma Cole, and Laura Moriarty are recognizably concerned with an art that delimits a rigorous anti-representationality at the same moment that it rethinks the limits and contours of subjectivity itself.

Obviously the influence of these forces—"The New American Poetry," "The New York School," and a poetry focused on the epistemology of language—will overlap within any given poetry. Part of the attraction of important poets like Gustaf Sobin, Susan Howe, Ronald Johnson, Kathleen Fraser, and Ed Roberson is their ability to resist categorization. Those poets in "mid-career," like Geoffrey O'Brien, Charles Borkhuis, Forrest Gander, Donald Revell, and Stephen Sartarelli, already seem to be at liberty to draw inspiration from many different sources and traditions. Just as clearly, the work of the younger poets this anthology presents—Elizabeth Robinson, Myung Mi-Kim, Claire Needell, Andrew Joron, and Drew Gardner, to take just a few examples—may cause us to rethink all of these antecedents or realize a more complicated picture of poetic source and vocabulary in them all. What I hope is clear is that the map of poetry drawn here does not lay out any simple or oracular set of poetic imperatives but rather seeks to elevate a certain poetics into view against the mainstream poetics that might obscure it.

Primary Trouble, then, strives not to define but to draw attention to some of the very latest tendencies in American poetry. While the anthology is in no way thematic, there *is* a common interest here in a certain vocabulary, a certain set of possibilities towards which these texts have both tended and been chosen. To call this interest "the sacred" would be too officious. To speak of it as "the spiritual" would be amorphous, too easily misconstrued in terms of belief and not imagination, unless "spiritual" be defined as a radical anger with the conditions of this world, socially and metaphysically. Or else it might be conceived as a critical detachment from the given—a detachment creative of the otherness of clarification, of a complex emotional and imaginary spark in the light of which metaphor and reality are constantly in question. To call it a new eroticism would also be reductive, but surely this poetry has an ample category for pleasure, a category absent, as Joel Lewis has noted, in the hegemonic mode of experimental formalism known as language poetry: *this* poetry sees sexuality as a crucial nexus between the body and the world, one that defies but revivifies words in their very effort to render erotic impossibility.

The spirit of seriousness, as Sartre pointed out, is a deadening one. As such, the area delineated by this anthology is not hostile to either the comic or the ironic mode. But we do note a break from postmodern irony, from the belief that anything and everything is and must be a pastiche of something else, and from the notion that poetry is a way of wryly manipulating these coextensive surfaces. Indeed, if post-modernism is ever to open onto something other than itself, it must be by leaving itself open to prereflective panics, angers, and ecstacies, to fresh beginnings which might momentarily hold off the critical apparatus, by affirming new

3

poetic forms. In *The Truth and Life of Myth*, Robert Duncan writes, "In the world of saying and telling in which I first came into words, there is a primary trouble, a panic that can still come upon me where the word no longer protects, transforming the threat of an overwhelming knowledge into the power of an imagined reality, or abstracting from a shaking experience terms for rationalization, but exposes me the more." The unveiling of a mystery, in which that mystery remains perpetually indeterminate, and thus the subject of further poetic presentations. . . . While it is doubtful that all the poets included in this anthology would embrace such a formulation, and while it would be foolish to insist that they should, the experience of living with words of which Duncan speaks was clearly our guiding impulse in believing this anthology to be necessary. At the very least we can venture to say that these are poetries willing to risk the panic of which Duncan writes.

Obviously this is not the only possible anthology, with the only possible poets, that might have been put together to feature new American poetry. (In fact, there are many figures whom the editors greatly admire whose work is not included, on the grounds that they could not be conceived of as involved with the particular tendencies counterposed here.) At the same time, this book makes no claim to speak for a new poetic movement, for a unity of views shared by all or any of the poets collected. To make clear the varieties of perspective as well as the points of intersection we have taken care to include a brief afterward of statements on poetics. "The prime abstraction of 'one' seems necessary / to hold the self in the frame," writes Clark Coolidge in *The Crystal Text*. "Much of my writing has been an effort to rearrange, rewrite the word 'God' by filling up pages with other names," states Fanny Howe. Gustaf Sobin argues, "The poem grows out of the poem, not out of one's own, particular intellect. The intellect is merely a guide, a gardener to those shoots, those roots: to that deeper set of imperatives which are first of all organic." Each realized in its poet's own particular idiom, these propositions all evidence the urge to go beyond the givens of subjecthood and objecthood, identity and commodity, experience and syntax. "The mind is never satisfied, never," wrote Wallace Stevens. Such seems to hold true for the texts of these poets, which, when taken together, hold out the possibility of a richer culture. In the final analysis, *Primary Trouble* proposes to provide an alternate focus, a necessary rethinking, of how our poetry works.

—Leonard Schwartz

4

H.D.

from **THE WALLS DO NOT FALL**

When in the company of the gods,
I loved and was loved,

never was my mind stirred
to such rapture,

my heart moved
to such pleasure,

as now, to discover
over Love, a new Master:

His, the track in the sand
from a plum-tree in flower

to a half-open hut-door,
(or track would have been

but wind blows sand-prints from the sand,
whether seen or unseen):

His, the Genius in the jar
which the Fisherman finds,

He is Mage,
bringing myrrh.

WILL ALEXANDER

from *Lightning*

Part II
Ball Lightning

During a thunderstorm I saw a large, red hot ball come down
from the sky.
—W. Morris in a letter to the *London Daily Mail*

Disk falling from negative charges, hissing from primeval lenses, hot
white thunder bolt spinning, dyed, binaural reverberation spinning,
mother, it's isinglass, it's the verbal variation of mica, its heated tentacles
like raging nose bleed colour, like a cloudy mass of hissing spiders, they
say, it's a pelican eater, a random aerial ferocity, its heart, full of nema-
tode resistors, encircled with shooting sparks from sinister tombstone
sticks, hemoglobin sutures exploding inside a nest of carnivorous, insatia-
ble crickets, whining like tornado blossoms, flecked with whirling cyanide
waters, mother, it's a droplet of fire exploding as bunches of bees, pulsing
like etheric solstice bodies, it is an axial flower of steel, a reckless astrono-
my, coursing through a maze of polysyllabic pitchblende, with its ghostly
integument melting pellets of darkness, this thaumaturgic sun boar eating
through meteoritic colours of wind, its centrality of blood, tearing the air
with crocodile omegas of blankness, with invisible Buffalo flames, with its
barbed wire grenades assaulting the potency of logic, hissing from the
depths the universal fire of explosion, devouring, consuming, average
corpses of people, taking light from the minds of the forgotten, taking
away their musculature, their mental realms, their idleness, bursting
across the atmosphere, like internal sparks revving up the flow of the lan-
guage of demons, and the protracted flower that it gives is magnetically
tied to the altar of panic, to the blind folded optics of Phobos, a mobile
crater on fire, a wretched double curve of sleigh spleens, bringing about
the deeper part of being, the more melodious increments of pontoon
tourniquets, of a gaseous fortress of greenness, a constantly erupting
furnace inside an owl's clairvoyant manikin eternity, with its night time
dawns, with its black spillage of roosters, with its nocturnal slivers
piercing the cornea with phantoms, with intense levitational whistlings,

which announce its deaths, its voyages, its body embargoes, its tubercular lemur interiors, its weight negatively encoded by zeros, by burnished astronomical bells sculpted in its motion of fire, its wrathful igneous knowledge, like a weightless floating cobra, genetically inscrutable, like a falling, undetected ozone egg

This disk, like flaming monastery science, like worms eating through a nunneries' birth systemics, as pregnant shellfish babies begin falling from its fires, glistening, in hawk white revelation, twisting around the incipience of salacious rhythmic intervention, their voices, as if cooking on a spectral appliance of blood, their faces, a blank algometer resistance, becoming backbone drachmas spinning from the unclean side of a compass, the heat that springs forward, like the magical hyperbole of Gondwanaland, its disaster spun, like the smoke of a fleeting altimeter beast

A beast inside its disk, minus pensive psychological cloves, minus tundra ejecting platelets, gases extracted from ostrich-coloured leper's applause, flitting along the skulls of deceptive x-ray gardens

And from this disk I see 30 blind water bulls raising marks from apertures of previously laid astrolabe contusions, spouting unforeseen unresolvable dangers, overcome, at the split second hour of a hatchless speaking song bird, destroyed in its singing by uplifted venters of shattered iodine illumination

Yes, the disk speaks of codeless narcissism archetypes, of nightmare ululation, of indefinite digital figurines, and the disk, with its savage treasure ship digits, with its carcass of suicide tapestry, with its circular Venusian glare, with its illumined chemical talons, floats along the terrified slopes of ultraviolet grasses, its destruction of insect mangers like the permanence of a proto-apocalypse, its explosive tumbleweed shadows eating through the atmospheric neurons, is like a brightly lit snowstorm of desiccated resurrection

This Ball Lightning, its spectrum of blazing rainbow instincts, trebled, by the inner explosiveness of angles, propelled by jets of iconographic sulphur, its kinetic ferocity shattering, full of space, blood, bone, and star, full of melted Dalmatian parabolas, full of subverted earthquake perpen-

8

diculars, sleepless, in its earthly parenthetical sunlight, in its circular climate swelled by heated floods from the rays of glacial firing tables

So this Ball Lightning, this disk, is a calendrics of golden lions floating across tornado foundations, soaked by Spanish sundial water, trampoline water, hovering in the air as a staggering vermilion ammonia, this fire disk in which I'm floating, with its levels of golden lions singing at shrines of cobalt, like hunting fish, like barracuda velvet, flashing formaldehyde signals, back and forth from the unknowable to the unknowable, eating roses from suspended tidal wave encirclement, their manes resplendent, like splintered mirrors of chaos, enriched by greenish nonformal gases, biting from the skies of southern suns oviparous anesthesia lapping like waves across filaments of an embryo, which swirls in the skull as a bottomless oven of diamonds

I see in its circular fumes, eyes, the colour of crab, boiling inside a bone crossed pot of imaginary mercury, light spilling forth from an imploded urine candle, the colour of a-vernacular litmus, seething, with glandular dizziness, its power engendered by precisely embattled spasms, which animates incessant magnificence

Suddenly I'm singing in my space ship of fire, suddenly my mind grows wings, I call myself the gigantic mosquito who sucks and gives blood to its mystery, who sculpts inside his spinning ambush denials, a scene of brightened tarantula embraces, a forest of eclectic volcanic contusions, spawned from a hypnotic ginger

To see this disk, I am cleansed with grounded facial negatives, with bone coloured writing, with vocal bone spur chemistry, with rapier crusades, with hunchback conjunctions, spurred by verbal star belt eternities

In this Ball Lightning saucer, I experience telescopic cranial euphoria, opening my breath to the timeless flight of universal demons, where my negative appendages, crimson crocodile slivers, are lengthened and stretched behind the smoke screen of existence, become a vulture's breast in orbit, become that dyke of bone at the farthest side of human blood, from this disk, I see the stars as imperial-sized maggots, discoloured by a definitive alligator blockage, stars, swarming in electron ravines, suspended, gorged on concision, like eroded Cherokee blisters sucked into

9

blackness, being eaten by vicious hydrogen eaters, by cosmic transfer gases, settling on the eye with the thick opacity of slumbering, the hair burned away by lymphatic circumference, then sharpened to flame throwers' mucous, my life conducted in tropic conundrums, in this Ball Lightning saucer, prophetically contingent with meteors

This circular explosion empirically haunting the fauna, spasmodically weakening the cacti, bringing up from the soil a mercurial ignescence, a leaking volcanism prairie, erupting and re-feeding its orbicular interior rivulets

I exist in this stunning orbicular containment, as it floats along the sullage, as an erupting suicide flower, its genesis bursting from star-like craniums of frenzy, spewing ferocious nightingale ammonias, above perfectly chiseled kinetics of lava

And it attacks, and emits spikes at random lovers, with its power to float through impenetrable revetments, with lightning strikes at the superficial levels of human bodily contact, contact no deeper than sensual facsimile, and because, such love is imitation, it takes on an emblem of blackened ribbon duality, crushed under smoke, heaving white cells and parrots, singing with a catch in its throat, its decimals soldered and re-blended by light

I am conscious in this floating fire furnace, speeding into imperative indifference, mentally turning to a wolf, into a rattlesnake shower of teeth, into a predatory jackal, lunging at the psychic component of the rib and the femur, at the chronic physical subliminals, at the crouching work day servant, the body reduced to red shift reduction, to a terror which fully transcends the wrath of judgmental delirium

To see from this poetic obelisk of nerves, holes, dense holes, blinking sweat mirages, eating into to inevitable duplicity, lies always co-mingled with truth, lies at the heart of historical damage, degenerate salamander powders, compound verbal degeneration synonymous with outmoded expression detached from the lungs by explosion, by galvanic arsenic floods, seeping into the perfect fires, unloosed by the power of detachment

My ball lightning saucer is breaking apart, a sun swept by the void out of existence, osculation with the face of non-being, negative phosphorescence, phlogiston, animation swallowed by the flanks of darkness, distracted by accumulating parsecs, by seismic glycerin effacement, by a stunning Lupercalian debacle, shifted to illusionary varix planets, where I vanish by degree, making laryngeal recitations of sonorous neutron decades, hatching above this shattered ozone egg, a lyrical recitation of acids, like a debatable neutron wand, attempting to burn within a self imposed existence of peril

fin

The Psychotropic Squalls

To peer into the obverse
into smoking cane field errata
as if haunted with the steamy colitis of whirling iridium
cancellations

as in the saliva of newts
one sees the intestinal raging of deltas
of blackened sea giraffes osmotically split into simultaneous alums
above a judgemental sea glistening with Richters

like a weakened neutron egg
its fissioning petrol mirages like spirals of irregular hunting geese
flying through flames of ulcerated smoke & gargantua
hissing a blank imperial greenness
rising above dense jetties of cobras

the shocking demise of the sea
the unlivingness of its winds
scorched by irradiations of shaking brine incisions
the burning gulfs of sun with a glint of explosive Mandean utopias
shocks against Old Testament linear prophetics
of Jeremiah
or Ezekiel
or the bony frozen finger shaking stunted alchemical missives
from a moon burned Judea
no more than a mechanically burning moat focused on smoky
spellbinder's disruptives
where the motion of the soul is delayed
reduced to flattened agnostic secular smoke
to a terrestrial rage which eliminates its sensuous heavenly fires
its stunning unreplicated angers
its sudden selenium spirals
its fire which staggers across the pseudo-faultlines of pre-replicated
judgement
its flirtation with spirits of enriched Draconian plankton

so that the soul with its amber of flashing microbe drachmas
with its wounded tourmaline divisibilities

12

flaming within a light of smeared tornado weathers
within a shower of black fish scales and spleen
is entombed
within a blank thirstless psycho-motion
falling from a furnace of stars
which both flares up and freezes
which inculcates a flawed microbial botany
as in hypnotic grammatical emulsions

within a hollowed elliptical opening where we witness old
Egyptian surgeries
where the dead magically rise up from mazes
& stare in a language of scorching totemic anomaly
spawned in heretical miniature
their phantoms
seeping from quadrilateral sutures
from brief
violent
renunciatory squalls

uprooted
armed with the weaponry of ghouls
& broken birch tree lizards
seasoned by the light of psychotropic angles
blazing in the middle of a green Venusian interior God
singing
as if
in the fumaroles of anguish
with an inclement bleeding
with a littered corona
of unstable altimeter reverses

Explosive Decibel Journeys

*for Javier García Sánchez**

Inside the catalytic mine field
there exists
the fire of antinomous poppies
the writhing of broken insect nodules
marshes limned with collapsing nitrate teeth
in an atmosphere
of kerosene & iceberg volcanoes

I am thinking
of dark obsessional blood edicts
of grainy migratory suns
spinning around a series of gloomy aqua tornadoes

spawned with the telepathy of ice bears
afire with fur & ancient Dionysian characteristic
with the blank specifics of a roaming cohesion
roaring
with an electrocuted mockery
into a bleak condensation of cobalt
flung into a dawn of broken intestinal ringlets

this dawn
explosively slanted with a fiery nautical intransigence
with blanched
stormy
meridian meteoritics
as if its smoke were Roman
bleeding
upright
contradicting
its anti-torsional eruptions
its sudden bloated carnivorous potentia
its protracted carnage by indifference
floating through rainy indigo explosions
floating through a palladium of "mineral ash" & anthracite & fervour

*Author of *Lady of the South Wind*, whose main character commits suicide by explosion.

14

a stoking pressure
of stone
& coke
& fabric
with an intensity linked to pulmonary punishment
negatively slurring all the bodies of zinc

the weather of Leeds & Sri Lanka petrified
by "hygroscopic acid"
by gassy ambiguous rain attack
by the in-vital foods of negative in-vitality
the whole world
an ozone of wicked calendrical debacle
an insidious metallurgical illness
revolving through haunted strontium mazes
weakened as a dysfunctional eclipse furnace

terra firma
becoming a dark enfeebled nightmare relic
asked to take on the weight
of unnatural suckling fevers
the grain spores screaming facing scarification by extinction
the mine field ruthless with inverted skeletal waters
pumping up scars
so that the rock fish swelter with wicked selenium error

because
there exists
acidic complications
fierce animal anomalies
hatched by a terror of blackened firing powders
so as to face an intermittent breeding
a smokey lattice work of angels
blinded by spectral anginas
set against the life force
with the rusty simultaneous core of statistics
always under the light of merismatic smoke
of merismatic compromise
in the mine field

in the wicked hydrogen ekstasis
no longer combined
with the smoke of simple Iroquois signals
alive with the truth of Indian burial law

I am speaking of clouded Euro-centric sulphur
of the Javier García Sánchez creation committing suicide by explosive
timed against
the aboriginal magnets
against the utopian sun angles
miming flightless strychnine ravens
ignited by great diagrams of blood
as if explosions were a song
of instinctive deflagrations
of degenerate human sparks
poised upon a shaky "nitrocellulose"

or translations from a synonymous kind of cyclonite
spreading through the plane
affecting
the power of waterfalls
the Gersoppa
the Kalambo
the Middle Cascade

yes
the Caspian Sea
the Peace
the Don
the Snake
waters prognostically poisoned
in this smoky litmus corral

a spiral of agony
illumined
by "Wood meal"
by "Aluminum Powder"
by "Dynobel"

"characteristics
of permissible explosives"
yes
dichotomies etched
like a sullen bread
of parched elliptical powders

blowing apart the earth
like a naked fish on an altar

a disastrous Nobelian hymnal
brazen
with purely creosote tectonics
like a ghost suddenly spiralling off to sea
with savage earthquake metrics
like flash points
with the treacherous teeth of elongated nightmare tigers

of course
an insatiable sea roaring
beneath a sun of territorial cancellations
as if suddenly shifted moons
had taken on the weight of perpetual solar expansions
like an exploded mist climbing Antarctic willows

in the end
an illusional jasmine furnace
in which doves are smelted
in which fingers
are detached & reborn
between a terrified calendrics
& the eerie decibels of an insolvent limbo

IVAN ARGÜELLES

from *"That" Goddess*

Canto the Tenth

the park where the small deer feed
    it is as much as anything an illusion
the dream of the Gardener the gardener
    who is an island or a precipice
        gazing into the space of his mind
or he is blind feels the deer's tongue on his hand
    which is like a salt-block
            a stone too will compare
the sun and trees combine to grace the park
        writing with grass on a page of shade
    a murmur extinguishes this summer
the cold a fleeting they flee the deer
    that was born then
           Sakyamuni
the known can never be perfectly determined
    aching obviously in a felt perception
the Gardener the gardener his music
        absence coming in great waves
    sky is all of a piece
        and night when the leaves talk
a margin to the right shifts to the center
    an island too sighted to the far left
on lawns the couples bare from the waist up smile
    "point zero" incandescence
in their eyes a tiny fire dances
    from which the torch passes
        to the invisible realms
to shape an idea until it manifests a photograph
    a glyph as well connoting flesh
reflect, good my Gardener on these matters
    the little albino deer
examining between the shadows What has been written
    winding between the soft anthems a wind

                              expels from paradise with its hot breath
the lovers illicit dreamed by my Gardener the
                                        gardener
            this edge requires a farther margin
to gaze into these silvery rills
                    of a noon near Isfahan
            inoperable during system quiescence
or a motor hidden in the dense foliage
                    feels strange this odd throbbing
            rubs beneath the skin to revive youth
alas fled like the deer into that small forever
                    no camera can ever capture
            clouds looming near brought by harsh aquilon
to have visited the sea once
                              "mine only you are gone"
            the palmers returned from jerusalem are blind
the franklyn's tale is corrupted by use
                    the first hour past meridian is all haze
dancing figures barely perceived the graces
                    three in number named also the Charities
            in earth's profound bowl Persephone lies sleeping
from this small park to Erebus is no distance at all
            my Gardener the gardener is in a swoon
                    the megrims have him
and he dreams he is Hölderlin in his last 35 years
            in error too the laurel-crowned poet
but let no sinister alliance join these in the park
            Sakyamuni
                              a flute of human bone sounds
not unlike that beautiful concerto by Telemann
            shepherds gather to exhume the monkey
            tufts of wadding drift in the august air
I am to sicily gone to prove the Republic
            no sequence provides the proper row
a country estate in the meridian hush
                    opium silence in the acres of turkish poppy
            added to this the few fingers of water
                    a suite of angels
whose present tense preserves language from narrative

just the signs for the objectified
or reified without causality
the nostrils suffocated with musk
honey allowed to drop naturally into several dishes
acorns gathered before twilight
a distant voice singing at the distaff
mellow golden as the reaped afric corn
"her" tones altering as the planets turn
by what fate we are drawn to this place
the green and the crystalline
burdened by black carefully trimmed
by my Gardener the gardener
who moves as one stoned on Bang
through lush verses of a Divan
he says that troy never happened
yet is bedevilled by Klytemnestra nightly
in the random furrows the red-eyed pigs
who cannot apprehend virtue
and see in every skirt an occasion for lust
yet the small deer on trembling feet
do return
to crop the new grass on the hillock
constant azure of a remote painting
contrasted with the waterfall's crystal violence
the chinese have been here to teach nuance
O Sakyamuni
bards grovel in the shade
"and I am by a tempest borne"
unconscious to the bower of morpheus
to in dreams relive Atreid horrors
staring off into "space"
what they mean dishevelling their hair
a community of nereids drying in the yellow weeds
one cannot guess clearly
the sun-dial has been removed
knows not what watch of day it is
generic for animal as in "Tiergarten"
meandering as the river out of its encyclopedia
yet their wet noses and enlarged pupils

ah, victim of sentimentality, strike them dead!
                    to the hash-house with their flesh
venison for merovingians and capetians alike
                         the chase but a royal aggravation
you defy the papal nuncios
                    cut off their nose and tongue
                    (for this is the dream of reason)
"Dear friend, I can no longer communicate my feelings"
          for the small deer have been flayed
              and left to dry rotting in the sun
while the tanner takes their hide to the medina
              where the stench will lift to heaven
          no court will accept these accusations
the veneration owed to the eternal fathers is defied
              the buds how do they know to open?
                    O Sakyamuni   a thought
              the velvet the inordinate a bit of sun
who has killed the royal deer of the Park?
              seated in the bliss attitude lids lowered
                    afloat on an irreproachable island
              to go after all only against the cliffs
              the dangers of sailing
                                   even is asleep
don't want to wake up
                    so who will repair this damage?
in all the newspapers photos of their strewn bodies
                    to say the hunt is "noble"
                         to say the hunter is "king"
aim an arrow into the middle of an eye
                    all sky explodes   shivers
          a fragment   and then what is
                                   less
minimalist activity in magazine pages
                    the route to the highlands to the watershed
the earth crisis on this little grass
                         cannot be borne and it is burning
nothing but the bleached bones or the black marker
              who will speak for the tanner?
              that he lives out of need in his craft

21

nor to dispose of each section as provided for by the law
and receive from the gods nothing
who disregard the "do ut des"
having slain in the royal park the deer
whose last fleeting glance captures pasargadae
the terrene-concept of paradise
for what else is a well constructed park?
let the sun glance on me its bright eye
the air be full of singing angels
my wish to die My Gardener the gardener
I wish to die Oh Lisa
stare me not down with thine aweful gaze!
and on the radio reports of corporate fraud
it is a still listener's day
nothing can be composed
the trees the grass the ghosts of deer
feeding on the humus of a god's mind
why are they so worried in the Baltics?
who speaks for the proles of Azerbaijan?
what! another dialect seeking nationalism?
in the slender hour when the heart surrenders its grass
how else does one address "that" goddess
but by epithets of violence?
"oh windy Ilion whither fleest thou?"
together we went to hades
nothing found but the lees
legend fails in excess the death
and the deer in the shade perplexed
as is the mind trying to ponder its riddle
mimic in the park the sun's rays
spotted hides regarded for their price
as the years pass more unkempt becomes paradise
a lesson to ignore the grass its growth
a pain to study in stark moonlight these weeds
the singing in the leaves is a sort of literature
Sakyamuni
your hands are withered petals
the sockets of your eyes are scorched
& dull as the nub ends of your thumbs

what can be taught on such parched dog-days?
        they wear styrofoam suits the angels
            they knock on the transept of delivery
      but it is not heard
          an inch is a hard lesson to learn
      they gather the few chairs
               and burn them to keep warm
on nights when the park is frost covered
      I never knew a solution that worked
    but aggravated assault on the monarch?
a channel too narrow to fit all these corpses
      together we went to hades
          "she and I in sweet surfeit"
    a canal is neither page nor ocean
but a kind of combustion for the kings of turkey
        to boil in their own rage
        in this narrow and watery defile
not to pronounce the tetragrammaton
      observing hieratic silence
    as the deer scurry quietly into the copse
    a wish to be "other" than the "other"
      miasma of the atreids!
concludes nothing in tragical dramatic declamation
      but that his head is to be shaved
        his testicles removed
      one eye excised and led
             to the monastery
     to record the days of his life in misery
impoverished but for memory of the Park
      startled by the small deer
    and what he did then and by whom seen
as suspected or not but ever guilty
        and the stains in the grass
      how high the run at that hour
then expecting night the spangled tenement
       should never come but silence
    in the bright mist of recognition
   the tall narcissi as if wounded by too much light
he listens for the hour to sound

as if infernal jove might suddenly appear
to deliver him of his terrestrial shroud
but nothing moving in the air
nor the hawk of horus

nor

breakdown

the skeletons of ordinary parlance
the fiend has a way of posturing
this darker resonance has less pitch
the antiphonies!   the antiphonies!

I am afraid   so alone
the fell thing
which cannot be named
and no solace in this deserted park
the small animals fled

day glancing into lateness
the empire all but dismembered
vitreous reality of the air unbearable
Sakyamuni
the declaration of an omen
and the virtues like the deer fled
together we shall return to hades

DODIE BELLAMY

from *The Letters of Mina Harker*

February 7, 1991

Dear Sam,

Quincey is absent, absent as you. He's been in Barcelona for twelve days with his wife. Hieroglyphs litter my computer screen, I look back over my shoulder: a messy bed, a bed devoid of Quincey, of me, of both our bodies. I swivel in my office chair to better study these vanished others those two naked forms on the bed rolling from pillow to pillow, silent and in slow motion like some corny film, gauze filter over the lens, shiny moments glinting in little star bursts. Twelve days is an eternity. My own ass is as good as anything, I suppose, to remember him by . . . tender, burning from the inside out *in this coffee-scented morning an invasion incongruous as Magritte's locomotive* . . . our last night together I wrote my love all over him: purple bruises with a flourish of red filaments, how's he going to hide that from his wife when he takes off his pants in Barcelona?

Writing has always been more sexual than sex, the sustained arousal of never quite getting it right.

A bit of post-orgasmic conversation returns to me:

      Me: And he lived to tell about it.
   Quincey: Who would he tell?
      Me: He tells the sunset.

I imagine Quincey flying all the way to Spain to try to forget me in the Mediterranean sunset—it's so Marguerite Duras. I underline a passage from *Blue Eyes, Black Hair:* "She looks at him. It's inevitable. He's alone and attractive and worn out with being alone. As alone and attractive as anyone on the point of death."

A married man who drinks by himself and sleeps on the coach. I tell myself I'm better off outside his life, his tortured take on the mundane.

He mailed me a postcard from Berkeley the day he left. His thoughts are elegant and black—a large passage is written over a smear of white-out—with the tip of a butter knife I scrape it away. A corroded message slowly emerges—I can't make out every word but the subject matter is Freud on cryptography, how it reveals the inner man. Quincey knew I'd excavate his secret, so well has he trained me in the labyrinthine pleasures of the hidden *pulling away from the toll booth Quincey says softly but firmly "I thought you were going to abuse me." I know this is a code but for what? Tentatively I pat his thigh, fumble with a shirt button . . . yes? . . . no? . . . then the waistband his zipper parts as easily as his lips and I bow my head to the inevitable . . . over the Golden Gate Bridge, down the endless expanse of Lombard Street . . . Quincey won't let me see where I'm going, my cheek brushing denim my mouth full of cock. From the waist up he's a model citizen of the road, observing the speed limit, smiling at fellow motorists at stoplights as he murmurs "Oh wow" or "This is great."*

My lover has lips as round and swollen as life preservers, but they don't make me feel very safe.

Slits of world peek through levelor blinds—Quincey's out there, maneuvering his way through a foreign tongue. The distance is inconceivable: thousands of miles, a handspan in an atlas. Is Spain any farther from San Francisco than Berkeley? Hours pass, days pass, but not my appetite, its impenitent accrual . . . I burnish my favorite moments like worry stones, superimpose them on the daily, try to survive their unavoidable dilution. Does Quincey flicker through these words like a summoned ghost—or am I driving him even further away with my insomniac urge to reinvent him *no wife, willing to slay dragons, etc.* no wonder I'm always surprised when he's through the door—suddenly— actually—rubbing his erection against me, all pleasure, or apologizing with tears in his eyes. The head of his penis is unbelievably soft, velvet without the nape.

He is flying far above me in the ink-colored sky UNREACHABLE. Days Without Someone. I should have asked him for something—something funky of his to wear. One seasonably warm afternoon he left a sweater here—I hardly knew him but I pulled it over my naked breasts—the sleeves hanging to the tips of my fingers were his hands holding me down, the rough brown wool his chest, his back *sheathed in his molecules I felt positively amniotic* . . . after I came I wiped the collar between my legs. And the magic worked—we were lovers in a couple of weeks. When I told him my ritual he wore the sweater to work the next day, idiotically smiling to himself, my secretions a necklace about his fine German throat.

His Lou Reed cassette, a poison novel by Albertine Sarrazin, a magazine from San Diego: Quincey clings to the things he loaned me *these fragments I have shored against my ruins*. High-strung and schmaltzy I play "Classic Film Scores for Bette Davis," a CD he bought in admiration of my intelligence and drama, the large gestures with which I snub him at parties. If he lit two cigarettes in his mouth at once, he knows I wouldn't laugh . . . graciously I take what he offers, suck the moist tip with a broad jerky movement *let's not ask for the moon* Quincey points out the constellations, the brown stars in my iris, Venus, Orion. "You look good." He said it whenever we got together. Sometimes he added a flourish of adverb, "You look really good." But sitting here at the keyboard in a flannel bathrobe without Quincey to look at me, do I look like anything at all? Sam, can you see me? In the vast black Beam Me Up Scotty, how's my reception? There's not an inch of me he hasn't licked—some residue of him must linger, an astral impression radiating from my body pink smeared with yellow trailing off into the atmosphere *his skin smells of soap, his hair like cherries* in public he blankly wavers beside the Mrs.—how do I pull off casual with this man who just that morning stuck his tongue up my ass, I strain to look past those pale eyes instead of burrowing. As he steps past me his body fractures into a galaxy of adorable touchables, and now, oh, Sam, all those pieces are in Barcelona with Lucy.

Quincey says we're Paolo and Francesca, a damnation so beautiful it made Dante weep. I'll never understand the ease he can come to . . . then walk away from . . . such pleasure. I've always been either not there or too eager. My writhing like grave worms moves in on Quincey destroying his last grasp on corporeality. I sense his spirit yearning for something to embody: the stiff daguerreotypes of my memory, a brace clamped to his neck for these unreasonable exposures: Quincey ravishing my armpit, his penis probing my mouth my ear my ass my cunt and then my thighs my breasts anything that can be clenched, Quincey brushing a lock of hair across his lower lip, holding my hand through his colorful glove. I'm growing antsy with this script of the remembered, nothing but theme and variation—I want to defile him, rearrange his history as easily as my hairdo. Quincey is a red brick wall. Before him a man in a brown suit is upside down in midair, having fallen from Quincey's window—the artist has drawn the man's scream very clumsily so that his mouth looks like Howdy Doody's, giving an unintentional comic air to the impending squash. Quincey as the red brick wall is impassible through all this.

The writing won't let me be—I have to keep pen and paper beside my bed—it sneaks up on me in the middle of the night. Then leaves. The world encroaches, Nina Simone on the jukebox, two glasses of red wine on a table the size of a crossword puzzle. Dion sits facing me, with blue eyes, black hair. As he leans forward his chest seems to swallow the table, he says, "The only thing I have under my wings are shadows." Occasionally his large hand wanders across a bit of my body: a stray I could easily fuck with affection, then walk away from. Quincey is off drinking margaritas with his wife *there is nothing in our situation to remain faithful to.* Quincey grows tiny, crushed with immensity, like the end of *The Incredible Shrinking Man* when the infinitesimal merges with the infinite and we know we're not watching any ordinary Hollywood schlock but a slice of Deep Meaning. Still, he won't be eradicated—as I make coffee Quincey's still wearing his demin jacket he lifts up the back of my nightgown pulls me to him biting my lips his cold hands cupping my ass—this memory inflicts a pang of arousal, a cramp in the groin, painful.

Late at night the phone turns tensile, surreal, an implement aliens use in their sex experiments: his wife just a room away, Quincey begins to masturbate through the receiver *"I'm going to tighten my hand around your throat so you can't move and then I'm going to stick my . . ."* Across the bay I self-consciously whisper, "I'd like that." He's amazed at the volumes of cum sprayed across his belly, scoops some up with a finger and eats it. He's so kinky, yet sweet, with a cleanness about him like a Cranach . . . beneath his dewy skin that fine chiselled bone straining . . . he asks me to squeeze his nipples, hovers about me a bright ecstatic angel eyes closed biting his lower lip, he quietly throws his head back then slowly brings it down chin to chest then back up again: this cum shot is precise, yet flattened and blurred like a color xerox of a collage; as I type it a frenetic neighbor stomps above my head. Sex, no matter how fondly recalled, comes across so generic. Only the spurts of conversation between gasps and undulations remain with me, the way he calls me "Babe" when he's excited—nursing my neck or shoulder he reaches up and sighs, "Anything you want, Babe," and I feel cheap in a way I want to go on forever.

28

We lingered in the shadow of the coastal highway, the salty breeze cooling my exposed cunt. "Suck my cock," yelled a man we couldn't see, exiling us to the beach . . . small birds scuttled along the wet sand as if animated by Disney . . . the onrushing waves left soap suds at our feet. Quincey reached under my black silk overcoat, under my skirt, his forefinger twirling pubic curls—the shore was scattered with city dwellers their features surprisingly distinct beneath the full moon—before their eager nocturnal eyes I felt like a potboiler, the kind of book read by people who shop at Walgreen's *let's fly into the sun let's fly anywhere these beachcombers can't see.* Last night falling asleep I looked into the shutter of a camera, a giant mechanical iris spiraled closed, blocking out the light, blocking out Quincey. Maybe I should call it quits maybe I should wipe my dirty fingers across this page, have his bastard baby.

His eyes are the color of my coffee cup he has two hands tendons form deep ridges on the top of his feet: a minefield of camouflage: if his wife sees through my writing I may never see him again. His name's not Quincey, he's not in Spain really: encoded in my language Quincey remains disembodied as he is from my life. His corpse walks in Barcelona—it is beet red beneath a peeling nose and baseball cap *desire that giant burrowing nematode sneaks up and grabs me* rattling my chest, Quincey's wormy laugh. He fucked me sideways while I fucked his mouth with my right hand, he sucked so hard I thought the flesh was going to fall away like over-cooked chicken—he said he was coming at both ends one long vibrating tunnel . . . what's inside . . . what's out . . . the hair on his ass grates against my tongue . . . when I lick him there I'm leaving more than saliva behind: sibilants . . . fricatives . . . a layer of soul . . . I removed the belt from my robe and tried his wrists to the bedstead—do whatever you want with me, he said, make it hurt *he wanted to be pliable, pliable as absence* . . . beyond a few entries in my diary, the gush of a schoolgirl, I never could write about Quincey *I was silenced before the undefinable thingness of his lips, his hands, his cock, all the insistent anatomical components . . . then he left and the words rushed in like vultures, picking away, redefining.*

I am aching. I am alone. If only I could give a bourgeois patina of meaning to this. Something French: "Pleasure is the creation of the mind, the body can't do anything without it." I'm lying on my stomach and Quincey is fucking me from behind—it feels pretty good, though I don't take his efforts seriously—I wriggle my bladder into the optimal position, patiently anticipating My Turn—then abruptly the flesh of my vagina crystallizes *the unsuspected is inevitable there is no stopping* and when it does happen I raise up on my arms and cry out. This is an ideal state of discourse—unmediated, with a totally receptive audience. Quincey, how could you throw me into this solitary confinement? Here on the inside we call it the "hole." I'm distressed by this lack of feedback. This silence. I jump out a window *wheeling around for one second which is long and good, a century* my foot breaks with the impact so I crawl on knees and elbows, dragging this useless lump to the highway *I am oozing mud, thorns scratch me at random from bushes—another century goes by, I can't recognize anything*—"Monsieur Le Truckdriver," I plead, "I'm a prisoner of love, the dark side of someone's double life. Please, will you sneak me to Paris!"

Eagerly he licks his cum from my mouth: I want to bring the reader this close to writing. Into a barely imaginable future I try to project this erotic reader, an incubus complete with organs that function and hands to hold my pages. This image isn't any more satisfying than if I were to tape an obscene message for my phone machine *sorry I'm not home right now but I'm hot for your* . . . it just isn't the same as having a body on the other end of the line, the bona fide heavy breathing.

Quincey, where are you? Wrap your phone cord around your cock. Remember me.

When he was aroused, Quincey turned monosyllabic, which really did it for me. I'd be chattering away and all he'd say was, "Yeah," his voice low and raspy, urgent as a wet tongue in my ear. Passion did a quick dissolve and I waxed silent as Quincey filled the frame, became the frame: his body, his emanations. "Yeah."

"Dear William Gibson:
    Right now I'm reading *Blue Eyes, Black Hair*. I'm afraid that Marguerite Duras is going to destroy my style—I find myself wanting to do all this frou-frou shit that I don't like even when she does it. I've been working on this prose thing about longing and absence, what it's like to experience a person who is not there. Sitting here at my MacPlus, I wonder about my main character—is he a sort of entity haunting the screen—*where* does he exist? Since I've so recently read *Mona Lisa Overdrive*, I'm reminded of cyberspace, how cyberspace is your metaphor for desire and longing, the

way we spend most of our time away from the loved/coveted person, and are frustrated by our unrealistic wish to have them with us instantly on demand. In cyberspace we can relive heightened emotional/sexual states otherwise lost to us just by their being transitory—at the end of *Mona Lisa Overdrive*, Angie becomes not a physical bride, but a bride to her lover's imagination. I'm hesitant about responding to your writing because you must have responses to your writing up the wazoo."

The present tense just won't stick to him—narrative has thrust him finally, irretrievably IN THE PAST. The tendons there are so pronounced his feet look webbed—I used to run my fingers in the fissures that extend from toes to ankle, daydreaming of roads carved between mountains, of running away. He said that entering me was going home—but what's home, Quincey—the couch in the living room, where you spend the night, depressed, after your friends leave? When he looked at his house through my eyes, he claimed his things looked interesting. From the little I saw of them, his things were simple, mostly secondhand, suggesting a lower socio-economic status than his own. One night while I sucked his toes and he sucked mine, we somehow managed to fuck at the same time, a sort of elongated 69 pivoting on his cock. I turned my head and smiled at him, said, "This is very Kama Sutra." "You're right," he answered, "But what would they call it . . . something like 'turkey clawing under bright moon.'" And then he fell out of me.

Quincey's flown into the sun and my heart is in a window display in North Beach—a valentine of dried roses and grass, it looks like a wreath you'd see on a pet's grave.

Before I'd ever touched him I wanted Quincey dearly—just the thought of him would get me wet. Once I had his body I was no longer moved by the idea, but by the thing itself. Next to him everything else feels bland and disconnected *maybe it's all been a dream, a very small and savage dream* his eye contact hypnotized me, leaning so close his breath flushed my cheek, peering *into* me, he learned every dot in my iris—he used them to navigate his way to my soul. He stole it. And then he went to Barcelona, carelessly tossing it back at me.

All I can imagine saying upon his return is, "I don't know, Quincey, you feel so alien."

31

Duras: "A swell surged up the wall of the house but fell back at his feet as if to avoid him; it was fringed with white and alive, like writing." Alive, yes, but at whose expense? I ache for the innocents like you Sam who try to befriend me. Bloodthirsty and iridescent, writing sucks the marrow from the unsuspecting then sits back picking its teeth with a rib. Poor Quincey never had a chance *do what you want with me, he said*—now he totters along the shore, his tortured features barely recognizable: a body pink and bloated from fermenting gasses—his pale eyes plead—but the damage has already been done. I've seen enough movies to not touch him—the slightest pressure of my hand would upset the delicate biochemical balance. A heap of dust or something more gooey collapsing at my feet, not even a shell would I be left with.

A shifting, a readiness—fear—my body is a mold waiting for plastique. Late this evening Quincey will return.

My mind is clear, clear as the night we parked in Marin overlooking the bay. There in the front seat of his car Quincey first made me come. He marvelled, the witness to a miracle—or, a child with a toy that finally works. I teased, "Quincey, it's a normal body function." The Golden Gate Bridge filled the windshield, gold and gleaming. "The tower of Camelot," he said. Craning his neck up at the heavens—boyish—he pointed out Orion, only visible in the Northern Hemisphere, only in winter. We huddled together, our clothes still undone, watching the crescent moon blink through wisps of clouds, and I thought to myself this is happiness. The last time I kissed him he was in a doorway, leaving. I stood on my toes to get closer and breathed, "I'll immortalize you." There's something Faustian about this story. I can invoke his name, his personality, but my loving descriptions of his body are bloodless, as though I were parroting another author. I remember his penis was friendly—just like him. But that's it. If I touch him again will it merely feel awkward . . . or good as a first time?

In just a few hours he'll be near enough to know . . .

Writing versus life—is the one flight, the other hot pursuit? I don't remember. I once was a nerdy high school girl with nothing much else to do than lie on her twin bed filling a spiral notebook with poems of isolation and black curtains a vulnerability so coddled it grew sentient. If this were a modernist novel, in the end I suppose I'd choose Life. The phone rings after midnight. A man's voice on the line, urgent and impossible. He doesn't identify himself, implores, "Can I come over I need to see you. Right now!" Without missing a beat I chirp back, "Well, Babe—what are you waiting for?"

Love,
Mina

TED BERRIGAN

Things To Do in Providence

Crash
Take Valium   Sleep

Dream &,

forget it.

*

Wake up new & strange
displaced,

at home.

Read The Providence Evening Journal

No one you knew

got married
had children
got divorced
died

got born

tho many familiar names flicker &
disappear.

*

Sit

watch TV

draw blanks

swallow

34

        pepsi
        meatballs
        . . .

                        give yourself the needle:

        "Shit! There's gotta be something
                        to do
                            here!"

                    *

JOURNEY   Seven young men on horses, leaving Texas.
TO SHILOH: They've got to do what's right! So, after
            a long trip, they'll fight for the South in the War.
            No war in Texas, but they've heard about it,
                & they want
            to fight for their country. Have some adventures
                & make
            their folks proud! Two hours later all are dead;
            one by one they died, stupidly, & they never did
                find out why!
            There were no niggers in South Texas! Only
                the leader,
            with one arm shot off, survives to head back to Texas:
            all his friends behind him, dead. What will happen?

                    *

            Watching him, I cry big tears. His friends
        were beautiful, with boyish American good manners,
                    cowboys!

                    *

Telephone New York: "hello!"

                    "Hello! I'm drunk! &
                        I have no clothes on!"
                "My goodness," I say.
                            "See you tomorrow."

                    *

                    35

Wide awake all night reading: *The Life of Turner*
                              ("He first saw the light in Maiden Lane")
                              A.C. Becker: Wholesale Jewels
                                                      Catalogue 1912
                              The Book of Marvels, 1934:
                                                      The year I was born.

        No mention of my birth in here.   Hmmm.

                        Saturday The Rabbi Stayed Home

                        (that way he got to solve the murder)

                        LIFE on the moon   by LIFE Magazine
                              *
My mother wakes up, 4 a.m.: Someone to talk with!

        Over coffee we chat, two grownups
        I have two children, I'm an adult now, too.
        Now we are two people talking who have known each other
                                          a long time,
        Like Edwin & Rudy. Our talk is a great pleasure: my mother
        a spunky woman. Her name was Peggy Dugan when she was young.
        Now, 61 years old, she blushes to tell me I was conceived
        before the wedding! "I've always been embarrassed about telling you
        til now," she says. "I didn't know what you might think!"
        "I think it's really sweet," I say. "It means I'm really
        a love child." She too was conceived before her mother's wedding,
        I know. We talk, daylight comes, & the Providence Morning Journal.
        My mother leaves for work. I'm still here.

                              *
Put out the cat

                              Take in the clothes
                                          off of the line

                Take a walk,
                        buy cigarettes

                              *

                              36

two teen-agers whistle
        as I walk up

                They say: "Only your hairdresser
                knows for sure!"

        Then they say,

        "ulp!"

        because I am closer to them.
They see I am not hippie kid, frail like Mick Jagger,
but some horrible 35 year old big guy!

        The neighborhood I live in is mine!

"How'd you like a broken head, kid?"
                I say fiercely.

        (but I am laughing & they are not one bit scared.)

        So, I go home.

        * * * *

Alice Clifford waits me. Soon she'll die
at the Greenwood Nursing Home; my mother's
mother, 79 years & 7 months old.

        But first, a nap, til my mother comes home
from work, with the car.

        *

The heart stops briefly when someone dies
a quick pain as you hear the news, & someone passes
from your outside life to inside. Slowly the heart adjusts
to its new weight, & slowly everything continues, sanely.

        *

Living's a pleasure:

I'd like to take the whole trip
                          despite the possible indignities of growing old,
              moving, to die in poverty, among strangers:
                                          that can't be helped.

                            *

So, everything, now
        is just all right.   I'm with you.

                    No more last night.

                            *

        Friday's great

        10 o'clock morning sun is shining!

        I can hear today's key sounds fading softly

        & almost see opening sleep's epic novels.

Red Shift

Here I am at 8:08 p.m. indefinable ample rhythmic frame
The air is biting, February, fierce arabesques
    on the way to tree in winter streetscape
I drink some American poison liquid air which bubbles
    and smoke to have character and to lean
In. The streets look for Allen, Frank, or me, Allen
    is a movie, Frank disappearing in the air, it's
Heavy with that lightness, heavy on me, I heave
    through it, them, as
The Calvados is being sipped on Long Island now
    twenty years almost ago, and the man smoking
Is looking at the smiling attentive woman, & telling.
Who would have thought that I'd be here, nothing
    wrapped up, nothing buried, everything
Love, children, hundreds of them, money, marriage-
    ethics, a politics of grace,
Up in the air, swirling, burning even or still, now
    more than ever before?
Not that practically a boy, serious in corduroy car coat
    eyes penetrating the winter twilight at 6th
& Bowery in 1961. Not that pretty girl, nineteen, who
    was going to have to go, careening into middle-age so,
To burn & to burn more fiercely than even she could imagine
    so to go. Not that painter who from the very first meeting
I would never & never will leave alone until we both vanish
    into the thin air we signed up for & so demanded
To breathe & who will never leave me, not for sex, not politics
    nor even for stupid permanent estrangement which is
Only our human lot & means nothing. No, not him.
There's a song, "California Dreaming", but no, I won't do that.
I am 43. When will I die? I will never die. I will live
To be 110 & I will never go away, & you will never escape from me
    who am always & only a ghost, despite this frame, Spirit
Who lives only to nag.
I'm only pronouns, & I am all of them, & I didn't ask for this
    You did

I came into your life to change it & it did so & now nothing
    will ever change
That, & that's that.
Alone & crowded, unhappy fate, nevertheless
    I slip softly into the air
The world's furious song flows through my costume.

A Certain Slant of Sunlight

In Africa the wine is cheap, and it is
on St. Mark's Place too, beneath a white moon.
I'll go there tomorrow, dark bulk hooded
against what is hurled down on me in my no hat
which is weather: the tall pretty girl in the print dress
under the fur collar of her cloth coat will be standing
by the wire fence where the wild flowers grow not too tall
her eyes will be deep brown and her hair styled 1941 American
        will be too; but
I'll be shattered by then
But now I'm not and can also picture white clouds
impossibly high in blue sky over small boy heartbroken
to be dressed in black knickers, black coat, white shirt,
        buster-brown collar, flowing black bow-tie
her hand lightly fallen on his shoulder, faded sunlight falling
across the picture, mother & son, 33 & 7, First Communion Day, 1941—
I'll go out for a drink with one of my demons tonight
they are dry in Colorado 1980 spring snow.

MEI-MEI BERSSENBRUGGE

Experience

1

The idea of illusion suggests that existences in different worlds, herself at different stages, or moving from one metaphor to another, can compare. She is trying to tell you the moon's color in eclipse, because she cannot reproduce a light in her memory with a pigment that is made, like a word, though seeing the moon enables a person to make inaccurate color. Think, if experience in her *is* time, because she gets to a state of being by experience, first. Experience is an interval in the body, but it also accompanies remembering.

2

Low sun from behind you on asters, chamisa. You find a space as wide as if time fell outside the stimulus of that glow, and her memory of it became space in her. Her body and will coordinate, like the relation of experience to seeing and experience to feeling the moon, which has no size.

Actual size of its color in her body assesses the vicissitudes of an aspiration created by seeing, so in this case, actual size became a piece of size in her.

3

You look on the plain from a bluff with him, and a point of juniper grows dark and dense of scattered ones, a piece of sieved material on your side of a membrane of noon light.

Seeing the object locates it like a cause in your body, for noticing a faint green around it as an underground stream. Seeing what had been invisible is a response to the object.

His presence, a cause or weight in nature, does not enter experience, but accompanies it, as experience had accompanied her memory of her, her features in her relative's face.

4

If she only sees with another person, what about the response is phenomenal, and what is

contingent, as a comet or virus, resonating to its presence in another human being,

but which could be a metaphor, like grass in light, or sunlight on distant yellow trees?

Nature, full of causes that never enter experience, contrasts to your thinking adjusting contingency

to contingency like a synthesis. Desire to know opposes, for example, desire for children.

It structures a branched straw in the snow, so its blue shadow is blue in a tiny armpit. When

he sees autumn grass, I tell him about its shadow on snow, leapfrog of see/know, to straw of light.

5

A sliver of cloud lights up. Not knowing where it is between you and the horizon

turns into desire to know this. "Where" is the secret of durable pigment. "It" is the part

hit by an angle of light that is moving, so each moment triangulates the space by way of the cloud.

On huge new insects after rain, light leapfrogs like falling. The vertigo analyzes a cloud, not

giving you to know it, the way knowing opposes wanting a person, or a person is opposed to an infant,

being inspired, not experiencing.

44

6

She is making the space during the day in an unanalyzed form, expressing it, using light, which as experience emotes a color, and one of the elements of making *is* the space, because she cannot see the light as a tool, while she is still figuring how to use it. Its use is his presence, or its end is, to which its use is a means. Her concentration obliterates time, like the relation of experience to a moment. It falls outside the stimulus of an absent person as a golden light in the room.

7

Seeing the light became a substance in her body, as knowing a ghost by seeing light in a room, a relation of experience to feeling. The metaphor of the light became an obliterating emotion, from one metaphor to another, so she got to the state of being of the light by knowing, first, a synthesis that put time outside her situation. She makes *that* into time, which can flood a plain, inside a leaf, a leaf of gilt on an image. Wanting to know as opposed to wanting a person is herself in a room flooded by light through yellow leaves. Each leaf like an ancestral feature assesses the vicissitudes of this aspiration. A consciousness outside a state of being is flooded.

CHARLES BORKHUIS

Inside Language

a silent wind
settles in
behind the motion of naming

collecting loose words
at the corners of our lips
where they masquerade
as things

a miniature world
talks itself into being
tiny trees and stones
created in the throat
twist out of proportion

a man's arms and legs
extend from the mouth
of an enormous sewing machine
a moment before sleep

~

bruised streaks of sky
a smoldering eye pulses
when feathers (the face)
signal this still vibrating second

are we brought to the edge of the cliff
only to crawl back

~

this shifting presence
aging in advance

midnight drips darkness into day
spots on the surface
of sight

again at the crossroads
each personal eclipse
describes another face

another street
that splinters into speech

~

how thought rolls out of the body
like a second "I"

leaving an accumulation
of linguistic traces
through dense foliage
and stagnant ponds

(the curtain rises slightly
revealing two feet on a dirt road)

desire to become the object
to speak directly from its sanctuary
(might as well try
talking to a mirror)

~

ripples of light out of each
tiny brown spore
landing on the page

(precarious seed)

moving toward and away from
understanding
at the very moment of
perception

~

mistaken ground of meaning

the words continue on without us

pebble and star
people the stain
stretching across the horizon

a rusted mechanical bird
blocks the sun
with one blazing sepia wing

(behind each received meaning
an entire language converses)

an old woman in the corner
peeks at us
through a handful of feathers

as if we were ghosts

~

the hand that writes
behind closing lids

slides from its moorings
into the deep
bell-tolling sea

(recurring shapes
within a changing field)

48

animals and objects
loosened from their names
stare blankly at us

(life among the transparencies
the stories we tell ourselves)

ice forms from the edges in
growing a second skin

in the distance
a solitary figure walks
across a paper-thin lake
blue vein of the sentence
extending out of each step

word over word in the dusk

Quartet

Wave

to say the thing and having said it
pass on through a maze
of paper boats vibrating on a lake

these are the words desired or else
dead water lilies
in the half-light that splinters
across the surface of what is

but language won't appear in the flesh
she's got better things on her mind
to be rid of you for instance
to inhabit flesh elsewhere

this ache this whole
inside that eats
you alive begins to grow
arms and legs
breasts that break
the surface of the lake
and slide back under

faces in the brine
distant battles
figures turned to stone
her voice
returning from nowhere
leaping a dark body of water
to the next word

Particle

seasons turning inside the egg
where the serpent's coil
tightens its circle of days
and the stone is extracted
from the belly by breathing
red sulfur through a glass tube

stone of your breath
the same stone that wears a hat
and walks into the sea
the stone that burns
in the eye of a fish
the trilingual stone
the stone that goes
disguised as a gardener
the detached stone
the stone in love
the stone that returns with no legs

the hermetic stone that burrows
through the sky like a mole
the amnesiac stone that reappears
for no reason
the hungry stone
the stone of concrete vistas
crumbling into words
the stone that lies to itself
the stone at night
alone and talking in its sleep

Echo

the sounds of space inside
the sentence a certain
disconnectedness
set to drift
through the static and thunder
of the synaptic universe
just below our breath

the sound of the oxygen sea
between conductors
the topmost creaking in the dark
awake in an ocean of glowing particles
you fold into the form
of what you inhabit
you travel the wires both ways
like an electron
dancing between searchlights
that radiate off the ends of words

you lose your name at crossroads
take in air as if
it were a secret flame
through which all is forged
you exist between thoughts
before they link
like loose boxcars in a yard

the finished phrase
is a wall against the night
we all stand behind it
with our flashlights burning
but you won't return
until the empire of the sentence
falls back into the alphabet
and the winds have blown
dark letters across these waterless skies

Spark

few embers
burning from within
bones blackened to carbon
charred skulls
distant hills of blue dust
dissolving into wandering herds
straining
towards the smell of water

the long shadow
of a walking-stick
stretched across the desert
warm blood drawn
from the neck of the beast
tales from the withered arm
the dried-up cup
that speaks in small flames
round the rim

tales of the laboratory
buried in the body
the chemistry of roads
that ignites in memory
sending sparks across the dark
mineral-coupling sea

Come go with me out to the Field —
To look upon the Rose
Whose glow — remembers once the Sun
Gave Garnets for her Clothes

Her crimson Cadence soon will Stop —
The music of the Spheres
Won't cease — but barely register
A Fraction of Earth's years

While Light still vibrates on our Brow
The subtle Minutes drag —
The Fly is droning with the Bee —
Our outer Bodies flag

The Lyric Can Snare

every whipped ideal save for
the one just mentioned

Legs flail under cover
waiting for birthday
or border to unravel
its quick hair wreath

Sound's armours teach moving verbal skills
Motor neurons pitch a fevered reach

The lyric still teases
us into a past perfect stirrup

Feed a cold
Starve a fever
You don't feel like earthly either

I'll be ready when you come
Bright red afternoon

JOSEPH CERAVOLO

Data

To indicate is to
turn off   in a world
away from ease.
Rotating in a mean format of oxygen.
First make and then
made all alone until
the end of a blank.
The smoke opens up and out
comes a word
in a new storage of love.
Turning off or
turning on the calcareous bases
we find our selves in
are set there by IT.
Divine and more
divine each day, no control,
but in another world.

Dangers of the Journey to the Happy Land

Talk of energy. Mayan sub-flower
Come to light and feel physically intent to
plasm
    Even if I don't share
    Instance the mother
Talk of energy or stolen from her
mother
    I didn't do that for
nothing   I speak as a wife to the
capsizing Both are once
Perspire like an autumn wind bakes. Mayan
sub-flowers.
    Am I allowed to go to
the tough section? That's tough.
    Mayan sub-flowers in
       the shade.

The Crocus Turn and Gods*

Toy for the raking gully
shame encore there,
sorry human posed working,
demeanor just helen as
garden comes, Music
o cotton unforgiven bargain,
chilly, gush, album in later manjun
embrace. Begs soon jamais
furious bungalow of
pour a boy. Scowl possess however
city trumped,
jumbles pity then, rum or
canto sleep in this eddy.
To a rumble Hour lo a grape
sleep   please graphic
to ours like ate
quivers place then float
came came wack ill of voices
god of
        Picnic lumin and
sake in Talk! Sort!
dose Ah slave and
premate Correo to
until of mades, asylum budding,
possessed sop churning,
woman tippling wings hill.
Young over ahoy
for the breathe

O targets! and sang   O timid of
among!   Off! Saying!
yellow shook then Pan! O

Completely leaf.
Yet prize!
alone aesop damage

*from Book III of *Fits of Dawn*

58

Night for the carnival
rummage of humans

O outside O nervous yellow
silo for the harm
        And soul
Really game smother nowhere
summit   Yes
    oar kill happen of enamoured

                Jungle
for my surely quake
smallen smallen stung of surged
    The birth
            Rampant! Bat! Perhaps!
    The drink   the whistle

there maybe
of the down
Not pine   Not scowl
prolific binge to wane,
orchard gyp afraid of
conch of frolick! Yes,
no fist, the soon trestle trestle fake So
malheure a shy for bunch

        "poseidon"
            Donné
Farmest ecoutez o meadow
        of pay

O shine of
    could
        Bark!
    Rooster for muffle
            Killed
O seem

59

                    begin poor
           serious Demeter   O
     hilly erg of
                              young
           being of otter being
                 apollo
     O Voyez!   O whelm
                       Succumb
              painty of dommage
           Bloom!   O tox
                 destroy N
                       oregon on motion

              Lore curious of milk
              O body   spill
                    degree enfance
                              cane of
     oaxaca.   Today
              force infant
           flowerous than earth

     Only the wand
              openly la playa
                 la plage
                          told
           winter aesop,

     behind october worse, worse than belts
        of caracas then
                 mind   O hunger   Livid
                    swish

                              bullet
           remind a reed o
              gravel connaitre
                       wack to doze

                    60

Dreamt of cheat
            cheat of
        suddenly soul dawn ocean
lasso for the
            Jealous!

Only violent elysium of
            the jetty
        saving ploughs   O
    lotus   O coon
            that grain
 . . . . . . O
    breathe

NORMA COLE

Saturn

'Body, divide-up, why'*

First the idea of a day's generalization.

Parody is made then attacked.

The skeleton is lying down as it should. The baby sat
on the edge of a skull as it must.

*Susan Schaller, *A Man Without Words*

62

Phenotext

A place invent and time.
All the old bonds and ties.
Our enemies stretched out.
Shocked but curious.
Different or not at all.
Language replacing.
Serendipitous little house.
The minds of the universe.
A shell game.
The room where I met my hands and face.
Black blood wanting.
Visual parole.
Inner crust.
"Our lovers are dying."
And flower hands.
Guess and unguessed.
Short but uncommon.
Stirring.
The name difficulty.
And need.
Not language itself.
Glazed over.

Sweep the formation
in the framework of its devices
there will be no remains
no signs of pressure
surprise is real
the belief that blood circulates
consolidation occurs in the response

Walk in beauty like the dead
the dark is at its zenith, etc.
a kind of iridescent
or even near blur
given for possibilities
forgive the echo

Variations on some of Dante's last lines

And move and hold back
entering by the highroad through the words
and fall like a person hit by sleep
arriving at the place without light

And fall like a dead body falls
and find there the great enemy
and come to a tower all of stones
such that through it the earth opens

We pass between the martyrs and the high walls
even up there water is pouring out
then turning and fording again
sling the noose from the roof of the house

And each and every vapor spent
over winning and not losing
in which it stands caught out
fleet then catapults like a stone

Filling our view
whereupon another valley is revealed

To raise discourse in the streets. Understand now her eating of history. The rest is futility.

Surely
shooting was taking place in the streets. She lies down in the gutter for protection and is yelled at by police. She goes inside the haircutting salon and Robert Lowell is still there having a conversation with someone who looks just like him. The city is unrecognizable. Her house is unrecogniz- able and so are the things in the cupboard she must reorganize. Napoleon had said not to put it all on one wall.

The crucial
tension the war is not separate from us.

The young child had been sucked up inside the vacuum cleaner and blown back out. Now it lay there dead without a face.

Structures
of indecision it was not always so. It befores,afters and durings. How privileges eat form. Transgressive responsibility

PETER COLE

from

```
        W
        H      T
S P E E C H ' S   H E D G E
        R      E      O
        E             N
                      E
                      Y
```

1.

The line coils seeking extension,
    seeking leafage and fruit beyond weeds,
        seeking wheat—
    whose flowers few recall.

    The line coils seeking inclusion
        beyond amazement,

the truths of attention within its law—.

The spikelets begin to bloom
    slightly below the middle of the head
        and proceed both upward and downward,
The glumes are split by the swelling
of two scalelike organs within them

        and echo in thought
like the hairsbreadth moon I wouldn't look at
    over the suburb after a storm.

    I'd deadened myself with the wood of shelter;

with the elegant wood I'd
deadened myself to the awn of sound,
to the splintering pulse,

and the flax in bloom:

with the dead
wood of the phonemes *soon* . . .

though the poem was an altar seeking submission—

shifting attention inside the rain;

and this was the month
of the voice in the greenness burning,

of the spirit wound in its claim.

•

Words are wood for the vanished altar.

Isaac the son who brings his own kindling.

The lord protects by concealing his name,

or laughing.   The line coils
escaping derision,
and coils again embracing abjection,
establishes shape charting conviction;

the sun in the sign of the Ram—

and the April moon of redemption,

of the great tabernacle to the glume and the law,
of the barley ripening, and the spelt to come—
though man can't live by bread alone—
whose flowers prefigure recall.

69

12. THE POEM UP THERE
"Ornament is nurse of pride.
Pleasure measure love's delight."
—Dowland's *Songs or Airs*
Anonymous

Nursing pride

in pride of place,

a trope's
loop of
central occasion—
equipment,
a slap in the face
to patricians of theme
and persuasion,

or civil (Horatian)
representation.

Unlaureate:

the poem *up there*

in the air of
any beholder:

the painted vase
a useless favorite
aunt bequeathed,

accessory,

and not our cup
of tea,

—her dominance—

70

defined our living
(warmest) room

in time,

  defines my life

with wife and loving

abstract lack and decor—

  not cure—

the offering of sweet
  savor exceeding prayer—

in the volume of splendor
I read:

  To forge links
    and make light,

  like Law,

  defines a practice.

24. SPEECH'S HEDGE

. . . where the honeyed
    combs of light resolve

onto a couch's blue upholstery,

    shifting with wind:

like spirit
    flinching in thinking

    as though in a gem,

or Byzantine dome,

but the onlooker backing off—unsure to his day.

And orange
        slits of escape nasturtium
        jutting his
    Persian wall of withdrawal.

Not images served

    but shards of an image—
        breakage's throne—

    reflection's
        text as homage,

    as place curiously home.

Nerve bridles
    before such a future floor

as though in the spooked
        childhood house

forever   on the wooded hill:

        planks
giving way to the story below
        and basement finds—

        the trap of stairs

        and libidinal
swill of spiral
        unknowing

or a corner turned

onto the
bevel of weakened roof

        forced by fear to climb—

for the forecast view to the jagged city,
        small   in the distant haze . . .

        •

Hives of midday light

through a window's invisible weave—
        and a barely registered

            breeze
                    on the skin,

lifting attention—

annealed,

ornamental.

CLARK COOLIDGE

In Nora's House with Rilke's Apollo

He cannot his unheard skull
could not turn on his sound gaze
so not ripe in his sever litter
but the rest of his body shows like a camphor
could slow then, remain, and turn down

His love which slows noise like a sail
though so much boats don't talk
as if someone told you, you must change
what does not see you
is this to feel the treddle clang of
fame, outside regard, a clay mast
sought out to pin your things to?
and then he comes back in, no power

A sex burst of no
connection to the other
(even closed-eye mother)
(everything else drinking by and chuckling at)
too much wind for you today, bronze bee
it pops and he drinks, throated in
orange reserve
Is he guarding? Do I smell myself shaving?
but wink little drabs of black on white
drop the other's book and leave the driving till night

These poems must rhyme, he said and dropped his shocking
I live in a shack, I thought and stopped watching
my task, let the bugs return
let one foot on the top step
receive
whenever whatever stuns the walls

His apparel shined in bee light
the converse powercell clad his battery jacket
in an oiled onyx blew over the mattress
thought of sex with tunes and wavered
just shortly, old guy on the edge of the
well once drilled, then easily launched
somehow an archaic torso, means?
I'd polish my forehead aside, I'd think
the environment thinner, crack in
the head letting paint through, light came visible
and it's Apollo, and there's the message of change

Birds threaten code from inside the chest
this is given, bargain of the chain-mail sentinel
you wouldn't bark in a museum, I would think
felt all out of a surface in eyes grown out
should not stop you, doesn't, and then
pretend to repeat everything not on the list
boat running out of (the whites of Attica)
and the lights within go to ground

I have inscribed, the message not to finish
torso to cease, the glowing stop looking, don't
stand up in the shell, heavy very slowly
when finally under weigh, down down
and away by the red and blue voice
perhaps fell far enough, had another mention there
only rubbed in the case of books

Will this be the back-ass of the case of failure?
Could you draw me down a vein of the entire torso?
she was the one in the third rank with the toes
over the fridge and early very early too, actually
what did "Nora" do here in this allday grey?
thread house habits? look out that
window for a change, reel in or back
as outsiders leave the habitat, at least
the red and blue ones, then the tips of his senses
to arise and alarm you

You must change without
within the will to, merely moment of
as much hill as nothing could be called here
and who to care where "here" is, romantic one
the winds blow, at least the grass seems

As the glass torso read out its pure lights
or poor lights, in which little is written
without which nothing could be seen to say
it's all housing up nicely today, the green
to blue that hovers, and shown I didn't write
this right

Sheer opticon, where birds could make a sandwich
Apollo goes, stretches to row beyond the nerves
go to makeup all this salvage here before us
inhabitants tending then loosing the pool by day
his eye piece trembles in brazen latches
caught as you'll be in no change beyond him
a berry patch could collect these things for you
that he has risen, you have stayed

Fog in a shot glass, cored the pen through paper
the landings get called verse, no butterfly
no remnants of clapboard stick in trim
tread the funnel's edges, all in the same
throat of rhyme, no endings as the sail goes
the wind does, in and out through this wet earthen throat
code note, beacon wink, cold betrayal
all those tolds of the real, all those icons
of pedal-back description, failing unction
you tapped him wrongly, you know, you child

Wet earth out of Dakota, the pen blade dips
his thin torso echoes, whites to the wind
no more messages, no backing round in toto
no friend stranger in the mentioning of trees
it keeps coming about that, and other
bronzen winters, how we laugh at their summers

Stop fleecing around and stall finally
behind the driven bush, your help's afire
your blame's abeam, I would have thought it saturnine
how out of light can you fret, still write?
those ones are having over water their saddle problems
in case I write, in window is a door
page by page might slam for

I made a date with the man in wheaten body armor
lest he make yawn, befriend beyond the boom we duck
it's sad to come savage then, don't you wind it all
bag around your prow, your sense of things ending?
a midnight laugh at dinosaurs or stones
whose head would fan loose and all the
muses come crabbing after? or a gull
lost hold on his throttle

Pieces of paper touched to the wall now
do stay, but the glowing firmament his chest
relaxes stops, send a call down for chimes
call me Harpo and extend my elbow
it's expansive this man standing upright
and his name equally, squall and bone
the sun finally tanned this sand
to a golden match for the sky

Hello, man the shadows, silence your salad kit
we'll get friendly later after the pin runs
those Barbary spiracles, the water's all going
back to where it'll leave soon, plasticene craft
leaves its color off, of, on
so you have me circle everything in repeats
torso for mast

Didn't he understand? We put these out
for stones at night, have to, not just paid for
to ounce out hardly in a heavenward do
clothes off, wrists locked, animal life over the side
that I made believe, what else got stirred
monkeys over the plantain marshes, wool by stripe

At least he had the sameness semblance never to be
a solace, heads up in the green window
feet up in a film, all they do is go by
and now it's what time after time?
somebody had elected us, truly house going up
shorts come down as a signal, shirt of an avenue
sense stripes, boats, wall of the water whistle
vanilla was the boat that shored my avenue

Shocking arcades, palace of the trebling dice
was deformed in the sails went around
that torso in the district middle invisible
you could slice off with a shovel, maniac
by maniac in clay-green drivel, the sands
not so far there but I can't reach them

Came by boat, went by perimeter
thought for a checklist in beige bent blouses
they nod as they kneel though I told them
house power only in that shade of blue
("back!" went the motor) (fairly gonzo
when a frog) then it's night time and the oils...

I came here this time by path, straight
by the torso, of an orange this way, they said
but I needn't have, sore and I didn't, no scene
at all, no redness of bronze on blonde planks
she ate what otherwise went for her dresses
pancake vision, lesser felt plectrum, old
as nose and just as ovum, the rearing heights
of Apollo Bald

This paper takes
well I
wouldn't say what
but night to come betide us
old will send and his clams, stride eights
that bird is doing
something to the shallows
frog stroke? or itch of deposit?
bird taken in an inch and flown

I want it all to jar together
whatever solid limits *and* the torso
here and even a makepiece there
an album memento of blurring fortune
to later get fogged in
lace and be spelled wrong
that jar with the teeth

This pepper leaks (better fix the felts on that axe)
lest later birds will call, and high in golden remedy
but the suction of the torso on the rest around it
nobody able to take notes, or rhyme an itch
the realm of invention squeaking 'round again
we'll have it summers, forget in winters
the black day of moles on the seating
headless could he even at all and eat us up?
(squeak)

And the breeze blows through his theramin toes
throttle by the threes using branches of trees
could peg his neck hole, stop this infernal seeing?
to get your number would know you have no number
about as fine as faucet failure and the threads gone

If his made-up nose gets thinner just hit the dimmer
have thought not attractive as you under sail
purple as the sea isn't and no letters came
(why do on rocks the cormorants rank so?)
don't ask for answers, merely lie
on your shell, sun

Morey Amsterdam showed then, purely blank to the torso
(I told you his cabin would be plain)
just as well the Wasatch as call him up
though maybe try his plume brandy, hats all off to
Jim the Failure used to know a few... no.
An event as stained as a purple bronze
a man as sure of his name as an answer then
what?

I came around again to blue fields with green blooms
an explosion mounting the Bark Casino
tuesday only, I could write anything (inefficacy)
these "chops" pretend around their own form of sand
as it's played out in yards of the bandsmen
granite mills matching the time
(I'd describe as a broadcast)

Settling down here, again no one to bother
the torso as a paid failure, field-stripped
so light I used up this month's vocabulary
merest attention to touch it off
thrilling as the bore of an open throat
(hot balloon sends up plume so cold)
lost his head I guess, the adages not to last him
just pending as the golden whistle and sand off all eyes

8VIII87
Chilmark

from *The Book of During,* IV

What we want is death. Not childhood, again for a second. A thing already here, unsorted. When we no longer face each other, cannot lock in, I can begin to see it. It begins to tell me. What is wanted is here so always now, tells when you are searched out. Look at the thin places.

This whole world is full of me, so I want to find the other, the death places. It is here so all around me, it outlines, too close I don't see it, I languish. Like when you fuck in a lock so close you want, but you want to see and can't, the closing body. The body that warms your eyes, that speaks through your bones. You lock in a sudden, and maybe the walls peel, and you *are* death for split. Amount is moment, not coincident, or coincidence is the call. And if your angel instructed you, you'd comply, no doubt. Or as if the dream rented the hall you now compulsively enter.

Washed dreams, hosed-down spells. Hanging the head all over again and seething up the words. Words to the traits, tends and muffled falls. That these ones must be washed out again and at all, I turn over turn you over to be fucked to be blazed then shorn of light. I sing you over the song to not repeat. And again the day the night. . . .

The spasm to squeeze you strong enough to remember your death. Shot back past childhood into the black. Turned out, if length tells, you were more at home there than in life. And I am moved to fuck again and again to recall it. The accompanying reverse toward a great series of successive rememberers is too well known to pursue here. And you have all spent more time saying it than fucking.

Well I realized we would go there where we know nobody, where we know one only. The world is divided into seines, some will pass through, some will remain held and surfaced away. Where you stop is where you begin. And in the night the whole lapidary outfit is turned loose on whatever joins. The surface at this point is far away. The nines in the mile book have broken. I dip my tongue in the ink and chew at this desk. Her whole body was covered, it seemed in one prolonged instant of ticking desire. Her skin scarfed in my subsidence.

Where I know one others seem to have known many. And the ones who have known death, everyone has known that pointless ebb. The angle of your arm is closer to it than most. The whole body's outline, why the tattooist wants to draw his lain body close with it. On the deck of the roof everyone watches for a twister. The inevitable hurrier will drop his edge.

It is I think that we are all strangers to this world, have come in a little bit out of the dark. Tell me about it at least, tell me your face if you can. If you could see what happens seeing yours. If you could let me tell you anything that is. The world is the only place where it is not dark. There are always lights on when you fuck. And the problem of seeing and then not seeing then. Picasso learned to draw. Writing as surely backing up from the subject. The poet should have written: So much depends *of*. You are the one who brings death. When I have you all so open to it.

For H.D.

1

trophies of pain I've gathered.   whose sorrow
do I shore up, in trifles?   the weavings,
paintings, jewels, plants, I bought

with my heart's hope.   rocks from the road
to Hell, broken pieces of statuary, ropes,
bricks, from the city of Dis.

encrusted.   they surround me: nest
the horror of each act from which I saved
a dried, dismembered hand.   poisoned

amulets, empty vials still fuming.   their tears
saved lovingly as my own.   to have
"lived passionately"   this secret

hoarding of passion.   Truth turned against itself.

2

Heart's truth, spat out of sleep, was only hate.
I caught it, on my pillows.   Tried
to turn it to diamonds.   Sometimes succeeded

so far as quartz in the hand.   Like ice it melted.
Heat of my will   burns down the walls around me
time after time.   Yet there remain

encrustations of old loves.   Filthy barnacles
sucking my marrow.   My illness:
that I am not blind,   yet cannot transmute

In body cauldron I carried
hate or indifference, anger,   clothed it
in child flesh,   & in the light

it seemed I had worked magic. But the stone
sticks in their throats. Night screams & morning tears
phantoms of fathers,   dead skin hung on

old bones.   Like jewels in the hair.

3

"I am a woman of pleasure"   & give back
salt for salt. Untrammeled by hope or knowledge
I have left these

in the grindstones of other thresholds. Now only bedrock
basalt to crack your breath. Beloved. To suck for drink.
I am not fair. But you are more than fair.

You are too kind. Still water   in which,
like a crystal, the phantoms dance.
Each carrying death like a spear,   for we die

of each other's hate, or indifference.   Draw blood
to draw out poison.   But it has seat
in heart of our heart, the hollow of the marrow

of our bones.   Salt for salt   & the desert
is infinite   it drinks
more juice than we carry.

4

O, I'd yet beg bread, or water,   wd lie
in the dry wash & pray the flood wd come
That my eyes unstick,   that I see stars

as I drown.   For 25 years, bruised, wounded,
I've hid in rocks.   Fed by hyenas, vultures, the despised
that chew carrion   & share the meal

which, sharing,   you lose caste;   forget
human laws.   My blood
tastes in my mouth like sand.

5

humiliated   time & again   by song
laughter from cracked lips.
power of incantation stirring to life

what shd sleep, like stone.   yet the turquoise
sparkles.   "happy to see you"   stars
beat against my skin.   what is mine:

cold prickles,   moving out
from spine.   pulsing skull
pushing to light.   burning bushes

that lie.   snow mountains where gods
leave laws, like stones.   Anubis in Utah
and tears.   and tears.   and tears

to bless my desert   and give back
song for salt.

Paracelsus:

Extract the juice which is itself a Light.

Pulp, manna, gentle
          Theriasin, ergot
like mold on flame, these red leaves
bursting
          from mesquite by the side
of dry creekbed.   Extract

the tar, the sticky
substance
          heart
                    of things
(each plant a star,   extract

the juice of stars
                    by circular stillation
smear
     the inner man w/the coction
till he burn
     like worms of light in quicksilver
not the false
     puffballs of marshfire,   extract

the heart of the empty heart
          it is full
of the star soul that paces fierce
in the deeps of earth
          the Red Man,
                    healer
in furs
     who carries a club

who carries
                 the pale homunculus
in his belly.
                 For you are angel, you call
the soul from plants

                 or pearls of ambergris
out of the grudging sea.
                 Extract arcanum. Separate
true Archeus from the false
                 the bitter
is not less potent—nor does clarity
bespeak truth.

                 Out of the heart of the ineffable
draw the black flecks of matter
                 & from these
the cold, blue fire.
                 Dry water. Immerse
yourself
                 though it be but a drop.
                               This Iliaster
flowers like the wind.
                 Out of the ash, the Eidolon of the world

Crystalline.
            Perfect

JOSEPH DONAHUE

Desire

Desire's green
and gold corona
in the wavering branch

and the shuttle of syllables through white light
and the pleasure of the mind of God permeating all accident
and no the guard cannot

shut the light from your cell.
The chasm of gold, spill of red on the river.
The black boat at midpoint and the island lifted in fire

or the incarnation
of color in a vivid field where
solitude opens toward you.

Not memory,
but its plentitude.
You awake from a joy

that trembles at the far end of time
unable to say what words have kissed you
in your sleep.

———————

Day's ferocity meanders
through the lack of significant feeling
(each watching

the face of the other fading,
each a ghost in the other's dream but only one is still alive)
and your thoughts circle back to Juan De La Cruz

89

his grimy dungeon when
tears still in evidence a woman steps from the shadow
of the psychiatrist's door giving you her number and the

prelude to an evening's
harmonic diaspora unrelated to
recent dark events.

———————

Words freshly tilted drift askew.
The aura of recent racial beatings touches the airy realm of the
fire escape where she talks about her diffidence

about the man she's "with"
and the city arrests its nightly glimmer
to attend her vulnerability and the rain mingles with

your discreet elation as
continuities in the lives of others rise
like land seen from an approaching ship

but then the ship veers into choppier regions.
You feel upbraided by the pettiness of your agonies
though you are older than you look and edging into a crisis

which seems both intermittent and perpetual
and partakes of the more sinister
of rationales regarding the presence of the poor

who lolled drugged
in broken boxes in icy weather as
further questions stir.

———————

Desire a city across the water which the attrition of leaves
makes visible or a time when place was simply the notation
of silence as through smoke and rain millennia exfoliate.

It's someone else's dream
this bewildered amusement left on your tape
the surprise party the world has arranged for you

and your life passes and you wait for the secret call
when the guests have arrived, you wait for
the one who will intimately mislead you through the rain.

Yes things seem to be happening
but far off and illegible like the bottom line of an eye chart.
You are frustrated in your search for some collapse of clarity

or deletion sufficient to break your
ritualized gestures of defeat, the way a sudden turn
toward intimacy in a conversation can resemble

a cycle of fire purifying your past.
But can you say what presses for entrance at the stern gate?
Now and then there is a flicker at the edge of things

cancelling all disappointment
lifting you in the wave of others enroute to work
as the world opens into amplitude and rushes into stillness.

You have lived in expectation
of some startling recompense, like some secret
Spanish Jew enduring the Reformation you have tended

this law in silence, amid adversity.
Meaninglessness was simply a mood which bothered you
but now you appear to shiver in this chaste defilement,

this voluptuous schism revitalizing all thought.
What was that shadow that flickered across the street?
Not a cloud, the living nightmare of a life, it passes now

as gold cataracts of light wash over the brick
braided and intricate as the portico of a Caribbean mosque.
There is no place you can enter and be safe at last.

Not even the raptures and hierarchies of art
or the luminous swath of rainclouds and blue mist
and the gold rooftop across the river

or the clusters of berries,
bare branch supple with raindrops
as the three sparrows rest and their weight does not

jostle the silver equipoise
of fallen rain tapering now
into exhilaration.

———————

At night the letters
recombine in hopeful bulletins.
Not promises, but the pleasure they give.

Flare or flashbulb as the speaker reviews the
abuses of a far off prison system,
her turban the color of early spring

yellow inside fresh shoots breaking into cold wetness.
As if you had torn up a snapshot of some
remembered bliss—

The kodachrome bits blow through the world
and incidents take on the color of that former time
though far from where you are.

Or as when the memory
of someone long dead brushes the mind—
You feel you have just seen a crucial part

of a life you can never know.
Where was that mountain town?
Why did the bare breasted occultist warn you so cryptically?

Why did you steal a car
and who was the man who died in the parlor
with such violent bravura?

An embarkation has been long underway.
(You dream of your brother. You miss him.
He comes in he's late for work but he wants to ask you

if you will give him a swimming lesson.)
Your routine opens into a sphere
colored with blankness and depth and beasts

from the scrolls of Renaissance cosmographers
and you discover that paralysis is part of the voyage
those twilit Sunday afternoons when phone rates are down

reconstructing daylight as night deepens.
Music cleansed of lament and
lutes and loved ones locked in earth as

from vast regions
facts bespeak an altered emptiness
and you sense a desire behind desire and to taste that

would be to know
the beauty God knew
the moment before Creation

when meanings mirrored
the need which evinced them.
No view of the river today

its threads of green and gold.
The man in the cell
turns beneath his ratty blanket.

He is a second
Jean Genet, equally
stroked and scolded

but destroying his books so that
his lovers can never be distracted from his whims
by the beauty of their image in the text.

————————

All things announce the hour
the plane's shadow cutting the cloudbank
ocean the fiery

splay of noon's winter mirror.
The cities of the earth glitter in the folds of mountains
and yet these dreams at last will lead you out of

famine and bondage.
You have no clear account of your route
except that a mystery sufficient to your desire

for comprehension awaits you.
Boat a fiery sliver toward what sea
its bowline script half risen from the froth

in the flux of inference adrift
in the echo of similitude across great distance
as in a notebook kept hidden for years and also filled

silver threads the
interweaving current
broken

by a black branch
held in a window that looks onto brick.
You cannot see, but you see.

You do not
feel at home, but
you are.

Transfigurations

for John Yau

I

Other lives, their jostle. The engineer
crumples error into a paper ball, hurls it
as I enter. Man in the locker room,
skeleton beneath pale ripples
of fleshless skin. At the corner phone,
the acting vice president, her son
beaten with a pipe in a drug transaction.
A girl in a skintight purple with a red sash
glimpsed through an elevator's closing door.
Hand on your shoulder, wrong number.
Other lives, your own, partaken of, or not.
In her white coat lamenting her difficulties.
A rancorous fruit eaten with ill effect.
The corpse upright on the median bench,
bits of bodies blown over the airwaves.
A sky-blue eye, clouded: a subway poster.
A swastika etched in the pupil.

II

Cruelties: Mayan priest: radio atheist:
Constantinople's walls and towers.
Mind crippled by doctrine. A man in a
motorized wheelchair questioned
with concern by a woman in remission.
Blue pool: the dead man's apartment.
Days at work with the boss not in.
No Summa survives the saint who writes it.
Message in red, left on my desk.
Bible with a nail driven through it
found where the convict took the girl.
The Grail. Fourfold method undone

95

by an envelope: noble ghost, you beckon.
Disparate myths: intertwined,
released as gospel. Days at work,
news of the suicide. Nothing done
but thoughts for the dead.

III

Misfiled at the precinct. A clipping
announcing a classmate's marriage, mailed
with bitter humor. We went at it for hours.
None of the old problems. Afterwards she slept,
but I was ecstatic. Newspaper cut, rolled
and tied in a handkerchief: disaster
followed when she followed her conscience.
Mount Tabor visible in evening light,
a deity revealed, and his prophets. Woman
in a blue dress. Her lost contact lens.
A snapshot once carried in a wallet
found amid the paperclips at the bottom
of a filing cabinet. The cop took the deposition.
Handkerchief full of money. On the mountaintop
with John and James. Fiery visions of spiritual bodies.
Unspoken cohesions as the data grows urgent.
The victim of the swindle opens the handkerchief.
Down from the mountain, far wall of the polis,
to sleep by an olive tree until dawn.
A postcard after they agreed not to write.
A table set with linen and silver.
Her entrance, nine years back. Asked by police
if a car was involved. Driven by hysteria to a shrink,
retelling the trauma with perfect timing.
You are not the victim of a swindle. You have
altered the terms of the agreement. Elijah, Christ
and Moses, etched in the pupil of an eye.

IV

Eye contact: refresher course on
symptoms. Realizing how you look.
A coat with stains from high school.
Summoned as a juror, expert in
feigned innocence. A friend you
give up on, an adversary you honor.
Colonial attitude of the mind
towards its residence. She allows
you to undress her, in fact she
encourages you. Plum blossom:
joy without repercussion. To think
of how you used to think. Anger
eases into languor. She leans from
the steamcloud, sips the cold beer on
the soapdish by the sink. To tally
the torments, that is not a full account.
Gold fleck: her eye: the flutter
preceding the mention of it.
Resented for the apartment's lobby:
had she lived here the attack
could not have happened. Reddish tint:
sunset on brick. Cluster of Jews
at ease on the street. We have half
an hour to get to the florist or
the plucked, bunched bouquet will be
bolted in, nightlight and alarm,
and we will arrive at the party
having failed in our promise.

V

Days at work, message in red ink. Phoned
long distance from a hospital bed. If I am
a living ghost how can I house the spirits
of the dead? Lavabo inter innocentes

manus meas: et circumdabo altare tuum,
Domine. Not that, but not uniformed of that.
Man draped in a Nazi flag, naked,
at a party after the performance. Conversation
with a puppeteer about the spirit world.
Dismal air quality, can't keep my lenses in.
Attached to oxygen. Infection abated.
The children wear masks when they visit.
Lord our brother has been dead three days.
The kidnapper called the station to request
a song, and shot himself before it came on.
Sky the color of tabloid print washed from my hands,
New York rinsed by rain. Deep breath in the silence.
Called by a voice both my own and not.
Adolescence in Egypt, acolyte
to an idol. Black horizon of a planet,
a narcotic flower opens. Dawn: the
unsettled dead on a riverbank. I sift
through manias, rigors, lapses. I hunger
to inhabit a living form. On the laundromat floor
the towel that Pil :e used. Golgotha. Sinai.
Tabor. Covered today by ash-colored clouds.

VI

This manual for a ballistics expert.
The jury clamors, no goddess descends
and Orestes condemned to scrub the
blood from his parent's house.
Beside the boarded drugstore the zealot
lashes the profligate teenagers.
At the podium: a senator lamenting his past.
All visible phenomena seem
evidence in a vast and unpublished
criminal proceeding. Reprieve
of morning crucified by noon.
Updraft up the avenue. Paper bag

clearing the girders of the new highrise.
Welder's spark, downward arc of slight fire.
Let love gather my scattered limbs.
Horror deepening the hope.
In corrupt versions of the legend
the gods welcome the murderer. Sunlight,
Whitened steps. A skull twisted like
paraffin left on a hot stove. As I unpack
my lunch: tales of a plastic surgeon on the
Amtrak to Boston. Disfigured,
restored, which face is the true one?
Scales. Banquet hall of the dead.
Questions still to come from the throne
I stand before.

Opiate Phobia

At times the real
seems no more than events passing

My clothes are clean
but I'm dirty

& these feelings of defilement
are not at all what was requested

verifying
citizenship here

among the esoterica stalls,
among the tears of the treacherous.

Though you are not
the earthly things you see

but soul
& intellect

exceeding the circuit of heaven
your words are drowning audibly now in a red

& irradiated
throat.

All's icing over
& the dream's recurrent

figures fly
away

STEPHEN ELLIS

Weathered Ides Grant Young Flesh
for Karen Driscoll

obsession is the mania dawn breaks blush
    across these eastern hills
                atmospheric
rise through flesh made pink at the tips
    of our inflammation
              upon a marriage bed
of grass grown out of imagining
    the winter's end
            an apex green
as search of hand in drift about the mantle
    of your hips now seized

(trees caught in light to a sparrow's grizzled song)

in folds of fucking straight through plush of pores
    dilated dark in brightness let
             as harsh to its flame
    drawn golden down each limb
               bestarred
and risen to our hearts' decanting
    song between our legs

attests the sap and salting down of spring

                the inapparent
grass beneath the snow
        as burns

as turns *into*, the green of touch *remembered*

on our passing skins affirms

Your Poems at Daybreak,
the Destruction of Knossos by Afternoon
for Jeff Gburek

The portent clear as ever be, brilliant crimson
petals stem the heart's twigs, each, Ozymandian
membrane of spring's taut drum the skein of green
within which hid, Hittitic archives spill from rim
this flowered flesh, its gnash unfurled as if miles tra-
versed within the rose, the heart's pelt, naked, mirthful
rise unto a flush of face, profundity begot as tactical
surprise, the pace by which each surface doth submit,
palms up, psalm laid low as thought, prismatic ever
place felt true, adjacency's tactile surmisings keen
indeed its rash, that space exactly where one's bred
obsession's bulwark 'gainst hearts' disguise, borne
each kingdom's come yet ever come to flower, desire
fleeting unto rise, similitude, person, flame & hour

NORMAN FINKELSTEIN

from *Track*

~~

And so was lost in the forest
among many others
derided or derived

with night coming on
with wolves
with nothing but the Name.

~

Emptied and emptied
at the limit of the zone
you have already traversed

having come to the limit
already
always already.

~

And so broke the promise
to the pronouns among many others
the idle promise

or promise of the ideal
zone or forest
among many others.

~

Wolf son of the Name
the fire in the forest
center of the zone

derided or denied
emptied and emptied
or burning and burning.

~

And in the fire is a face
And in the mirror is a face
And in the mirror is a fire

until the combinations are exhausted
and nothing is left
but a prayer for strength.

~

Blessed are the lines
from one to six
Blessed are the combinations

The thief
and the bride of the thief
and the home among the trees.

———————————

~~

Call this zone a forest
call this man a thief
call his wife his wife

so that all "falls into place"
And those?
—children of course.

~

Arrived or on the way
one said to another
what is that music?

or no more music
I stole it
said the thief.

~

Falling asleep
afternoon or evening
with no more music

though the house is filled with music
listen wife listen
listen children.

~

Listen to the children
who know their way about the forest
and return with stories

which the thief steals
exchanging them
for a kind of music.

~

Listen to the music
which knows its way about the forest
and returns with stories

which the thief steals
obsessively
thinking they're allegories.

~

Independent as any wife
or thief before his arrest
the stories in the forest

at home in the forest
wait there patiently
to be exchanged for music.

Morning

Done with trying — no one's awake — it's dark
Dawn won't be here — no feeling in myth,
this book, or anything else around you —
Only wait — everything will come
exactly as you planned.

It's the kind of language you remember,
Henry said, quoting Auden
        but mysterious at first;
a poem is memorable language.

That's sentimental.
You'll remember nothing.
There'll be nothing to feel.

Hermetic Silence

for Joseph Donahue

We aren't in charge, of course, and never were, and any caustic feeling, your regret or mine, becomes the sustenance, iconic presence that we harbor in this sign. I ask you here but do not speak what you intend — and in this way define regret. The room is regular, the entropy we could not find: we say we should not care. The room is singular, and now we watch convention flutter in disgust and discontent, refusing its participant, conceit. Not fear, at least no longer fear, but knowledge I could now become no more than what you thought, has kept me here. We watch that modern paradigm, the other man, the one whose head is gently brought to bear, and words that freeze in discontent will now bestow whatever grace we've got, remembering desire. He's everything I could not be; I take his form in mine.

So accusation, clement in dependency, is organized defeat.

Yet if this myth were half the truth, you'd be within the reach of my Adonic need, adverse to everything dispensed with Roman law.

I took your part within the sounds along the oily street, whose cancerous protection we identified and grew. Say this: one day I never loved the words but did love you, and so again remembered fear, for then I could distrust the word within the self, the tone within the ear. The other one had brought us both to bear. And then I thought I need him here.

The god delights us in his Orphic spring. When we're alone, his red roots fill us and we sing.

Apollo is our fiction, and we say we repossess the attitude that drives us in despair. The eyes of all around are glass, and none see you, or me, though in his finery they'd try to find their confirmation for that hollow sight: the roots within that run with blood and fear. This cheapened plastic land is colored up with flame. All things are roused when you restrain desire, or when some friend or friendship, like your own, learns through hate to please.

So gnosis lies in hiding, waiting. Deny me here. The only thing you can't deny is fear.

In Your Words

In time, we will not kiss, and your face given into fire will tantalize my dreams, and I will sear my hair as I lean close, looking at your shadow in the smoke. That much will rise, and singing for me then, as you can not sing now, it will emerge with other songs, in tight unyielding chords.

The Marriage of True Minds

The question keeps reflecting on itself: when marriage comes to nothing, promises insist on some intensity, and so you wait. In this sweet constancy, there's no more anger than a trivial delight. The lady gives the clerk his change and nothing more. She stands here by the bed in sullen majesty and is alone. Numerals begin their evolution, minutes move, but real achievement lies in lying still.

The vanity of joy in this cold jelly on your hands is colored like New England dawn, in guilt, anticipations of the past. For if we're men and married, we understand remorse through sacrifice, contrition waiting there, where you have never been.

And in this way, fleeing me, you fill my last demand.

Your image is the image you propose, but now you forfeit night and feel disease along the margins of my private room. Someone pries your arms apart, revealing to the rest of us the value of the air. And he arrives in secret where aggression can't recall these forms without repeated signs. All things exist, but none of them restrain the tedious sun today, and so consideration burns. In this, recall your thighs and anger, the yellow sores that run.

And so I waste our passion in its shadow, wanting mine to be some pleasure on the edge. I want to feel a casual remorse, not writing you, but custom, as you said, is never present in the dawn. And yet, dear lady, it is you who would not kiss.

In this, you are archaic speech itself, and even angels know where caged beasts dwell. And so upon demand, they tell me now. The snake, whose burrow is the cheek, slithers out along my tongue; I watch it find the sun.

The shore does nothing for the sand; nothing's living there. We watch it with the intricate release we get from books and tell ourselves that sailors are allowed what we can never see. And yet the boys wait silently behind the silver glass. Who's shattered now?

And this: not desiring what you most desire, you wash the walls, erase the images of rancor, spleen. But when they're bleached, then memory's a mirror, and mirrors without malice, angels say, are bliss.

So humor rises, becomes methodical with age, wiser than the minotaur I followed with your hands. The filaments of sunny afternoons could find you now, but you, at least the you I used to know, are locked in marble lands. I leave this room and find the blood is running through the sand. It is the god who takes us through the dead, and lets me kiss each face and find time measured everywhere.

Who's to blame? I sometimes wish to feel the final ashes of your hair, but as it is, in my New England way, I place these lips in stone, and, bargaining with mirrors for their skin, I reconstruct your ecstacy, alone.

KATHLEEN FRASER

Frammenti Romani:

"marks and evidence of events"

— for the photographer, Kenneth Josephson

Ache
drawn border's arousal

    Arise new radio gleeful
    to them

— these loud-struck ochre spaces —
re-heard and re-
sung little
motorscooter vices,

Repeat the fruited song
gone wings, what

    is farthest
    hear

Accede shadow able

   redoubtable cycle

   green when awake now

Noble hairpin

   spring's prong

   block-long cyclone

~

To accelerate

   (radiant outward from her)

radial's own wave

Porcelain light opens

plum waist, wool-sweet cape of

   thunder's borders.

Pulled out and re-drawn

"the relation of real color"

to soaked walls, a difference of
squash persimmon exteriors

— Michelangelo, given the choice,
retaliates —

in restauro's reserve
massive wave of Roman brick
and door

Yawn also
single balconey's coral geraniums

~

In thicket eyes as in
pollened
yellow streams of mimosa
given

(that flower stuck tile

ceramic-struck
field forever, some
nature's ideal)

bellowing leaves,
pared stems seeds skins make

noon's hollow noise

113

Now pried from hand's huge fabric clouds

        amorphous
        off-white
        awry

but   could   yet   see

could spot exactly where
to keep the illumined
alum honey hive-
ing

                            ∼

". . . put honeycomb there with
slabs of gorgonzola
on the bare
table, spread
the walnut bread with it
and a little
honey
and the Barolo from
Aldo Conterno . . ."

(How more
could you be

third-person
bound for scrutiny?

Barolo-dark sea)

~

Closest,
restored sections of

what is farthest

late drawn borders
re-examined

pulled out as "cuts"

     (resistant
     that tiny sweet "heart" of

oxygen's nerve)

Written in sleep's fore-glow
mid-afternoon
pallor struck light

    Light before dog
    rubber noise
    hose elaborate

street's papaya dense plaster
pessimism
    clarified surface duress

~

Aware. O here.

Be there, too, savory rattle.

Afternoon's little zipper
pulls you up each fruiting
rutting assault. Leaves contend!
Pips grow larger even. And figs soon.
Bend.

Tight fist that held you,
you entirely separate —

what is mortal
in this body.

Rome
July, 1990

Boot, wet sand and more white

Boot, wet sand and more white along the borders defining a trail of lush chemicals we adhere to. Your mouth, the cold ocean, these flecks of splitting light I never could paint. White silver nitrate. Blue breaking spilling. Show me the long shot. We sit inside its wide lens. Where does a sea wall ever curve again, with this patience?

Concrete arcs fall away from you. Full scale body throws its limit of miles out, to take in the tiny but animate species we cling to. Multiples of rough wet fur. Terrier leaping in waves each time her red hair flings forward with the pitch. Dives again for the moon still daylight floats. Every object on its stretching membrane, not hurried. You touch the little spots which rise and listen and slowly grow wet.

These labdanum hours

You couldn't find it in the bird's weight
pulling an arc through the twig. You must

catch yourself somewhere or fall anywhere.
Four cherries, red showing through

green webs. The surprise may not catch you
and that is the trouble. A whole new life

may be just another tree. Now the floor
is as clean as vinegar. It shines

from rubbing. Sleeping inside your little
and constant coughs, you could hear

someone helping you, finally waking.
The helper has her rags and tools.

With tenacity she hangs on to the dimming
vision. You are trying too hard

to enter this world. The door is open.
What can you find in this

that is yours, wholly? A belief,
not to be divided into silken strands

in air. This childish hope. I give you up,
each day, to another. Abstract acts

of generosity, as we dream in two positions
on the bed, with the softer, lighter pillows

just under our heads, some slight elevation.
Whole sentences are subtracted from

conversation. Darkness moves continuously
behind that line where the sun presses.

To let go of shapes held in peaches,
the bruise of a thumb and forced sweetness.

You were the lightest of all
the silver-white metals.

FORREST GANDER

A Table Laid with Horrors

I AM GOING ON A JOURNEY AND I WILL BRING:
flour and sandals, a fine-toothed comb and sourballs, this fish
hook and silt in my pockets. I take fibula and sternum, your
false pregnancy, a slip knot. Filtertips and soup du jour.
What I leave—
all things visible, light of the body, total number of my days—
are field notes and sheep's eyes, Fahrenheit
of sexual love, foreplay then your spotting, frost heave
and sugar beets,
the foster moon, twilights soughing. I let my face to the
screw worm,
my flesh to slugs. *There is a river the streams whereof.* . . .
Fair copy to second readers; to the fire ants my sputum.
I tender fire
opal to slop jar. Fill my feather pillow with skunk cabbage.
Forgive me
unfinished manuscripts, the burnt skillet, *the burthen of my passing.*
I bequeath fellatios to scarlet tanagers, fanfaronade
to my silent partner; in the flood plain, signs of the cross.
To my funeral bring spikenard. Place four scabs
on the first saltlick. A fait accompli in standard time.
The fire plug
among sego lilies. I only want this
footstool and my sign manual,
fascinating sideburns. I take fingernails sprouting;
from our kitchen floor
the sole prints. The front page plus my shaving kit. I leave
like a felon
with a sparring partner, famished and slakeless.
Like four horsemen
and their snake oil. Farewells in a saxophone. A flicker, a sputter,
faggots for Savonarola. Final stopgap. *My coming in my going out.*
Fresh heart and salt.

Fire Music

the broken glass of river
reflects the sky
in shards, as a flurry
of keeping, held out
ruins, present, like the gods
of the heart's edge

there's a humming bird
at the bottle bush tree
to burning wood, *there's always*
a face in the flames
though the foot slips

when I said *map* I meant
borrowed time
that scales the esplanade of moon
posing as a trick
aloneness as an originality
now worse or better
now sharp or winter

the grass is a green flame
under the blanket of snow
the underside of the clock's noise,
a muscle that soaks up the day

the color of a blade
as the flame passes over it
over the flux of waiting
where years skid

a mirror
no stone can crack
a shoe to walk in
an oar

that disaffects the waves, still
born gravity to lake's blackness

interfere for all stolen things
flying things the color of blood
is the affect in the machine

Near Hermes

your European son is gone, a trench
cut through to rusting iron
the smallness of the hours run
and sight becomes clearer
that is left behind

an eye stares back
from a cleaving in the mind, and walls
tumble on the floor
the hand grasps, from being
one thing and not the other
circumstances of its call
now into a labyrinth of care

I set out in a leaking boat
across a lake of ancestor's heads
to eat through walls of paper
with the solvent ink

mnemonic acid
just the distance between
one's own feet

music to question thought, thought
to question action, markings
on the wall where the ivy was
sheet rock dust and ground swell

fragments of an individual course
in the net of breath and syllable and world

the opposites of origin, to remember
the plant's shadow, shadow's flame
cords tangle, to grip the heart
seasons family are, mode of carbon
living in things of wood

JOHN HIGH

from *the lives of thomas— episodes& prayers*

mustard seeds in her field

the difference between those
coming&
those going
requires a look at the hands
alive in the world
the dog barks when one comes or goes
if a response is necessary
go to the bone
smell our blood
what is appearance
&absence combined
finds itself here
among the corpses

• • •

an open mouth
knows what is enough
look inside
the blind speaking
a possibility of
speaking   the body's fields
stripped
&calling in this ridge of hills

alone   look again
sacrifice of the stoned pavillion
listen for
the eye's flicker& these sheep
gathering outside the rain
expansive steppes   shallowness of the stream
                &then
sun& stars&
romance you want to touch
what strikes within   the interior
of the nose's hair/   breath& impulse
when anyone comes or goes

•   •   •

what we see is not at this garden's edge
black ants crawling
about the sleeve
into your socks
somewhere we possess
a nowhere
whose God& love present
can't say it
a troubled affair&
without language as the mirage enters
to live in the deer as she runs toward
the hunter's call
our drunkenness&
crossing between the crushed stones
dusted heaps of gone grasslands
though death
begins
past their fields

• • •

these are the unspoken details
born out of so many days
walking
the vanishing skies& what follows
as the rains close in
thomas, why have you come so far
to hear so little
only the drowned
fish remain
in the waters do we
find such articulate difference
nothing comparable to emotion
because we know that outside it
we have no being

          •   •   •

the
world   bends
the curtains
&converses the mirror
along the tracks
maybe her corpse
sustaining because
in this way
there is no shit beyond us
the test we set for them
they have passed
what country have they come from
find a moment
&smoke in it
if this is
all we have
celebrate the hour

ANSELM HOLLO

on the occasion of becoming an echo

the goddess stands in front of the cave
waves me into the drawing   eyes
like an afterthought
dotted in   green

gaia   drawn by a six-year-old
very clear

many more things in this room
books chairs a bed
at least two people
(how many more in their dreams)
but the signals are garbled
garbled

i mean (he says
who is i   who is i?)
mean well i want the whole world to love me
not need me at all

the goddess stands in front of her cave
not waving me in   just raising her hands
as if to say "well   who's to tell you?"
once upon a time
my head says   there was a man he got very tired
he went to sleep & didn't dream
didn't even sleep but was gone

out
& out there
all things were clear

mescalito

walked past
the back of my head
while holding
i was
another
equally hairéd head

he did walk past
wearing big rubber raincoat
& what are known as
"wellington" boots

slosh
slosh

&
out
the
door

oh, yes
*

sir arthur conan doyle & his contemporaries misunderstood the nature of
'ordeal poison', re-clarified by glover, leary, castaneda, & others: 'ordeal
potion' would see a less biased description, or pseudonym, for one of the
initial manifestations of spirit guides, allies, forgotten gods—as rilke has
them in his aphoristic "can you still play the old songs":
*
can you still play the old songs o play it again sam
the way they weave through my gloom like planes with silver wings
that toward secret casablanca sweep
over the evening sea
& as they come in to land   it is only just spring   spring
& there   on solitary paths   the forgotten gods
are no joke
though patient   & smiling

Argument for Resurrection

for William Rourke

The sum of two and one: a cardinal number.
Any symbol for this number, as 3, iii, or III.
Anything consisting of or representing three units,
as a playing card, team, etc. Being one more
than two. A circus in which separate acts
are carried on simultaneously in three ring-like
enclosures. Any situation characterized
by simultaneous activities, especially of bewildering
variety. To give a rotary motion to:
cause to rotate, as about an axis. To change
the position of, as by rotating: to turn the ground.
We buried him yesterday. To move so that the upper side
becomes the under: to turn the page. To bring
the subsoil to the surface, as by plowing or spading.
To revolve mentally: ponder: often with over.
We made a pact that he would come back briefly.
A situation requiring a choice between
equally confusing alternatives; a perplexing
predicament. An argument that presents a protagonist
with two (or more) alternatives, but is equally
conclusive against her, whichever alternative
she chooses, the third point being the angle
of observation. Having a cavity within;
enclosing an empty space; not solid; a hollow
sphere. Having a deep opening or depression
formed by scooping out: concave. A valley; basin.
A round, wide shallow vessel, often with sloping sides.
A vessel resembling this, as the scale or pan
of a balance. The amount that a basin will hold.
She carefully weighed the alternatives.
Toward what is ahead or what is in front; onward.
Out into a conspicuous position. The actual remains
of plants or animals preserved in the rocks
of the earth's crust. Some petrified trace

of the existence of an early organism, as a footprint.
One of certain inorganic objects or phenomena
of ancient geological ages, as solidified ripple marks.
To become slightly agitated on the surface,
as water running over a rough, pebbly memory,
or blown by a light breeze. To set or institute
a different cycle in: He is both absent and present.
An open way for public passage, especially from one
city, town, or village to another. Any way
of advancing or progressing: the road to release.
Road, highroad, turnpike, lane, and thoroughfare
are compared as they denote ways for interurban or rural
travel. Road is the general word. A highroad
is one adapted for fast travel, as by the elimination
of steep hills, sharp curves, frequent intersections,
and the like. Thoroughfare is a road accessible
at both ends: this word is now rare in specific names,
but survives in the phrase *No thoroughfare.*
To consider again, especially with a view
to a reversal of a previous action. A turnpike
is a road on which a toll is collected. A lane
is a private road giving access to a public thoroughfare,
or maybe a narrow road. Not fastened
or confined; unbound: a loose end. Something left
undecided or undone, as a task, decision, etc.
We negotiated the passage. The lane was open.
The act of bursting into leaf, or the state
of being in leaf. The arrangement or formation
of leaves in a bud. In certain rocks, a crystalline
formation into leaf-like layers: also the layers themselves.
The consecutive numbering of the leaves of a book.
A bound set of printed sheets of paper, usually between
covers. A volume of blank or ruled pages
for written entries: a ledger, register, etc.
Something regarded as a source of inspiration:
the book of experience. By memory.
To enter or list in a book. To arrange for
beforehand, as accommodations or seats.
Joining; connective. Serving to unite both meaning

and construction. The frontier line or district
of a country. A design or stripe in the margins
of a page or book. A bordering strip of ground,
commonly planted with flowers, as along the edge
of a walk. To lie along the border of; bound.
To strike and spring back from a surface, as a ball.
To leap; move by a series of leaps. To cause
to bound with joy. Made fast; tied with bonds.
Having cover or binding. Certain; sure: It's bound
to rain. Devotedly attached to. Having one's course
directed; on the way; destined: bound for home.

Drawing Room Drama

Concealed in the style of a late manner,
It was the spectator hiding behind the curtain
Celebrating the discrepancy
That the context of action conditions the illusion.
The desire to explore has tainted the evening
With a noiseless rush of jazzy agitation for three nights running.
Denial has sufficed to keep the story tame.
Show me the ingenious apparatus, you insist. All done
Zestfully, crowding in with invented imagery.
Ghosts drop by to pay respects.
You paper yourself with imaginary surface,
Paint the finish with pastel colors,
Endless varieties portraying the face
Required to play the part and figure out the play.

The spectator bears resemblance,
Tangles in detail, costumes herself in similar
Attire. The furniture has rebelled
In disagreement, stood its ground and said,
We no longer conform to function, we no longer intend
To furnish the enterprise. The architecture is drawn
Into the conversation, cast into the drawing room,
Vaulting through false arches of clever conceit.
A moon-struck illumination filters
Through the dust clinging to the window pane,
Spreads its blanket around the event.
How do we interpret these scenes, a simple sight-reading
Providing so few clues? Requirements lift
As the mechanical descends,
Directing the action from a repertory of contingent solutions.
An impenetrable self-reference locks the only door.

Deep Season

Discarded papers trembled in the sudden flurry
Of winter storms; the mail arrived later
Each day. We waited for the change.
Familiar streets were rerouted, old paths
Dug up to repair ruptured water mains.
The only change we witnessed was an instinctive loss
Of the actual extinguishing the visible
Terrain, your pointed finger
Directing attention to services drawing us out into the cold.
As the brass tacks of the literal come unpinned,
All frames of reference passing away
Into a white so blinding it pierced our eyes,
We stumbled dizzily through thin air, tracing copies
Over original intentions, duplicates, triplicates
Melting away until the very thing itself hung out to dry.
A coarseness of expression sufficed to say
It had its reasons for calling.

Seven Doors Away

A hinged, sliding, folding or rotating structure,
as of wood, metal, or straw, used for closing
or opening an entrance to a house. A doorway
often resembling an entire building or room:
to live seven doors away. Any means of entrance,
exit, or approach. Access. The doorbell rang
at seven o'clock. To draw or scribble
in an aimless manner. A design, figure, picture, etc.,
made in an aimless, preoccupied way. I was doodling
away my time when the doorbell rang, falling
backward at seven o'clock into various reversals
of fortune. Descent. A downward movement.
The fine soft plumage of birds under the feathers.
Down by the edge, the effects were carried out.
She had said something would occur to this effect.
Breaking against the edge, down by the water,
our conversation had come to cross-purposes.
A double stitch in the form of an X. Needlework
made with such a stitch. A note or reference
directing a reader from one part of a book,
index., etc., to another part. The faculty
by which distinctions are made between moral
right and wrong, especially regarding one's conduct.
Inner thought. An informal talk with another.
She had engaged me in strange figures
of conversation, opening the door to confusion.
To leave outside in an unsheltered place
so as to cause the death of by cold, starvation, etc.
To expose a feeling to the elements. I had left
myself outside unknowingly quite some time ago.
She had been taken to an emergency shelter.
Something had survived. I invited her to sit down.
A particular way of looking, speaking, etc.,
indicative of something known; especially
a particular cast of features. A serious expression
on my face brought her back. A clear choice
to resume our conversation. To assure the validity

of; verify. To render valid and binding
by formal approval or acceptance. I asked
for appropriate identification. Some evidence
by which to know. Any sign would do.
A small quantity of liquid, shaped
like a tiny ball or pear; globule. A very small
amount of anything, especially of a liquid.
A liquid medicine in drops. Something
resembling a drop of hard candy or a pendant
of a chandelier. Something designed to fall,
slide, or hang down from a higher point,
as a trap door or drop curtain.
A stage curtain that can be raised and lowered.
The atmosphere was pendant with possibility.
A slot or aperture, as in a mailbox,
through which letters, words, phrases, etc.,
are pushed so as to fall into a receptacle.
A falling off or away of a supporting surface:
a sheer drop at the edge of a cliff.
An incline or slope, especially when abrupt or steep.
To leave out; omit, as a word, line, or stitch.
To have no more to do with; have done with; dismiss:
to drop an unpleasant subject. She told me
supplies had been parachuted in for her survival.
We dropped the subject of our quarrel.
She had only dropped by for a minute, she explained.
Consuming immediately what is obtained; impoverished.
To bring into or set in a specified or implied place
or position; lay: Put the book on the table.
To bring into a specified state, condition,
or relation. To obtain an address.

Lost in the Galleries

But this view in the museum. A tear in the canvas
(*the upper story refuses weather, won't allow argument,*
transforms the difference
        Changing by the hour, by the season,
This face of trespassing on the preserve of ghosts,
        (*into a checkered floor, tiled perspective*
diminishing through all this resistance, or were they hosts?
So much depends on stones across the way leaning anxiously
Toward inscription, their only submission
        (*two horses circle the moon's shadow*
falling through an empty map implied by this absence of effort,
a flawless dream etched into the frame
Plain as the light of day, but now we've come across another corner
        Merely through this second explanation,
Prompted pleasure and a place to rest and reconsider
        what was inscribed in the stones: *you were once*
so easily convinced, charmed by the horses and their image reversed
A mere turn of thought, as the picture knew metaphor
Would turn from a place yielding neither rhyme
Nor reason, but enough for faith to signal a way
        (*— what beauty is if you have not been there,*
witnessed the long procession unravelling the way,
Casting a path through arcades of habit hardened into fact.
        (*only now the horses turn our way,*
        see we've watched them all along,
Two horses circle the moon's shadow
Falling through an empty gallery,
        (*witnessed what was inscribed in the stones*
        as our own picture casting shadows on itself
The upper story defines our narrative, dismisses argument,
        Plots our differences into a checkered floor,
Tiled perspective diminishing through all this resistance
        We've packed away, can't possibly deconstruct,
(*unwraps the rule around itself, leading provenance,*
        Builds long vistas of possibility.
But this view in the museum. A tear in the canvas.
An elaborate conviction grows all around us,

Willowed longing, blooming arrangements
Through the garden now submitting to reason.
      (*and then you turn into another gallery, only here*
time has diminished into another season,
            another introduction summoned quickly,
Yes, an acquaintance made swiftly, oh,
            But we argued anyway, wouldn't leave it alone,
Kept turning the issue over in disbelief, wandered through
Every leveled remark until the grounds were covered,
(*two horses graze, jump the fence framing the vanishing point.*
      Now, what was that argument about?
The argument surveyed and rendered into this vast form,
            (*filled with light, traceries of what we wouldn't agree upon,*
crafted into architecture,
A blend of pure faith and the landscape we were drafted into.

A Reading

You are impatient, says the oracle.
The weather has arrived cloudy, another day's conclusion
Shot with unraveling paths set back

From the shore. An ocean's breeze reshuffles the cards
Across the deck, disorder restored to pattern,
A chance you pattern yourself toward.

Prompted to rethink your question,
Which might, with grace, lift you above the determined
Arrangement currents have washed you against,

You play another hand. A chance you pattern yourself
Against lifts back through selves
You have assumed, fools sprung from oracle

Beginnings, framed inside the gold-leaf border
Of the cards played in patience
When it wasn't in the cards to share the evening

With another. And what of crossed destiny?
Teased out of solitaire, prompted by impatience,
You think you have been courted by the cards.

Strange, how this pattern unravels
Inside the tale arranged for the oracle's pleasure.
A link, after all, you think.

Torn Parts: the story

Was the discovery of a brother walking in a storm
Made one winter hot and sheets all sweat, lip and twist

This was the true love which you guys give up
For home as if beggars want to turn into candy

Awake was how we sat in arms, impermanent on a black
floor
Fear wormed into the rear of a room

It was not pink now but POWER AND LIGHT
Looked too near, you know

Every perception's an affirmative want
A memory? Or let's call it time. I'm pretty sure it is

Some word
When time and memory
Are the same, then I think I have a brain

Lace imitates snow on the nine panes
I wonder at all the winters
I survived without a human thought

"Imagination" sets off a glitter as hard as bitten sand

Relatives to numbers, trial and error
Unpossessable as pebbles

Children hold everything in, a secret between them
Who does not exist and

Between five and seven. . .
And as for good fortune. . .
The desire for enlightenment
And then children, judging my face

I have to wait

Lace babies dot the glass above the stove

Who fell into this grace: powerless without cause

Only by his silence knew his send-out
His face looked as if it had been visioned
In the sleep of a missus rushing with hairpins off her
head

He ran into a little bit of—machine, a yawn.
Made a cash withdrawal
Bought linen and ivory for the excitement of his sex

The Cross. One moment. Or meant. Meaningless

A he or a she. A he AND a she.
The little boy across my knees
Leaned back to sleep in his mystery

They graved out a way to dig deep holes from punches
It was fucking

At dusk a man called Criminal was calling to kill:
"You kidnapped the owner of this heart,
Brother."

You (we) guys got drunk from the fearful one
Chasing snowflakes into a face on the glass

Hate-water swelled into ice
All questions had a whatever to them

Better it be a paper boy

You hang in a tree
Than a feeling boy
I wonder if he felt sorry
Later, now, leaving

Us here (in the storm, outside, poor)

Who is the you, he asked
She:
There are lots of you

Madame Abandon hid herself among surprises
I was going to mention
Until I saw him standing by
The wrong-way water

Hiss of wind, ice in glass
Hits those who couldn't exist without their perceptions

She is the way. It's always been
Dry until the railroad is a riverbed

What I mean is:
establish ground from which we can continue calling

Can we quit the quiet imposed by sevens, a longer Lent
And penance when I don't know if I can ever feel

The same tale twice

Do you own land now but didn't suffer
Like a master never home from the forest, Mister

. . . but to forgive him for breaking his promise,
I've found no way since. But to never forget.

Impeccable as a north white house
I am the world, he said and left.

SUSAN HOWE

Thorow

During the winter and spring of 1987 I had a writer-in-residency grant to teach a poetry workshop once a week at the Lake George Arts Project, in the town of Lake George, New York. I rented a cabin off the road to Bolton Landing, at the edge of the lake. The town, or what is left of a town, is a travesty. Scores of two-star motels have been arbitrarily scrambled between gas stations and gift shops selling Indian trinkets, china jugs shaped like breasts with nipples for spouts, American flags in all shapes and sizes, and pornographic bumper-stickers. There are two Laundromats, the inevitable McDonald's, a Howard Johnson, assorted discount leather outlets, video arcades, a miniature golf course, two run-down amusement parks, a fake fort where a real one once stood, a Dairy-Mart, a Donutland, and a four-star Ramada Inn built over an ancient Indian burial ground. Everything graft, everything grafted. And what is left when spirits have fled from holy places? In winter the Simulacrum is closed for the season.

I went there alone, and until I became friends with some of my students, I didn't know anyone. After I learned to keep out of town, and after the first panic of dislocation had subsided, I moved into the weather's fluctuation. Let myself drift in the rise and fall of light and snow, re-reading re-tracing once-upon

Narrative in Non-Narrative

I thought I stood on the shores of a history of the world where forms of wildness brought up by memory become desire and multiply.

Lake George was a blade of ice to write across not knowing what She.

Interior assembling of forces underneath earth's eye. Yes, she, the Strange, excluded from formalism. I heard poems inhabited by voices.

In the seventeenth century European adventurer-traders burst through the forest to discover this particular long clear body of fresh water. They brought our story to it. Pathfinding believers in God and grammar spelled the lake into *place*. They have renamed it several times since. In paternal colonial systems a positivist efficiency appropriates primal indeterminacy.

In March, 1987, looking for what is looking, I went down to unknown regions of indifferentiation. The Adirondacks *occupied* me.

Gilles Deleuze and Felix Guattari have written in an essay called "May, 1914. One or Several Wolves?": "The proper name (*nom propre*) does not designate an individual: it is on the contrary when the individual opens up to the multiplicities pervading him or her, at the outcome of the most severe operation of depersonalization, that he or she acquires his or her true proper name. The proper name is the instantaneous apprehension of a multiplicity. The proper name is the subject of a pure infinitive comprehended as such in a field of intensity."

Thoreau once wrote to a friend: "am glad to see that you have studied out the ponds, got the Indian names straightened out—which means made more crooked—&c. &c."

Sir Humphrey Gilbert wrote in *A New Passage To Cataia*: "To proove that the Indians aforenamed came not by the Northeast, and that there is no thorow passage navigable that way."

Thoreau never visited the Adirondacks. His book about the wilderness and mountains in Maine is called *Ktaadn*.

Work penetrated by the edge of author, traverses multiplicities, light letters exploding apprehension suppose when individual hearing

Every name driven will be as another rivet in the machine of a universe flux

I

Go on the Scout they say
They will go near Swegachey

I have snow shoes and Indian shoes

Idea of my present
not my silence

Surprise is not so much
Hurried and tossed about
that I have not had time

From the Fort but the snow
falling very deep
remained a fortnight
Two to view the Fort & get a scalp
domain of transcendental subjectivity
Etymology the this

present in the past now
So many thread

———————

Fence blown down in a winter storm

darkened by outstripped possession
Field stretching out of the world

this book is as old as the people

There are traces of blood in a fairy tale

———————

The track of Desire

Must see and not see

Must not see nothing

Burrow and so burrow

Measuring mastering

When ice break up

at the farthest north

of Adirondack peaks

So empty and so empty

Go back for your body
Hindge

Dear Seem dear cast out

Sun shall go down and set

Distant monarchs of Europe

European grid on the Forest

so many gether togather

were invisible alway Love

154

at Fort Stanwix the Charrokey
paice

only from that Alarm
all those Guards

Constant parties of guards
up & down

Agreseror

Bearer law my fathers

Revealing traces
Regulating traces

———————

The true Zeno
the immutable morality

Irruptives

thorow out all
the Five Nations

To cut our wete

of the Jentelmen

Fort the same
Nuteral

Revealing traces
Regulating traces

———————

To Lake Superior to view

that time the Shannas & Dallaways

Home and I hope passage

Begun about the middle next

to Kittaning

Eating nothing but hominey

Scribbling the ineffable

See only the tracks of rabbit

A mouse-nest of grass

———————

The German Flatts

Their women old men & children

Numerous than I imagined

Singing their War song

I am

Part of their encroachment

Speed & Bleave me &

a Good Globe to hang in a hall

with light

———————

To be sent in slays

if we are not careful

To a slightly place

no shelter

Let us gether and bury

limbs and leves

Is a great Loast

Cant say for us now

Stillest the storm world
Thought

———————

The snow

is still hear

wood and feld

all covered with ise

seem world anew

Only step

as surveyor of the Wood

only Step

———————

Walked on Mount Vision

New life after the Fall
So many true things

which are not truth itself
We are too infinite

Barefooted and bareheaded
extended in space

sure of reaching support

Knowledge and foresight
Noah's landing at Ararat

Mind itself or life

quicker than thought

slipping back to primordial
We go through the word Forest

Trance of an encampment
not a foot of land cleared

The literature of savagism
under a spell of savagism

Nature isolates the Adirondacks

In the machinery of injustice
my whole being is Vision

———————

The Source of Snow
the nearness of Poetry

the Captain of Indians
the cause of Liberty

Mortal particulars
whose shatter we are

A sort of border life
A single group of trees

Sun on our back

Unappropriated land
all the works and redoubts

Young pine in a stand of oak
young oak in a stand of pine

Expectation of Epiphany

Not to look off from it
but to look at it

Original of the Otherside
understory of anotherword

Thaw has washed away snow
covering the old ice

the Lake a dull crust

Force made desire wander
Jumping from one subject

to another
Besieged and besieged

in a chain of Cause
The eternal First Cause

I stretch out my arms
to the author

Of the bare ground

My thick coat and my tent
and the black clouds

Squadrons of clouds

No end of their numbers

Armageddon at Fort William Henry
Sunset at Independence Point

Author the real author
acting the part of a scout

———

The origin of property
that leads here Depth

Indian names lead here

Bars of a social system
Starting for Lost Pond

psychology of the lost
First precarious Eden

a scandal of materialism

My ancestors tore off
the first leaves

picked out the best stars
Cries accompany laughter

Winter of the great Snow
Life surrounded by snows

The usual loggers camp
the usual bark shelter

Fir floor and log benches

Pines seem giant phenomena

Child of the Adirondacks
taking notes like a spy

Most mysterious river

On the confined brink

Poor storm
all hallows

and palings around cabin

Spring-suggesting light

Bustle of embarkation
Guides bewildered

Hunt and not the capture

Underthought draws home
Archaism

Here is dammed water

First trails were blazed
lines

Little known place names

tossed away as little grave
pivot bravura

———

Long walk on Erebus

The hell latch Poetry

Ragged rock beside hemlock
Mist in deep gulfs

Maps give us some idea
Apprehension as representation

Stood on Shelving Rock

The cold Friday
as cold as that was

Flood of light on water
Day went out in storms

Well structure could fall
Preys troop free

I have imagined a center

Wilder than this region
The figment of a book

Scarce broken letters
Cold leaden sky

Laurentian system of Canada

Tuesday the instant May

Elegiac western Imagination

Mysterious confined enigma
a possible field of work

The expanse of unconcealment
so different from all maps

Spiritual typography of elegy

Nature in us as a Nature
the actual one the ideal Self

tent tree sere leaf spectre
Unconscious demarkations range

I pick my compass to pieces

Dark here in the driftings
in the spaces of drifting

Complicity battling redemption

———

Cannot be
every
where I
entreat
snapt

Parted with the Otterware

R e s o l u t i o n

Picked up arrowhead

at the three Rivers, & are

hieroglyph

Gone to have a Treaty

battled

with the French at Oswego

At this end of the carry

islet

& singing their war song

neck

sheen

The French Hatchet

dusk

Their Plenipo   squall   Messages

disk   coin   splint   cedar

lily root   chip   grease   cusk

a very deep Rabbit

wavelet

swamp   of which will not per[mit] of

shrub

fitted to the paper, the Margins

mud

Encampt Fires by night

Frames should be exactly

waterbug

wood

canoes

c o v a r y

Cove

Places to walk out to

Tranquillity of a garrison

Escalade

Traverse canon night siege Constant firing
Traverse canon night siege Constant firing

Gabion
Parapet

Gabion
Parapet

Traverse canon night siege Constant firing
Escalade

Tranquillity of a garrison

Places to walk out to
Cove

canoes

waterbug   The Frames should be exactly   wood
                  Fires by night   Encamp't

mud   fitted to the paper, the Margins

shrub   of which will not per[mit] of

wavelet   a very deep Rabbit   swamp

cusk   grease   chip   coin   lily root

cedar   splint   disc
                                                      Their Plenipo
            drisk   Messages   sheen

                    The French Hatchet
                neck
        At this end of the carry
        & singing their War song
        iseler

            batteau   The War Belt   hieroglyph

            Messengers say   Picked up arrowhead

            over the lakes

            Of the far nations

You are of me & I of you, I connot tell

Where you leave off and I begin

      selving

      forfending
            Immeadeat Settlem
      but wandering
            Shenks Ferry people
      unhoused
            at or naer Mohaxt
      elect
            Sacandaga vläie
      vision
            Battoes are return
      thereafter
            They say
      resurgent
            "Where is the path"
      laughter

      ankledeep

      answerable   *last*

PASSACAGLIA   Strict counterpoint
  Moon wading through cloud   *reassemble*
                Union
           Stress
                    mighty
    distant day helter No *nd*
                 war lenght
                defiant   Premis
 Awake! top hill demon daunt *brested*
               on
              ce
             if
             first

anthen   uplispth   enend

   adamap   blue wov   thefthe

folled   floted   keen

                              Themis

thou sculling me
Thiefth

RONALD JOHNSON

from *Ark*

Beam 1

Over the rim
body of earth   rays exit sun
rest to full velocity to eastward pinwheeled in a sparrow's

eye
—Jupiter compressed west to the other—

wake waves on wave in wave striped White Throat song

along the reversal of one
contra-
centrifugal
water to touch, all knowledge

as if a several silver
backlit in gust

All night the golden fruit fell softly to the air,
pips ablaze, our eyes skinned back.
Clouds loom below. Pocked moon fills half the sky. Stars
comb out its lumen
horizon
in a gone-to-seed dandelion
as of snowflakes hitting dark waters, time, and again,

then dot the plain
186,282 cooped up angels tall as appletrees

caryatid
to the tides of day

wide bloom the pathed hearth yawn
on purpose porpoised pattern
this reeled world whistling joist its polished fields at sun
pulse race in a vase of beings, bearings
all root fold forms upon
to center eternity
or enter it
instruments of change.

and bareback as Pegasus guess us

Beam 7

Sound is sea: pattern lapping pattern. If we erase the air and slow the sound of a struck tuning-fork in it, it would make two sets of waves interlocking the invisibility in opposite directions.

As the prong of the fork moved one way, it compressed the air at its front, which layer in turn relieves its compression by expanding the layer in front, and so back to back. As it started the other direction it left the air in front (opposite) immediately rarefied. The air beyond this expands to the rarefaction — itself becoming rarefied — forth and forth.

Compression rarefaction compression rarefaction: these alternate equidistant forces travel at the rate of 1,180 feet per second through the elasticity of air, four times that through water (whale to singing whale), and fifteen times as fast through pure steel. Men have put ear to earth to hear in advance of air.

Pattern laps pattern, and as they joined, Charles Ives heard the 19th Century in one ear, and the 20th out the other, then commenced to make a single music of them. The final chord of the 2nd Symphony is a reveille of all notes at once, his The Fourth of July ends with a fireworks of thirteen rhythmic patterns zigzagging through the winds and brasses, seven percussion lines criss-crossing these, the strings divided in twenty-fours going up and down every-which-way — and all in FFFF.

Both tuning fork and Fourth are heard by perturbations of molecules, through ever more subtle stumbling blocks, in spiral richochet, to charged branches treeing a brain.

The outer earshell leads to a membrane drum — and what pressure needed to sound this drum is equal to the intensity of light and heat received from a 50 watt electric bulb at the distance of 3,000 miles in empty space. (Though sound cannot travel, as light, through the void.) At the threshold of hearing the eardrum may be misplaced as little as a diameter of the smallest atom, hydrogen.

This starts a 'hammer' to strike an 'anvil' which nudges a 'stirrup' — all, bones — against a drum known as The Oval Window. Shut to air, this

171

window vibrates another windowed membrane, tuning a compressed fluid between. *Here, also, is couched our sense of the vertical.*

A resonance is set up in a spiral shell-shape receptor turned with yet another, also spiral, membrane. This is the pith of the labyrinth, and as sound waves themselves it trembles two directions at once, crosswise and lengthwise.

The mind begins early to select from the buzz and the humdrum, till most men end hearing nothing, when the earth speaks, but their own voices. Henry David Thoreau seems to have been the first man to re-learn to hear that *Moto Perpetuo* of the actual: the Greeks strung their lyre to the planets, but Thoreau heard his stretched from first dark sparrow to last dog baying moon.

While a bat uses its ears to see, its optics overtones, the fly hears only in frequencies of its own (and other) fly-wings. I know the housefinch singing outside the window just now heard its own song with slower and lower ear than mine, but I do not know what this means, or how it rings in finchskull. (Though all animals have an auditory range which includes hearing what they can eat, and what can eat them.)

A man once set out to see birds, but found instead he'd learned to listen: an ear better unwinds the simultaneous warblers in a summer birchwood. There, he came upon an Orpheus, all marble, holding a spiral shell to the ear of his Euridice. Turning the other way, he saw Orpheus again, listening to harmonics of midges in sun, the meadow like a nightingale around him. Cat's purr, moth-wing.

The physicists tell us that all sounding bodies are in a state of stationary vibration, and that when the word *syzygy* last shook atoms, its boundary was an ever slighter pulse of heat, and hesitation of heat. Matter delights in music, and became Bach. Its dreams are the abyss and empyrean, and to that end, may move, in time, the stones themselves to sing.

ANDREW JORON

The Birdsongs Are Aging
Translated from the German of Yvan Goll

The birdsongs are aging
A stone falls from time to time
In the courtyard of the forgotten

Towers of mourning stagger over the city
The wind from the green ocean is blind
& no one tells it the way

Jackdaws scatter their broken wings
Across the marble plaza
Seeking the protection of prophets

In my skull are tolling crazed bells
They have forgotten the cause
Of both their lament & the eternal name

Baring the Device

Presence behind words
    manifest as someone (neither sender
Nor receiver)
Breathing gently on a mirror

— fog of experience
Whitens the plane where parallel lines converge

The song's archaic medium
Playing through (s)hells of degenerative grammar

"The Universe is a private place"
— heart wrung from the bell-curve of noise

Unpaid labor in a world without objects
"Waiting to receive the blow"

The moral of the tale
Masses hugely as the timescale
    condenses to a point

— a single ray
Emitted from the candle to the floating eye

Blood-tip
    of the solar nebula

Zirkus

Mother — that was (the violence that was done)
A slave wind

   like weather inside a glass

   "faceless" in
   the mercantile slang

   many words (Are contest upon a fallen cipher)

Compounded of tin
& used for the reckoning of distances

See *Amphitheater-eye*. White
Terrace
   descendent
To long-buried center

Opens a lost treatise on "the male womb"

   his reason *plucked by the senses*

Rings proportional to silence
& the town, depopulated, becomes a temple

   (hidden there, a boy's heroic
Torso)
   conic section turned
   inward to Doubt

The accident of beauty: that ravaged
Integer
   closed on itself

See also
Space, the opalescent pearl of — sinking

Shade of a Grammarian

1.

That is a black sunrise
& that
    a tongue unsheathed of words

I, to gauge
Radiant thistle-in-tautology
    did stricken tense
& chorus

That termless
    music leaks, & I collect its ink

Prise apart the dazed imperative
    spelled in matter
Correction. / "spilled in *mater*"

    teach neuters to
Divided labor; I, flensing the Alone

[Love] each consonant as rhyme-of-blade
    & mirrored absence; each vowel as contour

Field surface — wraith — reverses
Depth

2.

I am the Chiurg upon such smoake

Who asks for a man-made body to ascend
    in coils of red calligraphy

    (as if this vellum were ancestral skin)

Gravity pulls down its gloss
In English. "Flammation" caused by iron gears

What else unwinds the sign?
Let signs be wounds denuded of my flesh

Authorial my tooled
    denials erect their cavity here

    the brazen head
Insists: *You must tell no one*

& I, hypnotized by the pendulum
Swing from sense to nominatum
    reply. *No one will ever know*

ROBERT KELLY

from *The Loom*

[passé défini] ". . . the preterite . . . is to reduce reality to a point of time, and to abstract, from the depth of a multiplicity of experiences, a pure verbal act, freed from the existential roots of knowledge, and directed towards a logical link with other acts, other processes, a general movement of the world. . . . Through the preterite, the verb implicitly belongs with a causal chain, it partakes of a set of related and oriented actions, it functions as the algebraic sign of an intention. . . . It presupposes a world which is constructed, elaborated, self-sufficient, reduced to significant lines, and not one which has been sent sprawling before us, for us to take or leave. Behind the preterite there always lurks a demiurge, a God or a reciter."*

                    It is here that music
                    resists the division
                    into time or tenses
                    Is present. Unison
                    to which each man brings
                    his qualities, his "style."
                    Dividing (*scheiden*)
                    must be inside. The own
                    pursued & subjected to pain.
                    Putting the devil in hell,
                    Boccaccio calls it. Rains
                    on the hill. All the ordeals
                    begin in her, cave-oven
                    barred by grate, the interlocked
                    desires, too focused, too
                    goal-directed, make an iron
                    network. The fire must be puffed
                    hot enough to melt the bars
                    or he must bring to the oven
                    an instrument not connected
                    with his feelings.

*Roland Barthes, "Writing and the Novel," in *Writing Degree Zero* (1968), 30.

Crowbar, brute lever,
much tempered steel & a little
cunning, pry it from the rock.
Every virgin was a harlot once
& knows how to aid
his analytic. The mortar
of the oven dome
is the weakest part, pry it
& bricks can be pulled out.
Leaving the original gap,
filled with the fire
he brings there
to warm himself with.

No, his hair wasnt black,
only the charred heart passage
turned black. His hair was brown,
he hadnt been to the moon,
only a friend of his, now lost
from record, came from that district
teaching this skin dance
in new places.
Modern glass doors to the cave
where the oven waits, cold now
since the dream is ended. Beside
the oven, a niche in the wall
with gentler heat, where bread dough
for instance could rise.
The mortar in old
New York buildings,
weak now, sifts out
almost at the touch.
Put up a century ago
with sand & long
human hairs, jet black,
oriental, mixed
in the mason's trough.
The water has dried out.

That's where the hair
is black. No water left
I can learn even from this.

I am slow,
my hands are far away,
the music
closer than my skin.
Peripheral blurout.
Ordeal of earth.
These are ordeals—
to tear her veil
in the fury of his pain,
tear away the pain
that veils his heart,
burn heart, beat the heart,
beat the endless women of the heart.
The ordeals
are all day long.
Every day
is a dream, every dream
an initiation—
to reach an irrevocable
He Did,
absolute deed
snatched out of context.
Silence of that,
our strife
is not with upper air
but the potentates
of our own despair,
our *complicity*
with the way things are.
We put up, & go down like flies.
Like grass. Like whatever
you choose,
till the rice is finally harvested
& we clear out of our houses

the dark furniture of pain
consequent upon the time,
implied by Balzac
& begotten
on middle-class proclivities
for sticking pins
in little girls. Bayros
in mind, his knives, the axe
the witch rides
with its blade
inside her,
inward razor,
ultimate reprisals
a man makes
against himself.
Congested city
of our conflicting wills
set so often
to deny or self-destruct.
Circumcision. The cut
off sacrifice, to start
life with a loss.
The woman carves
her lover's initials
in her skin.
      A tree
can surrogate, its flesh
bears the testimony
of what we wanted
to carve into ourselves
to make some knowledge stick.
I cut my arms once
slowly with her knife
to prove
      something,
what was it, I didnt gouge
deep enough, the memory hazes
& the scar is gone.

Why did I do this
to myself, what was on
my mind?
       Sun Dance.
Self-initiates. The veil
of the body torn,
inner meat
the only Isis.
That the mind
be banished
from the streets
where it too easily
lingers,
       the way things are,
the star of the likely
giving his comfortable
light. But wormwood
is the star
where knowledge grows,
not serene, bitter, more
bitter than any sea.
Pain makes howl. This
speaks.
       Mescalito,
turning the body inside out.
All the Sacred Emetics
of the desert, to empty
the body that it be filled with light.

There is no cunning
in our ways, we fall
for the old way. Hurt me.
Hurt me in her. Confuse
subject & object, reverse
the current of gemütlichkeit.
"Love what you hate,
hate what you love—
that's the way."

And this is our famous
technology of ecstasy,
read it
in every crime against the person,
read it in,
encapsulate the pain
& make it live
always inside.
Morbid fester. That's
where the Star Wormwood shines
on the bitter sea.
In its light
we see that the street
is not the street,
my hand is not my hand.
Tree not a tree.
Flower an emissary
from the Kingdom of Torture.
Bee sting. Spasms of childbirth
so that some new thing
can come out. Its turn.
Burn her arm, hold it
to the candleflame or lightbulb,
the years change
but this does not,
the opening eye
of agony
when what we suppose is real
shivers
to dream. I do not see the street
I see the pain.
It is raining & I love the rain
& I do not see the rain.
I see a newspaper:
sailor seized for burning
with a cigarette
his initials
on his girlfriend's rump.

What was she doing
while he did that?
What did she learn
while he, with her pain,
tried to experience
some hint of his identity,
to read his name there,
to make her him?
Old dimness of it, old
death, that a man
could find himself only there.
Stuck pins in himself
deep, would walk around
all day long with the
pins in him, hidden
under his clothes, all the time
knowing himself in the pain,
carrying it like a chalice
of awareness, this thing
stuck in him no love could give,
something inside, making
him himself. With every step
he knew
it is not ordinary
where I am.
We are silenced by the way things are.
Against the silence
pain clamors,
Artaud's cruelty, friction
of the alchemists,
hairshirt, Thebaid,
stimulus amoris, oxgoad of love,
to prod.

Pain teaches nothing but itself.
My hungry eye
is on the world & knows no patience,
& in the brittleness of hope
guesses there's another way.

Not pain, not the stoic
refusal to feel pain as pain,
not an equanimity
that becomes indifference
to your own flesh & others'.
Something else. I call it Work,
not knowing its real name.
I call it Work, it may be
another kind of torture,
this time not done on me or thee
but on the currents of Time,
as energy, bending it
to our use. Making.
Man is compromise
& I refuse the terms.
Animals are the teachers of pain.
Not be animal. Be
the other thing. The extreme.
The outside chance. Making
something somehow. Making
time to shape itself
around the wood or word or cloth.
Riding that. Be the other thing.
The afterbreath. The placenta.
The feeling that does not feel itself
but only other. The testicle.
(Homage to Artaud
who refused to be man!)
The staircase. The statue.
The object. Be the other
thing. The no name. The that
that is this. Not artful,
not a thing produced. Not a mask.
Be the other thing.
The ether. The new syntax.
The wall. The ridiculous.
The frenzied. The hidden.
The eater of food. The rider.

The goer. The thing
that makes experience. The man
in woman & the woman in man.
The conundrum. The trivial answer.
The lawless seed. The plan-less.
The map itself. The difference.
The wine glass. The magnet.
Be the other thing.
The broken sword. The dead tree.
The snow. The listless pond
covered with fallen leaves.
The wheatfield. The springtime.
The artery. The doorknob.
The grammar-book. The flame.
The outcome. The space
inside a house. The bird
on the roof. The underfoot.
The miracle. The inaccurate.
The crack in the wineglass.
The charred paper. The ruins
of an old church. The chimney.
The cow. The distance between
the tips of her horns. Her horns.
The mountainside now in sun now
in shadow. The interval.
The zero. The blind man's mirror.
The coin. The empty bus.
The desert. The saguaro. The palm.
Be the other thing.
The ink. The hairbrush. The needle
of acupuncture. The alkaloid.
The beachcomber. The friend
who does not stay to supper.
The star. The crayon. The this.
The compass. The man who just left.
The hose. The smell of something.
The what I forgot.
The other thing. The process.
The god.

The Bounty, II

Mother confused with earth
Ankles leather bound
Henceforth return to the position of the seed

Upon her feet two sons four daughters
Head a bent a foul rhythm of elbows and knees
Shell once spoken (speaker) recognize by fin by frond

Left for dead the penetrable body mothers
Stories to crust abeyance
Divested wander white bespoken

~

On that recounting with bulbs and flowers woven
Rendering afloat recognition the mill
Who will know us embankment out of sequence

Preparedness state of preparedness on behalf prepare
Material compel it fixed and evident
Site of denuded trees

Absence charged with hand and foot chest and nipple
Upon the thr—
Who last ate sitting down anticipate his mouthful

~

Enter woodland and waste perspective thumbprint worn
Weapon affront lungs out
Demise detail weight of a head insupportable

Called to attention wooden capacity leap
Fruit bowl leap stand at counter at readiness
Thinned to white foam recognize it as ocean//scrape

Commerce complicit undifferentiated
Riotous blood to its root betrayal when
Milk mother boy to bone plumb plunder thinking

~

Outheld outlandish property skew mud
Imprint wail time and acre
[As well as his eagerness to despoil us of our property]

Face for nations albeit feathers fathers masked ones
To protect our heads from falling projectiles
Sword slit sixth month pregnancy held to command

Slew bayonet Kwang-ju sister pumpkin spill lantern world
Carnations red for mothers living white for dead
In each school room repeated white blooming

~

Owned random slipper streets made to appear wet
Bales of hay in the incinerating field
Grip of iron in the children's throats

Because the face was hidden and the money was painted
Manipulation prevent what emergent story fodder
Rank and degree speak amiss stunned have

Hasty hemisphere issuance guttural meet time
Conflagration dividing cells their imprison
Tools and adjustments called family in the habit

~

Dominion hankering position
Vain lain barrow burrow
Ripe melon on grindstone

Serve affect yoke stamped
Material responsible for temperature
Features enslavement slung over shoulder

What and wet nurse and institution
Concave freshly slaughtered chicken every rising
Couldn't recall agency by which to relate

~

Admonishment arrive sooner rather
Witness attendant authority
Brack bracken lichen slip word this bare arms current

Paper lanterns pulps of teeth fir exact amount of profit
Rough approximation relative
Superfluous ownership skirts ballooning under water

Mutter call it was flurry fury
Scale wrought minimum
Pressive [ruin]

~

Tend attend log by log premise
Nameless indeterminate climb fence and pole
Subsume white generational white

Malice so turns matter of this matter proceed
Firepath vestigial
Point blank inner written last abode

Number of live births
Radial amid intone
Every locuter world of particular

~

Mother's daughter born/ /
Ton a designation fluent full
Inflection rooting variegated

Emblazon affirm infinitive
Form and door variable green vestry
Forage fervent reclaim

Sword to method
Let diligence still standing chimney
Register derivative

ANN LAUTERBACH

Subject to Change

Those of us who are there will never leave.
Given our inability to make a version,
One that does not twist
Off the ground, the same ground we have
Imagined, separately,
The thing casts itself into being.
Such impediments cannot be altered.
Other ideas are lost.
Are they ideas? What thing?
Once there was possibility
But now that too is gone
Predicting the river.
Is it all, and will it stay
Longer than usual,
Gathering hesitancy only because it
Is new, until, heavily absorbent,
Boundaries fail, as if of ash?
The sky was something else, massive
But kind, leaving nothing in its wake.
Often I have thought the linear
Duplicitous, mapping outer and inner,
Showing us core and enclosure
As it helps itself over destiny's rail.
The difference is the air's lunar kiss,
A residual, if despondent, bearing.
Those of us who leave were never there.

For Example (1):
Stepping Out

*It has been easy to say in recent times that everything tends to become real,
or rather, that everything moves in the direction of reality, that is to say,
in the direction of fact.*

—Wallace Stevens

If everything tends to become real
then whose trial has ended
on a scale of one to ten
in which three is a dream
on a floor
no one can see.
              Also, perhaps, maybe
elicit the shard from its fervor
to display amnesia: one person in jail
another walking across a roof
where what is written on the sky
brings formality to the event, as when
we first ask, *What is it?* The world,
loosed like a hem, is
what we step out on
and are pulled along away from our doors
not so much appeased as grafted
onto the long dark pause.
Pointing, not seeing anything, not knowing
the name for what isn't there.

But the prestige of a moment is not its name.
After all, we sleep among secrets
and wake to their burden.
If we could pay attention at all points then
theory would be what really is there. But then
another intimacy begins
while a chorus of male voices
carries the bar away/raft
of flowers brought into a girl/her body

emerging from the story as a new link
on an old sheet/ignorant single ambition of one hero
listening to another but not listening to this spring's snow.
Only the women speak of war, for example.
"To be prolonged in the first place
so we dream of escape," she said
in the midst of history.
                              The dictionary
is part of the clutter
lure, decoy, bait, snare, trap
and so to cross the heart
might make us *only here* or *here only*
depending on the translation.
Was one aflame? Is this a lake?
And why is part of the flower
mentioned at night
when she finds these love knots
in another dream she cannot recall. And
around the sinuous thread the doctor
with his pen
draws a line across her abdomen like the general
in the green room with his green map and stick, his
war game of war under the strong light of the canonical:
Kafka, Freud, and whatever girls might make an example.
Festering green bar, nothing on the menu available.
Et peut-être yes! now she understands why
she would rather not mention names
but what was it said of the singular? The wall
could be a *lining* or an *inner partition*
if everything tends to become real.

It's true, I was sad all day
for no good reason like a forgotten task
attached to too many site-specific verbs—
to want, desire, wish, require, please, try, attempt—
you get the idea. Only the finality of rhythm
on which to insist: rhythm as the example.
Now the resourceful writer becomes a drunk
as she stands against a church wall

under clear light.
Nothing is early enough, for example.
We are not located in the world but in its
particulars: what's done is done, the show is down.
Tyranny comes naturally to the dead. Was that
the perilous night
mentioned by the composer and copied
onto a page? The fat belly revealed, the wound
similar but not the same. Indifference
spoils what is real, for example.

So we find ourselves in the excess
of what is already here
and want to speed up to the good parts.
Some noises are glamorous, like dance, the
discipline of celebrated silence,
but love moans and collapses
under a saturated roof
and we admit to being ruined, at least once.
The glassy eye is anointed by its tear.
If you save everything that has hurt you, you
might come close to saying its prayer
passing the basket from hand to hand
not having to memorize the empty gaze
where you just were. Then
survival could be negative space
where what might be reconstructed
has fallen away beyond erasure
to the small case before travel.
Get back in your room.
Is anything in childhood mutual? The lifted
parameters of touch mingled with the stung
as when reaching up above clover
to the magics of another season
which might be serene. They danced
under an awful light, and her shoes, her gowns,
twisted in shadow; only the shadow has lasted.
The clasp of his hands on her back, for example.
The limbs of the corridor could not speak

195

but were folded under
where wet hair was out of sequence
on the black floor. The train
pulled its litany across a populous tread, torn
into geography and a wish to stay up later
than time, when whatever *wisteria* was would
bloom and hand down its scented ladder.
On that side of the street the boys were
always ready, but the stairs were dangerous and locked.
To protect what is new, to laugh without ambush or cartoon;
to sleep safely. It is a matter of listening, and so
learn how to depart. What is dragged behind is a
sound that is not understood, as the city
gathers and gathers, near
as what will not come back.

From up here in the bleachers
things seem real, but provisional, like a day
in which only paper airplanes sail by
to eventually cover the field.
Unfolded and flattened, they reveal
notes and pictures in colored pencil: hearts,
trees, flowers, rhyming couplets, and other
impediments of the age. And perhaps the game is
halted on account of their weather, which is only
the missing voice and truant litter of desire.
The athletes' faces hiss with sweat and rage
and Mom is picking up socks
and spare change, paying bills, lifting
the nearly empty carton of milk
off the shelf in the fridge. Her task
is to remember whatever comes next.
To her, time is an all too gregarious
protagonist, not so much eager to please as
insistent and daft, adept at charming the room
full of anxious initiates into voting his way
without knowing the facts, for example.
She thinks how rain on the roof
does sound like applause as she closes the windows.

By now the airplanes are mush
and the fans have departed in their vivid multicolored slickers
and hats. It seems strange to think
each knows where to go, although some may not get there.
Whereas all stories seemed false now
all seemed true; the confusion
was arbitrary. This spot, this
dime. She turns on the shadow of a breath
like a bird on a branch. *Touch me not*
was how it sounded from across the field, a page
torn from a journal in which she confessed
she could not wait, writing into the wait.

Maybe all absences should be excused.
The banquet, in any case, was dull;
the soufflé never rose. But things
fall on a regular basis, especially in spring,
and sometimes we hear them, petal by petal,
as when we put our ear to the chest
where the letters are kept.
Be sure to put the broken glass
in a brown paper bag so it won't cut
someone's hand; there's enough blood
in the carpet and in the sand. Even
the mattress is stained and, like sand,
indented with the shadow of weight.
This represents a decade of dreams
which also should be put in a sack or box
and shipped to a new address: strange,
how the body takes its dreams with it
like a city buried under the rubble of ages
never to be found. Strange, too,
how what is and what is not
make a quixotic braid
which, like weather, has no end
other than those we invent
to measure change. Rain again today.
You can hear it too, sloshing through the gutter
like a rope of sound. Instead of falling

you could walk downstairs
onto the familiar street, but be careful
and take your umbrella: remember, the street
won't miss you. It goes one way.

For Example (5):
Song of the Already Sung

1.

The situation is not going to change.
Which situation?

Anecdote of the moon.
Held there, cast in a blitz of lopsided gas.

Or say a row of trash cans.
Something set to music, then lost.

Four wasps on a sill; some stench.
The last thing said. Say that.

Smoke inert, leaves
frozen at June.

To do with a lock
with the other side of a bridge with

another familiar strand of hair.
The body's epilogue: *not you.*

The confession stone turned
before the applause.

2.

Because it reminds me of amber.
Funny how you move them from something, the bones.

The bugs that you find in amber.
They don't look like real bones.

The something of time past—of someone working
as if they were all broken, like the mugs—

has gone awry like Icarus in his machine.
But you want to hold on, a fondness

tentative, not followed through.
Different theatrical situations

whose absurdity doesn't lead the mind
anywhere right now. More complex

replicas. Diagrams. Maybe fossils.
The amber piece, the photograph

that won't change. Speak
of another kind of time

pressing flowers in a book to
remind you of what you don't have—

controlling the bones. Each has such—
I mean an example is a sound.

The tip of it, a
very extended kite.

The challenge of the thing.
An average pen, for example.

Its relationship to these
pieces of light: the smallest piece.

Is it a model?
It doesn't touch bottom.

A distinct velocity, a
quivering line when

absence of color becomes color's
harmonic particularity in air.

A lot about America:
real people, real objects

fashions in color, partial statements;
a meandering, vagrant line.

3.

In the midst of a phantom inch
wild and beautiful simultaneous competing tunes
an immense scattering
to picture dissonance
among the rushes
this excerpt
the horror of our kind
say an image, facedown,
never to be lifted
touched for the sake of it
the shine
and those who are not clumsy
the advantage of that
yes scooping water from a pond
child with broken net
standing at the threshold maybe

As someone's father
elicits recurrent gaps
net of the fallen through
of the unrecovered
attached to that
singing that tune
between desire and the actual
a theory of response
the spectator's knowledge
now's edge
inscribed, instructed to sing

that lullaby again
tell a story
put the sock on the doll
pull the dress up over her head
immersed in yellow
iconicity of a scream.

4.

The situation
is not going to change. Refrain
etched above the song.
Erudition of a rat.
Mind of a turbine engine.
Luck of the draw.
Examples of what?
                    To watch as the reference

floats away. Away
as nightmare or game.
Glancing across the table at another's—
the confusion distance is.
A beseeching gap as in a harbor
or panels left uncertain, occupied by
weather. What cannot be
transformed into something else.

Another in another room.
It's a bright day in a small Egyptian town
but the birds here are nervous.
I can hear her voice
but I don't know what she is saying.
A time and place for circular action: this
ends in some kind of secret
some kind of occasion
an abandoned pier
the far end of a pier
alone at the far end of a pier
some kind of bargain is drawn up

an occasion for meeting
face to face.

Downstairs, downstairs

a person decides.
Talking to myself (himself) this
basement in retrospect is mine.
I am always installed on a still point
a potentially dangerous spot
a seed bed
I can build sexual fantasies.
                              Maybe
I can say good-bye.

A clean white space but no space is neutral.
Thumbprints. Something to
acknowledge, bring back, shadow
thrown out, cast, dragged across the gravel
repeatedly. Wanting all said all done
to save one or two—
an urge to get up, go.
No particular creed, the girl now walking
across the grass, some pages in her left hand,
I can't say what in her right.
No space is neutral. There's a man
a kind of cult figure, a kind of hero.
Sound is replacement for him (me).
A house is what everyone knows by heart.

Then the real is a convincing show? Of course
the beam looks real, but is more melancholy
an inhalation of breath moving across
to a charged little image.
It's like looking at a forest
through the eye of a needle.
In a shop I found a dirty white vase. I washed it;
now it is clean.
There's a form of dreaming in another form
and there's the sacredness of common objects.

203

NATHANIEL MACKEY

The Phantom Light of All Our Day
for Jess

I wake up standing before a scene I stood
    before as a child. What bits of
  it I see no more than seem they were
      ever there, though they'd
  someday blur the broken paste-up
                                  world
                                        I saw
        would blow itself apart . . .

  My back to the wall whose beginning
the day of my release brought forward, so
    unlikely a start, I stand watching the
  brook I stood before as a boy, no sweeter
      tooth but for boundaries, bite
                            off more
      than I can chew . . .

                Bittersweet kiss
of this my tightlipped muse, puckered
    skin of the earth as though
                        its orbit
    shrunk.
        Shrill hiss of the sun so
  much a doomsday prophet gasping voiceless,
                              asking,

        When will all the killing
                    stop?

  As though the truth were not so visibly
                        Never.
      As though the light were not all but
    drowned in the Well to the uncharted
      East I sought . . .

Let its blue be
my heavenly witness, I resolve before
                              the brook
            I stood before as a child . . .

            Up at dawn every day these
      days, I'm learning to look into
            the lidlessness the North Wind
                              wakes . . .
            learning to gaze into the sky
            my invented eyes unveil under
      acid rain, chemical sunsets, blush
                              of a
shotgun bride.

            The grass blowing east at the
      merest mention of wind where
                  there is no wind, no place for
            a horse in this the riderless
                              world.
      I'm learning to paint. I repeat
      these words as an irritable mystic, my
            would-be hum, neither life
            nor limb not on the edge of
            dislocation, some such
                              dance
            I dare . . .

                  But still I stand before
            the brook I stood before as a boy.
            Thicknesses of paint, as if
                              the eye
looked into its looking, let the skull
            show thru, show the Kings of
      Xibalba play with poison gas and me
            among the, 1940s' chemical
                              warfare corps . . .

I'm learning to see, says my enamored mage, what's
    going on. I hear the rumbling in the music I
paint.

        Luminous breezes locked in the nucleus'
        inmost reaches echo Atum's vow. These
                radiant winds obey the abandon our
            learning sought.

    I stand watching the brook I stood before
            as a boy, the painted echo of
        a snapshot my father took. The oils
                                    thicken
    my sleep,
            the unuprootable oath I wake up to,
                                    the earth
    a part of Ocean
                again

Memphite Recension

So night sits me down be-
fore braided Isis, I
see the moon behind a cover
of clouds.
Exploding light all around us
nibbling our skin
like fish, ointments
oiling
the air, all around us like
eyes of a religious
ghost looking
down above the body it leaves
behind . . .
All the times
I'll eventually
recall but won't
reclaim it keeps alive,
the cracked
interstices of dust . . .
The crushed
coaxialities of dawn,
their lack of thunder's
earthen mesh,
the earth
itself turned upon
an absence . . .

Each ember of light outlives
any likelihood of touch, each
previous burning's rub of
ash plants a rasp in
love's
voice . . .
We set out across time
to what reminders of
haunts we left the
comforts of work loose

                                        of an
almost tasteable remorse.
                        Above us black
                                        revolving
                wheels turn an earthy grind, we go
                        down on all fours, back
                        uppity others adrift in
                                        gutters
                                                of light . . .

                Lidless, walking in thru one
                another's eyes, waterbabies
                        both, we meet at our
                                        booth inside
        the Long Night Lounge whispering
                        dreams and regrets, eroding
                                        witnesses
                                                yet

"John Coltrane Arrived with An Egyptian Lady"

—belated prayer—

no sheet of sound enshroud
the Fount of this fevered
      Brook becoming one
with God's Eye, not
      a one of these notes

      come near to the brunt
      of the inaudible
note I've been reach-
      ing towards

                  To whatever
            dust-eyes giver
      of tone to whatever
talk, to whatever slack
      jaws drawn against bone

                  To whatever
            hearts abulge with
      unsourced light, to whatever
            sun, to whatever moist
      inward meats
                  of love

            Tonight I'll bask
      beneath an arch of
                  lost
      voices,   echo
      some Other place,
Nut's nether suns
                  These
      notes' long fingers gathered
            come to grips of gathered
      cloud, connected lip
                  to unheard of

      tongue

Slipped Quadrant

As if by late light shaped of its
arrival,   echoed announcement
       come from afar,   loosed
       allure,   the as-if of it its
       least appeasable part.
                                    Rich
       tense within we called it,
              would without end,   seed
       within a seed sown elsewhere,

                                    somewhere
              said to've been known as
Ttha.
                    Wrought   surfaces, putative
       soul,   cheated heart.   Shot
              body borne up to be looked
       at, learned from, one
                                    heretical
moment's reprimand. . .
                           Something a
       Sufi said in Andalusia.
                           Something
              said to've been said before.
       Ominous music made a mumblers
                                    academy,
              vatic scat,   to be alive
       was to be warned it said. . .

                                    And of
              loss long assured of its
                    occurrence,   echoed
              agreement grown more remore,
                                    long out of
              reach,   not as yet known by
              name though not nameless,
                                    swift,
       uninterpretable design. . .
                           In oblique

league with majesty,   secret,
unannounced,   came to where the
        flutes of the Afar spat salt,

                              limbs

under loosefitting cloth. . .
        Came then to within a stone's
    throw of Ttha,   very far,
        weary, felt we'd walked with

                              weights.

    on our feet.
                    Saw the in we sought
        ran on, some said stop, some
        we'd barely started.

                    Stood us

        up within sight of Ttha, strewn
        kin, sat us down sipping hog's-hoof

                              tea. . .

    Trashed ecsatsy. Impudent if.
                    Said
what but wind on our stomachs fed
    it, whim. Felt for it falling away
    from it, called it "Calling it the

                              earth,"

    unsprung.   Shied away might worry
    cease, drew near, bud bursting out
out of earshot, wind out of India,
        three-digit heat.   Scratched

                              air

screamed reparation, strung spillages
    fingers pried apart as they

                    struck. . .

    Running start without which no escape, with-
    out Rasta's far-eye squint   not

                    see. . .

    Numbed comfort.   Lungless bellower.
    Believed it.   Faith gotten back,
                              as if not,
    broke in on its answer, made its caught

mouth twitch. . .   Grew numb,   having
      nothing to say, said so.   Glum,
   though if need be not.   Encephalic
                                 blow.
Hollow emblem.   Blocked.
                              Heads wet,
   many a midnight soaking. Slogan-weary
   sleepers. Dream of a just world.
   Saw the in we sought ran deep, sat us
   down with chills, polyrhythmic
                              shivers. . .
   Pinched earth, outrun by longing.
      Whimsical inlet.   Renegade
                              wish

Song of the Andoumboulou: 12

Weathered raft I saw myself
adrift on.

Battered wood I dreamt I
drummed on, driven.

Scissored rose, newly braided
    light, slack hoped-for rope
        groped at, unraveled.
                    Braided star
    we no longer saw but remembered,
        threads overlapping the rim
of a sunken world, rocks we
    no longer saw by extinguished,
Namoratunga's long-tethered
                        light.

Breathing smoke left by the gods'
    exit. Scorched earth looked at
with outside eyes, burnt leaf's
                    Osanyin,
        raffia straw beneath
        coatings of camwood
                paste. . .

Saw myself bled, belatedly
    cut, inverted blade
    atop Eshu's head,
                sawtooth
cloth of an egungun,
    thunder whet the edge
                of a knife.
    And what love had to do with it
        stuttered, bit its tongue.
    Bided our time, said only wait,
                        we'd see.

Tossed-off covers.   King Sunny Adé's
wet brow.   Four twenties on the dresser
   by the bed. . .

   Cramped egg we might work our
way out of,   caress reaching in
   to the bones underneath.
                              Not even
looking. Even so, see
                    thru.

   Watery light we tried in vain
   to pull away from.   Painted
                                 face,
   disembodied voice. Dramas we
      wooed, invited in but got
scared of.   Song so black it
                        burnt
   my lip. . .   Tore my throat as I
      walked up Real Street. Raw beginner,
                                    green
         attempt to sing the blues. . .

Tilted sky, turned earth. Bent wheel, burnt
                                    we.
   Bound I. Insubordinate
                        us

KEVIN MAGEE

from *Tedium Drum*, Part IV

What exactly the date was is not what was thought about is
held unabated, unthought. One page might include a list of
arbitrary, they would have to be arbitrary, unexamined verbal
impulses, social bits of language. There are no more proverbs.
Every night a crowd milling, doing the talking, the room not
even a room with four walls and a fire escape. We followed
them around with great disappointment and even greater
concern, the news of the decision to restrict directly looking
forward to this date in view of the blows from the batons and
news of the roving begin to compose I admired his composure
enormous moral authority liable to not exactly justice but my
survival. When there is nothing in front of you there can be
nothing inside you, the thought disappears and all that is left
is this ghost of the matter in my head, the ghost of the matter
instead, It was a saying of ours, a saying of ours for years.
We may be goats, but we have our rights.

The sound came in waves, wave of liquid lapping, lap.
Insatiable. Trajectory of daylight, warmth, heat, dazzle
and beam bright agitated bouts of energy, integument of
purpose, swathed. Increments. Clemency. Yes, you are
forgiven, you may go free. The sign of election, and just
when they least expected it, the child took the clock apart.
The child broke the clock. The heat curls the paper, melts
the flowers. Writing carving its course in the clay over
time. Hard look of the sexual disavowed, disallow,
importunate in nothing but in Thee. Noon, the exquisite
hour. The heat releases smells. Write with your hat off,
it is that hot. Does the body smell because the air is moist,
or is it the sudden shifts in temperature? She wept at the
wedded tendril of the dog's entrails. The dog was dead
and decomposing. The absurdity of the bicyclist at Balbec.
The miracle of photosynthesis.

The sky is perfect today, just like yesterday, a virus. The
worms lift their weary heads. They have been digging all day
and the dirt disgusts them. At times it seems as though they
cannot breathe. Candelabra. Embrasure. The sun shines on
the page. Hagiography, socio-souciant. The brother of bay
leaves. The big dumb dogs bark and bark at their boredom
of barking. They are not theatrical. Trickle. Now what is
left. What is there than for. Anywhere what had been, was,
or was it—why not. Why not won't what, what then. Redact.
With or without. A shout. The mere thought. Is that what it
was and if it were was that how it is, now? Withering. The
motor of. There is nothing more to add, nothing to be said
for: kiln, milk. Possibly the edge or contour, expectorate or
rind. The clay was fired. Per perhaps pillow. Bear nor got
that right or wrong. Stipulate field. The full inside spread
of a folded page. The binding is panel-stamped brown leather
over boards. Parchment fragments from an unidentified
manuscript serve as filling for the spine.

Instrumentum Vocale

The failure to write is a personal failure

or pick up a pen that patently

disfigurement accompanying deteriorating

times   infuriated by the interruption

but in remarkably good health

shut in a book   a single Book

rests on columns where through gaps the Master

the calendar and the feast of kings

quicken the shade   as on the shores of Sidon

where there are reputedly few trees

~

an inexact expression not a falsehood

not at least a deliberate falsehood

had said I had read what was the name

and there was one   the name of the book

when she entered the room

what was the name of her book with trees

there were obviously no trees in the book

only what I had said I had read there

on that ride and crushing ground

217

~

Reaching across to find

was looking for your book

and in the book could find

no trees. except for the

concept (her work in Egypt)

wandering off with rough

script, what had she kept

~

not thinking this
she was listening to her voice in his
hand held forward
to the maligned page

there was the candle
exact circle of light
she drew back her hand
usurping, in the full

regalia of her calling
figurines of the demons of fertility
the soft knock of oars
trees cut into cones

~

(not a song but

scratched

accretion   there

are even birds in L.A.

at daybreak and it

was cold by the curtains

was told behind curtains

parted on to   a gift

parted on to   parallel

columns)

~

Brevity
else the barrel burst

throw stones at a stranger
immersion in skins

inculcate
this legitimate wish to make a choice

whatever initiative may be salvaged
will not find identity

uncultivated spatial concept of
centrifugal mobility

like the floating uterus in the Greek theory

219

~

Both my parents illiterate to the last degree

leaving to me betimes the hut and hardship

adam and eve incurring curse from god of laboring

therefor in such extremitys

I must seize the one remedy

reading on the road of a sacred day

saw standing above the height of my head

an author of full great reverence by semblant

unlettered luxury

TOM MANDEL

from *Prospect of Release**

"Ich bin, auch hier, in Ihrer Gegenwart, diesen Weg gegangen.
Es war ein Kreis." —*Paul Celan*

1.
That one is conscious and not know why
like cleaved rock or two that never joined
eyes blue in life become brown coals
silent as the Kodak into which they stare

from the rear of a backyard family gathering.
Brothers-in-law caper in the foreground.
Seasons, months, weeks, moments flatten

against the horizon, forgotten. To whom
now do I belong? An infinity of numbers
whose factor is three. I saw it was

a volume. At sea when I met him, light
poured in unrecalled, he offered no answers
to the questions I asked whose answers
were obvious, and I did not know why.

3.
Clothes surround the body's points
to underscore its battle for insight.
As they are dressed they stand ready
in a time of distraction. We had not

prepared this story but gave ourselves
instructions. 'Place my body in a valley
gather my bones into a cedar box

*a book of fifty sonnets.

221

without your hands touching them. Put
a linen sheet over them, tear your
garments to the navel—all you are wearing

the suit that surrounds your frame.
Shovel dirt on me. Do for me what I did
for my father.' And I did for him
what he did for me. Do this for me.

4.
As a full cup slides across thin ice
a wave somewhere stuns a shore
in the trembling world of names
a petal of wind blows his my way.

In profile, waiting to return, tell us
of daylight and darkness. Is it lonely
at the top? To the dying does a world

appear to begin again? During day lie in
an overturned bed, and right it at dusk.
The category of person straightens.

I followed your body to the grave,
as I will to my own. Where tragedy
studies us, fear its inheritance,
honor mother, father, the single name.

5.
No paths lead among graves to articulate
our perplexity. Walking and thinking,
male, female, dust, frost and preservation.
No truth outside creation. Only truth within.

To praise you in bewilderment my soul
knows well, counting up ways as things
go wrong, as if the rest-stops along

a King's highway, without model of love
would lack commitment to meaning and fill
as traffic flows by, for how else should we

go on if not in these roles, enslaved to
meaning's delicate sense, identity and
difference our trespasses press upon us
as repetition transforms our route.

7.
Study the esoteric text, don't turn
your face from it. There is no proper
articulation of what confronts *'the teaching
of oneself,'* leaving only *'a trace*

on the soul.' Encoded in desire
tragedy studies us. *'Some significances
traced on the soul of a perfect*

*individual, if articulated linguistically
or expressed in metaphors would turn coarse
and elude one's design,'* wrote Maimonides.

In the time taken to articulate a letter
we live and die in syntagmatic opposition
to God, the ultimate (escape of) meaning.
To deny anything is an act of perplexity.

10.
To one who dies the world begins again
followed by words to describe it.
Youth and age, luminous with restraint
cleaved rock or two not joined. The dead

unite the clods of dirt that cover them
with instruction, their bones without
bare hands. I will do for him what

my father did for his. Landscape is
imperfect, moonlight to make it so.
In unwitting contribution the scientist

has taken to himself with love this
dead thing, vibrating the conscious use
of his own social maladjustment to
reveal the living act of revision.

The Shade

Asked to explain his suicide after a brief creative flurry, the shade replied, "only pretending to be silent, just pretending. Too many fleas in San Francisco. The sense of an order is its effect on an obedient man; give me something else." You and I, we are like two eyes in a profile. It is my supposed property to be naturally crude and effective. Allow me to point you toward some trees which are too well-bred to talk. In place of our complex of flesh tongue time, they have been provided with limbs pointing in every direction at whosoever may pass including birds through nearby air, though if such a one settles in your branches it may be too much like a scratch you cannot itch to be perfect. What do you think? Myself, I feel more like one of those natives in Wittgenstein's examples, holding up a red slab of blue cloth with a sign on it that reads, "wrong way, turn back, you're already there." Pretty lush for a wrong turn. Although I don't remember all the details of my past, my life has all occurred recently, and I'm not going to grab that lovely red-hot coal; the past in which I burned myself is real. The dark is a colorless object. What I say to myself in it is set over me in the same way as the past. It was then that I changed, now I'm only getting ready to. Most of what's around has actually never been anything but context, always a background never a fore. The Greeks didn't separate words as they wrote, so the only crucial thing is to arrange the letters in a way that sets up camp with what you know. For example, I know myself so well that if I relax for even a moment I realize I am waiting to change, and I do change—immediately. I don't have to look up dust in a dictionary of dirt. People say a verb involves action: let them talk. The next change is actually the picture so that the objects I depict will surround me and they and I look back out at you. A frame appears around your head, a wonderful patchy luminosity I dub intention. But really when I describe something it's just that I wish it were that way, and this I share with Wittgenstein, a fellow Viennese. The earth was once a ball of excellent gas, and now the Danube flows, etcetera. If reality is declaring itself via language it certainly is taking the long way around. In the poet's tool chest: favorite tools may seem poorly maintained, spotted with grease, indications of use and wear. A very few spotless items also, bought and paid for but never used. Naturally their untouched brightness catches the commentator's primitive eye. So now I'm in the picture as I was saying I wished to be. Interestingly enough there are no laws in this domain despite the magnetism of ideas, so nothing really happens in the room (it is a picture of a room). Our role is merely to maintain its state. Whenever the paint fades we repaint it, a different shade of course, and this necessitates rearranging recovering or replacing the chairs sofas tables run lamps and hangings. Because so many visitors are eager to observe a room where nothing happens, we hold our meetings here and set up chairs in the corners for observers, who may actually spend most of their attention in distraction, for the view out the windows of the room where the picture hangs in which nothing happens is magnetic, and a line develops daily as people wait to pass before the picture and before the windows. If someone in the crowd stands still to linger, tarrying too long and not wanting to make way for the next in line—well, I've even seen shoving and wrestling, real violence. Sometimes the room has to be kept empty for a while except for private services, memorials and such. But let us take this matter up once more when the ray of light bounces back from the mirror. A scream is a pretty dense formula. Tomorrow zero, the shade had just vanished from a place that can only be reached by means of a work, and I have given up forcing myself into the place I am now. The further ahead our destiny lies, the more we can know of it. I imagine myself on my deathbed. I imagine you all looking at the air above me. I hear you say, *"you have an idea."*

BERNADETTE MAYER

It Moves Across

It moves across and over
across the ground
it moves across over the ground
under (by the bridge) the moss
lover the moss
across the grass the
grass moves across crossing the
blades of grass into
larger fields
of grass crossing over the
mounds and hills of
nothing but grass on top of
roots of grass
it moves across slowly
slowly into
another field or further
through the forest still
moving by
and by emerging from
the forest small enough
moving
the same rate
under the bridge next to the
trees next through the
trees missing them moving
around them still
crossing like the trees
the trees over
like blades of grass the
grass over as a bridge goes over
bridges
bridges over the trees
it moves across the hills
like a field over the fields

like field on field
of a hill of a hill
as if the forest
into its forest
on the ground like the ground over
it
stopping over
near a patch of grass.

from *Midwinter Day*

Stately you came to town in my opening dream
Lately you've been showing up alot
                            I saw clearly
You were staying in the mirror with me
You walk in, the hills are green, I keep you warm
Placed in this cold country in a town of mountains
Replaced from that balmier city of yours near the sea
Now it's your turn to fall down from the love of my look
You stayed in the hotel called your daughter's arms
No wonder the mother's so forbidding, so hard to embrace
I only wait in the lobby, in the bar
                            I write
People say, "What is it?"
I ask if I must tell all the rest
For never, since I was born
And for no man or woman I've ever met,
I'll swear to that,
Have there been such dreams as I had today,
The 22nd day of December,
Which, as I can now remember,
I'll tell you all about, if I can
                    Can I say what I saw
In sleep in dreams
And what dreams were before your returning arms
Took me like a memory to the room I always return to
When thought turns to memory's best love, I learn to
Deny desire from an acquired habit of vigilant fear
Till again to my nursed pleasure you and this love reappear
Like a story
Let me tell you what I saw, listen to me
You must be, you are the beginning of the day
When we are both asleep you waken me
I'm made of you, you must hear what I must say
                            First I thought I saw
People all around me
Wondering what it is I write, I saw up close

229

The faces of animals, I slid down a long grassy hill
Past everyone doing everything, I was going faster
There were no streets to cross, no dignity lost,
A long story without pausing
I was racing, no one approved of what I was learning,
I saw a woman's daughter, we met on the stairs
I saw everything that was ever hidden or happening
I saw that my daughters were older than me
But I wanted to see further
                                    Nobody including you
Of all the people doing things, was approving
Of my sliding like this down the long tilting hill
Past the place to play and all the past
                                    I saw the moon's
Last quarter in the southern sky at dawn
                                    Then I saw
The shawls of the dream as if they were the sky
And the dream's dark vests and the dream's collar and cuffs
Of black leather on the dream's black leather jackets
I was alone in the dream's dressing room trying on
Different styles of tough gang-wear or raingear
In the dream my daughters Sophia and Marie
Are always with me
                    Then we climb
A mountain to the Metcalf's house, Nancy's fixing us
The eighteen intricate courses of a Japanese dinner
We sit at a counter curving around the kitchen
Like what they call a kidney-shaped pool
Eating hearts of heads of wet red and green lettuce
In the most high and palmy state of friendly love
Then Paul takes us all on a trip
                              A while ago
The Japanese lady who lives next door smiled
When Marie smelled the fragrance of her cultivated rose
Sometimes dream is so rampant, so wild
As to seem more luxuriant than day's repose
So without riot spreading everywhere
How can I be both here and there?

                        Then I found
A message in an over-sized book
On the way to Allen Ginsberg's nursery school
Where Ken Kesey was conducting a big picnic
                        Then I saw
All the buildings of New York drawn to look
Like the illustrations in a children's book
                        I dreamed
The road was so slippery from a truck's oil spill
We had to stop at a truckstop
Though our friends who were ahead of us might lose us
All the food in this place is served in a big dollhouse
And the salad's in a hatbox, they're catering to us
It's hilarious, suddenly we all crack up
                        We say
You don't just eat from the desire to see a vine
Which today is called a chicken sandwich
You do seem to eat because you wear a hat and so
The hat's box is empty and must be filled with food
Do you see what I mean, it was a special restaurant
I was with Grace Murphy
                        Then I dreamed
I was ordering pompoms
Not those ornamental tufts on hats and not chrysanthemums
But a kind of rapid-firing machine gun
Really I can't figure out what's good and what's bad
I know I want to awaken feeling
Some remembered perfection
For which I crave a homeopathic dose of evil
Like the hair of the dog in the proverb
To offset the unsteady state of memory
                        What man or woman
Could this be involving, so fleet it is indulging
In not quite flying but dreaming, flaunting
The short-lived continuity of a sound like hummingbirds
What is a story
                        Can I say that here
Or should I wait till later wherever the question

Of life's chronology of satisfying the favored senses
Might better qualify the falling course of the grave day
As I must come closer to inevitably waking up
Like a dying man is dying spoiling the favor
You might grant me to extend this liberal time
And remit my punishment due though I've confessed already
And been forgiven
Are you going to convince me
There's nothing more to dream up
Like sins not committed but related anyway
To cover innocence
Always listening to everything you see,
Watching the sounds of the day

ALBERT MOBILIO

The Third Kind of Interior Word

A contemplation, a furtive act
hung false but vividly up —

My mark is found
resemblance to a ladder,
a secret, because the rungs
are sudden proof

how intelligence believes
its touch, some question always
bleeding through
Dreamt rain of one

made kindled sound, made choir
out of bodies
Strict letter striking pure,
its alto shears me miles

across this private tense
of cadence doubled hard
Pidgin threat, dyslexic flux
that gear the actual bone

beneath the human gown
Devotion is a winter loom
burnt sexual,
a darkened wax I've flawed

with gas blue match
Corona of my smothered wish,
a violent mouth & untaught page
The killing cure is talk

as if *said* could column largely
from the radio shade
of mental things a world
that climbs to climbless slow

Step One

And what a cremation that was. Now I can mark my exact place in the etch-a-sketch bible of conclusions. Only then will I be quiet about the lack of shade here. There's always some way of heading off alone to where the cover's good, some way of saying this is not an ordinary way of talking. The exact is often found torn off from the rest with edges sharp enough to cut tolerance from skin. Exact collapses upon itself with the din of a spontaneous chore. That's what I'm doing, stashing the verb *to be* behind a couch and calling it a place to sleep.

In the mountain towns they gather to trade calendar beads and decorate the thorns. High voltage wires criss-cross the cemetery where the cigarettes have gone unrolled. Chronologists sabotage our murmuring. Divided up and spent, this braille cannot spell my airborne name. Among the rocks and below the gulls, I'm aimed toward a collision with the sunglass novel that's waiting out there somewhere.

Snow fell. He sold death and dismemberment insurance over the phone, and sometimes he worried, and sometimes he sold psilocybin mushrooms. He believes in emigration anywhere for everyone. Once he unfolded the serpent in his heart, his laughter was recorded for playback by border police. They taught him with a slide show how thinking can be deformed by the prospect of travel or sexual expectation.

Nauseous right off. The bus trip to the airport takes me through the midtown tunnel, the occasion of some head throbbing claustrophobia. It's like having your mouth affixed to a two-mile exhaust pipe. My stomach gets jolted into spasm by the stop-start driving and I'm battling down this morning's coffee. At the airport the air is soaked in lavatory detergent and jet fuel. Worse, it's begun to rain. I feel like I'm being wrapped in a grey, noxious gauze and the nearest fresh air is in Greenland.

Welcome to this multitude of sand. The cactus garden's in the upper room; the dancehall features a black light portrait of a tearful Stalin. All of our guests thrive in cabanas wedged beneath the ambient talk. Taste the vibratory scroll of things, what's just beyond the mailbox continent you roam inside. If you could look closely, and get your antennae quiet enough, you will discover how it all hums like a tuning fork, how it shivers without stopping.

Step Seven

The last stroke tells of the decline of the sugar house. Our sweet feed gone for good. Behind drawn shades, her cinder dark eyes fix on a tangle of dogs in an asphalt lot. She listens to the streetlight's crackle and imagines herself some kind of equipment. This is a fervid world of constant noon, spliced with intervals of wax classicism. When she shows me how to use my spoon, I see she doesn't know herself. She lacks, it seems, a direct link to the body.

Welcome back from where you've been. We played all your records and took turns soul kissing in your bed. One night we threw a party and invited your ex-lovers. Before they left we told them to take something they thought you would miss, but no one touched a thing.

Blown off course, driven down among the feathery stalks. There among the genealogies, our shoes rot, although we keep most of what we earn. Friday nights we ride into town for the special kinds of stains they sell there. Mornings find us bewildered as we stumble out for another gunpowder sermon underneath torn clouds. A semaphore seen from the satin-wood prow. The ship that left us here smacks against the dead horizon.

I took my gloves from the glove compartment and found the ignition. The rear wheels spun in the slush as the smell of gas filled the car. From the dash, the heater blew cold, stale air. Furious height I'd fallen from. Precision overwhelms. After the tires had burned themselves a black gutter in the ice, I began trying to rock the car free. People passing saw my head drumming the headrest and they leaked dirty smiles into their scarves.

And he said, *You're elliptical and self-reflexive, but so what, nobody reads you.* Then more drinks came and the thought thickened around the one open window. Inflected bone, taxonomy of white. Someone quoted Richelieu. The level of magnification enabled us to be frightened by the appearance of our own skin. *Cigarettes,* he said, nudging me, *are the last graceful sentences.*

LAURA MORIARTY

Rondeaux

Each page a day
Each rectangle outlined
On the sky there is movement
We are under it it is raining
These days remembering back
To that day actually the present
Streets meeting already writing
As if divided I write you and see
Each page handing it over directly
You at the same time in a speech
Make writing into life
Paper in hair and eyes
Mixed with the general storm
Inundated with each other
Each page says anything

Naked still on the second day
A current goes through my handwriting
My diary overcome the sea
Is like silk today There is
An unusual situation with us and the sun
And the moon big on the horizon
This is the story of the birth of Diana
Of your creation of a lover on paper
Naked but keeping track I write
To wish the season upon you
From the middle of my life to the middle of yours
In this rude outdoor existence exposed
Writing that I realized I missed the floods
As they pulled away revealing only mud long covered
Naked at last again as I write this

As I taste it's warm almost hot
If quiet I can hear as well as see
A woman chopping celery in a bright
Kitchen from the back window
But she doesn't see me watching
Her movements are precise and quickly
She has everything laid out One must
Learn how to cook or how to drink tea
As I taste as if I were made
Only of the ability to taste
As if I were taught to stop with tea
And to wait to turn on the lights
By one whose experience retains heat
Like a day that was warm or a cup
As I taste it seems to stay hot

Aye, rarely said But you have said
When long When days have gone on
A week spent and leaning against
Some booth or bar say Aye and stop
Not for yes or always though yes always
You put a word to a long even
Breath I have heard you say
With some awe at the slowness of time
Aye, rarely said But you so often
Offer this equivalent for sighing
Named for a vote or forever
Each day a law that passes finally
You number yourself in the tally
You make a perfect total with your
Aye, rarely said But I have heard you say

Let's stay or you said go
Someone running not unusual
To have to go to work at dawn
Glad for the job happily gone
So let them take our places
And not as we did go but stay
An hour completely red not
Reckless though unearthly
Let's stay you were so
Flushed the way a night will
Make you vague and permeable
Nonsense that you or I should be
En route Look someone running
Away and not unhappy to
Let's stay but you said no

Though you complain about your bruises
Among cushions even here even you might find
Some edge to fall apparently against my will
Though not everything is as soft as I am
And not every impulse toward sympathy
Needed or received or not each attempt
To fit a plug into the wall doesn't explode
In your hand and wounds will come
Though you can hide them well enough
You complain meaning I do since it was
You said that though no one else heard
Nothing can be proved but for those bruises
Which even as you complain are both
More or less than you deserve to have and
Though you have them now are fading

Why am I divided from him?
A continuous line begins with the brow
And becomes the nose by agreement
A piece of linen simplifies
The features of its women like
Masks or any other kind of quiet
A beautiful arrangement by convention
Only if accepted or if not
Why am I divided thoughtlessly?
A stylized head bisecting two scenes
Of life or its embroidered equivalent
House man clouds a child suspended from
Parentheses that by balancing unite and yet
Why am I silent in the foreground divided?

He takes off each shoe with the grace
You sometimes find in drunks ones who
Dress well despite lapses in time
Giving out with a frequency that would be
Alarming if heard or if heard understood
He favors a discrete red and allows
For repetitions in a scarf or even picks up
The theme in trousers or an extravagantly
Open-throated knot as if we could see his heart
He takes off his coat drops and retrieves it
With the elegance of a single move full
Of intent just to show off the deftness
He possesses with a surprising fervor
As you do when it's what or all
You have left or so they'll say when
He takes off but then I'll always see him

And to brave clearness I'd have given
Almost what I did give Nothing
That wasn't strictly speaking mine
Wanting only what was blatant
Giving into the available restraints
With the same passion I might
Have resisted or perhaps I did
For it was the same damn thing
And too brave or too grand for anything
Like what I should have done or been
All things reduced to the absence of these
Same things They rush me to return
On time or even before I've gone and said
Here is to all we are not lamenting
And to brave clearness or to what we have instead

So then as I say I begin again
These days it's always four a.m.
Before I drop off the night's morning
Almost and almost dusk and time
To begin again and again I've missed
The morning approached wrong-
Endedly but then if one end is more
What you want to do then do so
So then offering itself begins with
And remains awake tilted up until
Blood runs to the eyes and it's time to consider
How like any of our mornings is this dusk
The beginning and how I began to say
I begin again exactly as when before claiming
So then as I say I begin I began again

240

Which thinks only of itself
As a naked woman writing a book
She is in love with you
My mistress he said to me
The same flowers which grew then
We write at random
We go to bed in the sun
What we know to be true
Which thinks only of itself
Or he of herself like dominoes
She spills over into you
He is me
A version of anyone
We write it for them
Which thinks only of itself
A fully grown woman
I am in love with you
She writes everything down
Arguably
We write it out

Before it disappears the implication is strengthened
We are our own audience
I am forced to move in a certain way
By the other members though this place is familiar to me
They are strange transforming everything as they
Go loudly not deciding to I also go
We excite each other
By our multiple presences swelling the parade pushing
Before it this emptiness tends
To disperse in circumstances which
Close in as when cops with sticks
And masks worry the lingering coherence
Of potential events we submit to them
Yet our complicity meaning to have itself lays open
Before it the spectacle of our dissemination

On the borders were prophetesses and scenes
Of liftings one by the other
And climbings effective and not of barred doors
And pilings of groups on roofs of any
Description being stacked too near to see
The progression and its counter filing
Oppositely as much of a sight as if
The intended might have been going on
On the borders inasmuch as the borders
As urgent as the center seemed
To order the disarranged elements
Repeatedly fixing and loosing
The attentions grown expectantly
Keen of their advantage
On the borders finding the complex sufficient

LAURA DE SADE

"To wear binding like binding" she wrote
Also "my name as the title shows
Is Laura" a common enough situation
To be bound as oneself to admit
To unpardonable pride or unusual
Desires "to court sensuosity as if it were
The judge of truth" as its own renouncing
Stands against men in the old sense
To wear down in the arena
Of full view the libertine regalia
Imagined upon a rigorous silence
As when turning back to a woman
Entangled in leaves an animate
Becomes a sentient piercing willfully
"To where a man's heart beating . . ."

242

Chandeliers were existing but I
Decide to say goodbye to my flesh
Apricot walls with what was left
Of the days
Extrapolated
As they already were from the decadence
Of calendars or gardens, fountains
Made to display
The divisible symmetrically
Chandeliers depend upon
The pendulous fullness of someone's bride
The facts of linens fastened with ribbons
To fat beds
That celebrate being stuffed like
Chandeliers we use up the light

The year forces itself out of me
Much as the remaining days
Drain unmercifully the resources each measure
A full measure takes just that much
As can be born by the taker
Whose confession starts a new life
Whose time is identical with
The year we are having
Though we can't have it
The name of the present is determined
By its numbers as if naturally
Because I do the year seems to exist
Consecutively because I lose the count
Doesn't fail to encompass me in
The year's reckoning

Where into the floor were drawn
Fishes and other saleable creatures
Assembled into a flatness
Whose plan enhances
The singularity of each tile
Along with the overall drawing
Of coins from passersby
Making purposefully for stalls
Where in bins the catch
Oiled and made to shine like
Whatever would be freshest
And desirable as the instant
Of perception unites the impulse
To spend with the seller's intuition of
Where she can get her best price

By ending on Saturday the thirteen
Hours and minutes to be determined
By season that interval
Of light in which we find ourselves
Like any other burning complete
With unalterable change
The sameness of ending blackly
By ending on Saturday
There might have been a Golden Age
A bursting treasury
Or only a name
To end it though
By ending here we've ended nothing

Last winter in Florence
A costume drama in progress he writes
Strangely narrow yet embracing
I described him noting suddenly
What my handwriting as an old woman
Will be he continues I am that now
Inside devising a man or woman
Who is manly outside
Last winter fingertips barely
On the street one overcome one
Twisting inside made for the purpose a cloak
Or other garment against time against
The body they were the same constructing
These memoirs out of nothing
Last winter sending them back to me

SHEILA MURPHY

from *Pure Mental Breath*

13

Road becomes so instantly metonymy,
It sings when tires grind over it
With new firm grips that hug each chunk
Of cinder, gravel stone.
Road mentions politely that you need not stay
Inside your lovely or depressing home.
For to remain in motion is its own libation.
Being free, its own libation. On the road
Semesters feed into the novel you are making
Of the movement. Cities flicker by
Like little dots of charity, they feel so
Numb and harmless from this distance.
Only the whine of motor against pavement
Furnishes a lovely humming noise
We say is roadnoise meaning it sings
Under our touch as we would want
The town to do, the house,
Even if holding still possessed the same intrigue and magic.

22

Tender knows the power of its hand
Requires restraint like justice. Pulls back
Against the grain
Of wanting to intrude because of need
Or excess energy. The quiet promise
Being so much even feeling
Rotates give and take again.
Until the layers tuned to intimate exchange
Run deep enough to reach the soul.
The purest center that must never be approached
Without a quiet reverence. Lines
Drawn without the hand
Of understanding. Or they never are
Acknowledged. The less attention paid
To boundaries, the more natural justice
In a combination of attracted souls
On the brink of letting go of artificial markings
To allow true melody its voice.

Maxfield Parrish

Often I turn on people
in rather strange &
inexplicable ways.
The source of
the irritation
escapes me.
It always has.
Sometimes
my heart just
opens and
all the lions
get called
back to some
other corner
of the cave.
You'd probably
laugh at the
flowers I
bought tonight.
Bluish purple
& they don't
even have
a name. "Name?"
pronounced the
man at the
fruit stand
he shook
his head
& laughed.

These purple
flowers have
no name. &
no smell. But
the room
smelled & looked

different when
I brought them
in with me.
For instance
I was gentle
with their
stems while
I thought
about how
many lovers
have told
me I'm
rough. These
are hearty
thick stems
yet I slipped
the elastic
off their
limbs as
if I were
a servant
undressing
the president's
child. Just
thinking of her
for once. Oddly
alive & being
touched by
me in this
practical way.
The whole thing's
off-kilter the
way my purple
flowers grow.
Something that
makes sense
in February.
I have enough sense
to buy flowers

now. But such
strange ones.
Sprayed. Their
eerie color
is not real.
At least not all of it.
Maybe none of
it. The eerie
little branches
from which
piney green leaves
grow & I guess
that's real. But
the 287,
no I mean
thousands
of faintly blue bells
I can hardly see
I must be getting old
up close they make me feel dizzy
the fineness, the wealth of this pseudo-life
tiny balls, pale blue
with a sliver of a tongue
sticking out or sometimes
everything's teeny & sexual
it's sort of like underpants
a cover or a case
that's purple & the little
ball is blue.
I don't know why this wave
of a plant belongs in my vase.
I needed something fake to
start me up. Something
I could be gentle
with just to try.
Looking hard I say Baby
I don't know why I can
give you everything
& I'm dazzled by your frown.

CLAIRE NEEDELL

from **Reaches the Body**

Boundary

Color, even whiteness, reaches
the body as a name.

Nakedness, "river",
drives blue from it.

Domesticity

Blur of whiteness,
self, incandescent clue.

Who, brought into
such a language.

Jettison

My dream is
this fall from one
side and the other.

An object falls against a slope
my body.

The language beforehand; body
in the language.

Seclusion

Light, assumed eagerness,
passing through a wall.

It isn't living.

Witnesses, by all counts,
leave.

Not the body the act.

Propagation

I want you to think
me hollow.

Intercourse suggests
an artificial point.

Head On

The dream which exacts the body,
excludes nothing from it.

There isn't one sound,
one color, that your name
cannot claim as content.

Passage

An object passes through
tight significance.

If I await consequence,
nothing will end.

Submission

The self *is* doubled.
Inescapably inside
the other's
language.

That retrieval is
seizure, say if
"swan" comes out

of "girl",
catches her.

Judgment

Breath in unison.
The use of a syllable, in battle.
As would
enlarge.

Wave

Voice the red flower
dismembers.

That even echo is not
repetition.

In Spite

Your name, nullified
by desire.

And pity doesn't
people the foreground.

ALICE NOTLEY

Jack Would Speak Through
the Imperfect Medium of Alice

So I'm an alcoholic Catholic mother-lover
yet there is no sweetish nectar no fuzzed-peach
thing no song sing but in the word
to which I'm starlessly unreachably faithful
you, pedant & you, politically righteous & you, alive
you think you can peal my sober word apart from my drunken word
my Buddhist word apart from my white sugar Thérèse word my
word to comrade from my word to my mother
but all my words are one word my lives one
my last to first wound round in finally fiberless crystalline skein

I began as a drunkard & ended as a child
I began as an ordinary cruel lover & ended as a boy who
         read radiant newsprint
I began physically embarrassing—"bloated"—&
        ended as a perfect black-haired laddy
I began unnaturally subservient to my mother &
        ended in the crib of her goldenness
I began in a fatal hemorrhage & ended in a
        tiny love's body perfect smallest one

But I began in a word & I ended in a word &
        I know that word better
Than any knows me or knows that word,
        probably, but I only asked to know it—
That word is the word when I say me bloated
        & when I say me manly it's
The word that word I write perfectly lovingly
        one & one after the other one

But you—you can only take it when it's that one & not
        some other one
Or you say "he lost it" as if I (I so nothinged) could ever
        lose the word

But when there's only one word—when
                              you know them, the words—
The words are all only one word the perfect
                    word—
My body my alcohol my pain my death are only
                    the perfect word as I
Tell it to you, poor sweet categorizers
                              Listen
Every me I was & wrote
                    were only & all (gently)
That one perfect word

from *Désamère*

Overhead at night, above the planet
Identity gone to sleep . . . Look what I've done
End of century, world so human
It may become a desert
Doesn't it feel like one anyway?
Approach a desert then, in a prophecy
An America now and later
Flat and cut with washes
What nondescript hardy little bushes!
In the distance treeless mountains
Then a campfire, someone's here
Small orange-haloed, a flame
People sit around it
Two, man and woman, well-lit
A third standing, distanced from the two,
Tending towards them nervously
'I dropped the shell,' he says,
'But I'm not responsible for the misaim
Someone else set the sights — '
He's speaking to the woman
She's middle-aged, brown desert face
'I believe you,' she says
'When you die, I take it hard'
The man who sits with her's different
Wears glasses, a somewhat mid-century suit
His eyes are closed,
He seems to talk in his sleep
'You're both caught in times separate
From your condition now,' he says
'Still causing it, you can't leave your pasts
I'll try to dream you out of them'
Faceless people at the fire,
Further back from it, hard to see,
Murmur to each other, sometimes say things to the three
And one says to the dreamer, 'Who are you?'
'Robert Desnos,' he says, 'dead and happy

My intention is to be happy
Even if our world should disappear
I see you better than you do
Because I'm foreign and because I died
In nineteen forty-five,
The last time things seemed clear'
He's quiet now, and the others
Are focused on the fire, waiting to hear
The voice of Desnos again
And wondering where the world is

~

Desnos addresses the woman,
'I dream your brother's bike's been stolen
Out of a smalltown home, how can that be?
An extinct bird called the Stalin-bird
Now appears in Hawaii
Brother on R and R joins your family
A vacation from Nam in Honolulu
He shoots reds at night, that's to say, injects seconals
I can't make this dream stable
Your times are too nervous
Now you're riding a dirt-bike of your own
You ride it over a low hill, on a secret path,
Into the desert
To this campfire, where I await you'
Desnos stops and sleeps
The woman says to the others, 'You're all trembling'
'We were the vulnerable,' one says
The woman's brother's shaking all over
'But you kill everyone! Are you vulnerable?' she asks him
'I'm shaking so hard can't talk,' he says
The fire in the center seems steely
Has blackened mechanical flames
Another woman says, 'We loved each other:
Why's the world so bad? Where are the animals?'
Desnos sits and dreams, eyes closed

'Oh I'm dreaming,' he says, 'of
John Kennedy's pain, it's
Virtually nothing, quartz pebble'
'I remember,' the woman says to her brother,
'In Hawaii you nodded out into the salad
I gave you small money to score with – why
Didn't I give you
More, more of anything, why didn't you tell us
Stay with us, anything?'
Desnos says to her, 'I'm dreaming of a zoo
We're in barred cages like a town
Everyone's there, small monkeys are there
I myself look like a monkey
Who's there are the vulnerable,
The animals are vulnerable'
Brother's shaking, says, 'The desert's full of me!'
Desnos says, 'The future's this desert
I'm dreaming
The future, there's nothing in it but spirit
There are no animals
And then no people, it's so beautiful
White and empty like dissolved bones of a carcass'
Someone says, 'Don't believe we won't
Fix the future'
'Fix the future, fix it,' the woman shouts
Desnos says to her,
'You must enclose it in your largesse
It's in the desert still, a speck, it lives'

~

Desnos says to her, 'I'm dreaming that
You read a biography of me
Simply told, was it written by a fool?
In it I'm a soldier, not a poet –
I try to take a hill, you know, *that hill*?
There's one in every war
I'm a toy, hill's a sand-pile

259

You look down at me, you're playing,
In a desert lot,
You and your brother, now in the book
Your brother says, "He isn't me, why not?"
A sunset-color cast to the sky
"Let's put the hill in a jar," you say,
"Let's re-organize the world
If you can read a book you can do that" '
'. . . But you can't!'
The woman's speaking now, 'My name's Amère
See how it's short for America?'
'Were you a soldier?' Amère then asks Desnos
'I killed a German in a poem,' he says,
'Il est mort dans la rue déserte'
'Sand's better scattered,' Amère says, 'I'd
Dump out that jar now, and say, "Each
Speck of sand is a poem,
Eat it, and grow sandy, for our future" '
Desnos, back to dreaming:
'A vulture, white-headed, approaches
The concentration camp,
In my biography, as wide-winged
As an angel
They say I'm noble, but that vulture exacts nobility
Until nineteen sixty-something'
'What do you mean, Desnos?'
'Nobody got to have my death in Vietnam
Now I dream,' he says, 'that in nineteen forty-five,
Year you're born, year I die,
There's a map formed out of a spiderweb
With holes, empty torn places
One's "Stalin" one's "Nam" one's "eighties" –
The map's spun from the ass of a man
He speaks:
"We had to collaborate with Monster S,"
He squeaks. . .
You made Cold War with S's heirs afterwards
Created both sides in each of you

Included S's evil
In yourselves as experience
Now the world's dead of competitive economies
Of Science, cars, the Human Spirit
When the planet was clean, we thought ourselves
No better than it
It can't be written clean
With poetry, dear Amère'

~

'You're agitated, your face is scratched,'
Amère says to Brother,
'Please let me take you in'
Doesn't hear her, circling fire, says
'After a while it seemed to me
What we were doing was just murder'
'My dream,' says Desnos, 'is of an elephant's
Soul, large and purple,' Brother repeats,
'After a while, it
Seemed to me. . . ' Amère says, 'I'll help
You finish. . . What we were
Doing, was just murder'
Something flies close, spectacled
Owl, Brother says,
'Like a goddamned raccoon, isn't it cute?'
A red parrot lights on his shoulder
'We'd precede the Phoenix Program
They'd a list of people to kill — you know
Pull up their hair and shoot them'
Desnos says, 'The effect of war
On all wildlife is unimaginable, I dream
How Americans kill the elephants
Who provide the Viet Cong transport'
'I have to keep reading this book,'
Brother says, holds up the book, 'Tells how
They left us in Laos, in seventy-one,
All but two died

261

We ate raw fish and survived
The two of us walked back to Quang Tri'
'More animals arrive,' says Desnos,
'Unaccountable in our desert,
Chévre de Perse, ours de Perse,
And the sika, dark eyes, of Formosa
Why, isn't it just the old zoo!'
'We go back to Quang Tri, takes seven days
Hilly terrain,' Brother says
'*Instantly* they send me back out!
Into North Vietnam, they must want
To be rid of me, the others
In my sniper unit, never come back
I have two records but one of them is blank'
'Look how the stork
Comes near you,' says Amère, 'it likes
You, it pokes your ankle'
'. . . Want to be home with animals forever,
Cockatoos, burro, pigs,' Brother says,
'Not all night in Quang Tri. . .
Civilians, I killed lots of them'
'Look,' says Amère, 'a civilian, a Chinese
Jaguar, gold and dark'
'That orangutan's ridiculous,'
A shadow round the fire says
'You people haven't spoken for days,
Where have you been?'
'Quang Tri's fallen, we've pulled out
Some of us are ghosts of the French
We're heading back down towards the south — but
We know we won't pass our urine tests'
A large white Himalayan vulture
Ruffed neck ruffed feet
Face fierce in white softness
Alights with rush and flap of three-meter wings
'Beauty,' a ghost murmurs, 'such beauty,
How can we keep it alive? Look
All the animals are gone again'

~

'I know what an animal's like,' Desnos says,
'Sweet, educated, unassuming
A man fits out a Terezine:
Torture chamber, gas chamber, crematorium
Men destroy Laos and Cambodia'
'Brother's shaking again,' says Amère
'They rehabilitate Nixon, but *he*
Manages for only a moment
To be rehabbed before an O.D.'
'I dream,' says Desnos, 'night's blackness here
Is produced from the eyes of a Cambodian woman
Who's gone blind in refusal of sight —
Won't watch it any more, the
Extermination of her family
In a genocide of which Nixon's part-entrepreneur —
Bombs Cambodia, finances the Khmer Rouge —
He's in my dream too: as his advice
Is being asked, as he counsels politicians,
His published memoirs in front of him,
Cracks form in earth, trees wither,
But his face grows younger, hair actually
Lightens almost to blonde'
'I keep going AWOL,' Brother cries suddenly,
'That's why they give me a Dishonorable Discharge'
'Is there judgment for Nixon?' Amère asks
'In the judging of Nixon,' Desnos says,
'Perhaps everyone's judged, to the extent that
Everyone tolerates him:
Trees disappear, animals die, don't they?
The same laxness results in global warming,
In a world where it's difficult not to be guilty'
'Some people are more vulnerable, less
Free to be good,' Amère says
'I was vulnerable,' says Desnos, 'and I was free
Whole countries of freedom inside me
During my abduction by the Nazis, watching

263

The anonymous soldiers so unlike animals,
I knew everything, didn't I?
Auschwitz Buchenwald Floha Terezine
Reading the palms of the others
Foretelling for them long and happy loves
'*La passion de la liberté est une passion
de l'âme*'
To be free and to be good
Are almost the same
But why should only victims be free and good?'

GEOFFREY O'BRIEN

Scroll

The body of the saint
Is rooted in gravel pits
And warrens. The angular sun
Tilts back
And settles into its blaze.
The shoots rustle.
The law was made
For worms. The fallen hammer
Gleams under the leaves.
The women in exile in the mountain
Learn the corpus of fragments
By rote. The flowers
Force their way out of the rock.
The border is invisible,
Almost unheard of. The fog
Lasted twenty years.
Forests were eaten. The soil caved in
As if to swallow itself.
There are murderers out there.
The voice in the wind tunnel
Instructs the abandoned and delights
The ghosts. The charred reeds
Thicken into a paste. I balance
My arms to describe her emergence
From the blood lake. The broken roof
Interrupts the sky. As near as the bones
Is the dwelling of the inventor
Of sentences. The fringe
Excites, the absence lures.
The curving stream stirs envy
In the rotted heart. A column
Painted with vulture eyes
Guards the prohibited music.
In the fire he lost his name.

The branch
Studded with dark birds
Trembles. She has dreamed of a cave
Where she gave birth to her father
And where with huge pawlike hands
She disarranged waterfalls. The smoke language
Is part of the arsenal. The children
Spy on the priests. Palisaded interwoven
Groves are watered
By captives. The merchants
In their parade bells
Forget when to stop. She speaks
Of sand bars and they recoil in dread.
Even in the plague quarters
Hollows can still be found
From which the signal flutes are audible.
Where the earth swells
The harrows are laid to rust
In anticipation of whirlwind.
The brambles flex in their sockets.
The light unravels.
The shuddering of the granite
Warned her of sacrilege.
The purloined hair
Poisons him. A music
Of uneasy intervals
Combs the silence. How dusk
Invaded them they concealed
Even from themselves. The unshaped
Suggestion of a spark
Corrodes the attempt to gaze.
A mottled hide barricades
The aperture. The rain is empty.
When you fold the words inside out
You enter a sacred cavity.
Its transparency
Peels itself away from itself.
The mask is displayed only once.

They dwell on the memory of a splash.
Mist is depicted
By a black rectangle, the pond
By a footstep. The interior is limitless. The animals
Change shape. The shell scratchings
Force them to stop moving.
The pauses between the sounds
Diminish or expand
As if pulsating. The hard part
Is going back through the thorn patch.
The line of stakes divides men
From woman. The child's nicknames
Were discarded. Ownership
Adheres to the dead. The cup
Annihilates them. A radiant opening
Promises to make a center.
The rusty striation
Mimics ambush. The breath
Retreats from speech.
They recite the old story:
"As if he had ingested caverns
He saw blue stains everywhere."
The hours are kept separate from each other.
She never goes near the tangle.
The chipped eyes
Dominate their niche. Whoever was killed
Was hidden. It leaves a hole
In the network of sanctioned embraces.
The world can suddenly be burned.
They watch the smoke from the sea.
The walls are designed to disappear.
We guarded the morning.
A lizard twisted
The ledge into view. The leaves whistled.
The layered glitter
Sloped away. A field
Fell. The melody had begun
Before the playing started.

The bundles click. The furred ears
Stiffen. The magical body
Imitates the concealed maiden.
The brushes creak with language.
The woven animals
Catch fire. The sandy edge
Harbors animate voices.
The target flees from itself.
In the flow of the grasses
The trees erode. Its river
Washes it free even of water.
The leap is rocky.
Hollow
The sky drips.
In the shadow of its shadow
Tensile
They have strung together
Blots, sun spots, blood drops.

Ornamental Syllable

Almost without a way to bud it creases the netting.
The hole airs its root-hole.
Air's its root.

The crack jubilates. The folds unpeel.
It edges out:
coil-hauling, caul-holing, keel-hurling hail-curl.

The jays' jazz flashes in jasmined haze.
The dome's a medium
amid a dim "I made, I met, I'm at"—

a meander undammed. A nub of pulsing sockets.
Hisses skim pond mist.
A larval harbor. Other levels unravel.

Radiant ardors card the garden.
Sandy haste, a drained boat. It keens
garbled prophecy—"I saw a sky in that pouch"—gnarled thatching.

Any weevil's eave the lip of its shadow.
Wood-ash, staff. Pile out the vessel. A few near
A new evil. Save the last puffs. Shiloh,

oilish sapphire, devious lava.
Wounded rain,
detritus of wharf ear.

A cone
cyanated.
A trill haloing cumuli.

Schismatic bandana
mirroring
me or roar or ring.

The grain
stretches
from within its frost,

pockets of resistance
gallop
toward a fiery alphabet.

The Prophetic Child

The gardener's daughter
Looks over the rim of the well
And God looks back at her.

He is blue smoke
Riding a lion,
He grabs hold of the light.

The women
Walk down from the hill house
And transcribe her raptures.

I have come
To damage the gate.
The bees hum in Phoenician.

She receives a vocabulary.
Every scratch and pebble and wormhole
Has a name and is a doorway.

The fence post
Is the Agony of Noon,
The cloud is the Death Pearl.

The well bursts apart
Into expanding necklaces
Whose throat is the Tree of Life.

The lady on the cocoa jar
Gave birth to a palm tree
Alone in the desert.

The outcast
Slaked his thirst under it
And of her bones made a ladder.

The chariot
Is welded with groans
So as to be heavy enough to fly.

In the splintered light
Of the milk wagon
She hears a choir.

The piano master
Will publish her melodies
And the women will sing them.

Their favorite is the hymn
That says we are all made of sunshine
And are now returning into sunshine.

There are other and more perplexing songs
They have not yet wished to copy out.
They have not yet penetrated

What she understands by "nailhead"
Or "the fly is shivered"
Or "he commands the cities to drink blood."

At the gardener's gate
As her face at dusk becomes indistinct
They are thankful for her silence.

Theory of Climate

The air mass
Puts pressure on the playground

So that the fault lines buckle
Into chaotic ridges—

In a gentle sliding movement
They give way,

Like an earth tremor—
Or as a mountain would hiccup into labor—

The world is greased—
The continents slip from their moorings—

The land bridge rolls apart
As if on ball bearings

And with relief the ocean
Overwhelms the valley—

Undermined by the tender
The creatures find safety in roughness—

They bless shell and thorn—
They give praise to the inventors of curses—

In the paradise of weaponry
The monotony of the perimeter

Is camouflage—The razor wall radiates
Around the nest on whose linings

Pictures of sacred massacres
Blaze and zigzag—

the playground forms a natural system
Of dams and hedges—

In self-defense
The robbers build terraces—

The insane farmers
March off in search of vengeance—

Down in the wood road
The goat pen shakes with radio—

There is a registry of places
Where people failed to make payments—

The world is blockaded—
The car tip dangles in the scar—

The family burns slogans
In the plywood fence

Shored up with carburetors,
Fans, chair parts, disconnected bolts—

In the piles of wires
A girl skips barefoot—

She invents a story
About the bent handle

Of the grist bucket dangling
From the rusted spike—

It is the cave where Saul
Met the prophecy woman—

Where he ducked under the hood
To check for rain damage—

There is a registry of places
Where people deposited money

Or identified victims
Or where winter left flood marks—

The man who drives the bus has a voice in his groin
That recites the plots of movies to him—

Two strangers drove up from the harbor—
They argued about money—They shot the owner

By the door of the bar—The car was not found—
The door took another twenty years to rot utterly—

By the tarred border of the drained swamp
An out-of-work gangster torches the tire dump—

Barges came downriver
With whiskey and machine guns

And women for the warehouses
Of the waterlogged city

Of bought cops—The ballad
Is defunct, that went

"My body was a ladder
I climbed to the roof of the sky

And when the sun got thirsty
I knew it was time to die"—

The inhabitant of the attic
Wakes by owl light—

The absent landscape makes noises—
In the bottom of the water table

The houses are changing shape—
She hears the walls melt—

In her spirit body
She wants to skim the tree tops

Like the helicopter pilots
On weekend maneuvers

Tracing the concealed body of the creek—
Past the half-finished house

Where the family threw everything in the van
Last week and just cleared out—

The government puts pressure on the air mass
So that the playground is scarred

By a metallic folklore—
The children eat the brains of dragons

Or imagine they are a burning ramp
Climbed by armies of dogs—

Land where the dead do not talk—
Loop of radio menus

Transmitting hardware prices—
Color-saturated films of abrasions

With music under them—In the black shed
They excavate remnants of gasoline and vodka—

After the poem is over
The man who walks on the road every day

Pulls his words back over his head—
He finds the word "sun"

And takes it to the darkest corner
Of the garage, and buries it—

MICHAEL PALMER

The Theory of the Flower

I will read a few of these to see if they exist
(We will translate logos as logos)

He swam in the rock
I am here from a distance

"Now kiss her cunt"
"Now take his cock in your hand"

The film is of a night garden
There is nothing meaningful about the text

There is nothing meaningful about a text
She

brushed away the sand
She brushed away the hand

This is Paradise, an unpunctuated book
and this a sequence of laws

in which the night sky is lost
and the flower of theory is a black spot

upon the foxglove
(These words have all been paid for)

He turns then to shade his eyes from the sun
She edges closer to the fallen log

This is Paradise, a mildewed book
left too long in the house

Now say the words you had meant to
Now say the words such words mean

The car is white but does not run
It fits in a pocket

He slept inside the rock,
a flower that was almost blue

Such is order
which exenterates itself

The islands will be a grave for their children
after they are done

You may use the paper with my name on it
to say whatever you want

I promise not to be so boring next time
never again to laugh and weep so much

which is how spring comes
to the measured center of the eye

The mind is made up
but you forget who it was first spoke

The mind is made up
and then and then

This is the paradise of emptiness
and this the blank picture in a book

I've looked over the photographs and they all are of you
just as we'd been warned

How strange
The winged figure in tuxedo is bending from the waist

The metalion addresses the mirror
and the music of the shattered window

falls unheard past the window below
How strange

but not so strange as speech
mistaken for a book

The phrase "for a moment" is popular in the world
yet not really meant to be said

This is the third or the fourth world
where you can step into a tremor with your tongue

I do not drink of it myself
but intend a different liquid

clear as the glass in which it's held,
the theory of the flower and so on

or the counter-terror of this valley
the fog gradually fills

just as we've been warned
It isn't true but must be believed

and the leaves of the sound of such belief
form a paradise

(pronounced otherwise)
from which we fall toward a window

Notes for Echo Lake 2

He would assume a seeing into the word, whoever was there to look. Would care to look. A coming and going in smoke.

A part and apart.

Voices through a wall. They are there because we hear them what do we hear. The pitch rises toward the end to indicate a question.

What's growing in the garden.

To be at a loss for words. How does the mind move there, walking beside the bank of what had been a river. How does the light.

And rhythm as an arm, rhythm as the arm extended, he turns and turns remembering the song. What did she recall.

It was of course the present the sibyl most clearly saw, reading the literal signs, the words around her, until a further set of signs appeared. And to divine the fullness of the message she uttered would demand of her listener an equivalent attention. The message was the world translated, and speaker and listener became one. Her message was the sign itself.

Hermes alike as the bearer and concealer. Hermes as the sign.

Who lives in the speaking and unlistening, wild onions by the river, roses in the garden a hundred years old, lilac, iris, poppy, jasmine trellised above the kitchen window.

They walk beside departure and images of a dry riverbed unfold, voices through a wall arm in arm. They walk beside an answer typing each letter as it appears. A large white room has a beamed ceiling. The poor live in long rows.

While staring at the sea he paints a woman's face, requests more light and time. Is there ever an image that appears, word inside word, skin blue as dust, nameless hills beyond. Is there an image if there is.

To be at a loss and to return there, saying things and speaking, it's started to rain. He paints a woman's face the color of the sea but portrays someone else as an empty chair. Then he learns to erase four words each day.

As an arm folded might mean 'to flow'.

They collide near the cafe door, smile politely and pass. He watches the philosopher turn the corner and disappear.

There is agreeable poetry.

There is poetry like a white cloth.

There's a poetry licking its tongue.

Let me lend you my fork.

Voice occurs through a wall.

As song divides itself, she explains with a wave.

We have never been happy here have never been happier.

Untitled

O you in that little bark
What is the relation of the painting to its title

The painting bears no relation to its title
The tiny boat bears

nameless people across
water that is infinitely dark

darker even than snow on paving stones
darker than faces in shadow on a boat

The boat is called Blunder, or Nothing, or Parallel Lines
The poem was called I Forget, then Empire, then Game of Cards

a game played yesterday in milky light
light which played across the players' faces

and the arcane faces of the cards
There is no relation between the painting and its title

The painting came first then its title
The players are playing cards in a little boat

They are asleep and it is dark
Their dream is called The Orderly Electrons

One traveler dreams she does not belong
Another dreams with his eyes wide open

like a solemn philosopher
dead from an act of thought

Two more lie with limbs intertwined
The painting has no title

though it has been signed Keeper of the Book
the signature obviously forged

for D.S.

Untitled (September '92)

Or maybe this
is the sacred, the vaulted and arched, the
nameless, many-gated
zero where children

where invisible children
where the cries
of invisible children rise
between the Cimetière M

and the Peep Show Sex Paradise
Gate of Sound and Gate of Sand—
Choirs or Mirrors—
Choir like a bundle of tongues

Mirror like a ribbon of tongues
(such that images will remain
once the objects are gone)
Gate of the Body and Gate of the Law

Gate of Public Words, or Passages,
of Suddenness and Cells, Compelling Logic, Gate
of the Hat Filled with Honey
and Coins Bathed in Honey

As the light erases
As heat will etch a d, a design, a
descant of broken lines into glass
Exactly here

between thought and extended arm,
between the gate named for lies
and the double X of the empty sign,
a kind of serous field,

fluid scene or site
peopled with shadows
pissing blood in doorways
yet versed in the mathematics of curves,

theory of colors,
history of time
At Passages we peer out
over a tracery of bridges,

patchwork of sails
At Desire is it possible
we speak without tongues
or see only with tongues

And at Lateness we say
This will be the last
letter you'll receive,
final word you'll hear

from me for now
Is it that a fire
once thought long extinguished
continues to burn

deep within the ground
a fire finally acknowledged
as impossible to put out,
and that plumes of flame and smoke

will surface at random
enlacing the perfect symmetries
of the Museum of the People
and the Palace of the Book

Or that a Gate of Hours speaks
in a language unfamiliar,
unlike any known,
yet one clear enough

clear as any other
and clear as the liquid
reflection of a gate,
gate whose burnt pages

are blowing though the street
past houses of blue paper
built over fault lines
as if by intent

Annul

"Gold? What, *real* gold?"

O golden yellows and browns and still resistant greens
of hardy urban trees so different from country ones!
O   how   laughably swaying the tips of your branches are,
how beautifully autumnal your russet hold on me please
don't   let   up. As violence is to be seen in the outside
    world . . .

mad lady on the steps asks if my father's on the street
I tell her No, he's in the air.

She doesn't understand and persists
casually pursing her lips.

The cruelty she manifests,
an absent-mindedness, has its origin
in others
so,
    We walk away   (from her)

beating of despairing wings.

Rose Garland Sonnet

After Lorca

Eat! Gyrate! Quick!   that condition called Death
I Despise!   Song!   Give me Song!
That which brings me down the most,
That which shall otherwise come
To me a million times, come, light up my nerves!

Between that which is queer and that which is even
More queer, like trembling plants, we straddle
The air. We rise up! Posies of sea-anemones!
Shimmering with heavy-metal kisses!
God is a fresco painted on my heart,
Casually thrown away, like succulent watermelon
Rinds   It's the truth!
O   Jump   Now   before balmy death
Time shall not take away <u>our</u> breath.

288

Mevlana

Turning round to discover that
Though your feet are on the ground
Naturally, your head's in the air.
Elongated your spine is
All the better to climb to heaven with.

Make of me Beauty a Ladder then
(It has already been granted)
Dissolving at every step.

Echo

Drink no more
From that pool wherein your
Fat face stares
back. What is this
pompous self-regard. It is
nothing.
Tho' it has been continuing
Lo these many years
and will continue without you
as others will stare
at the glasses on the table
at the emptiness
of your poor pot
sit back
breathe deep (and)
Consider the fountain.

STEPHEN RATCLIFFE

from *space in the light said to be where one / comes from*

40

Blue saw in the voice and, suddenly controllable beneath the weight
of leaves thought sparks as it wakes speech, one hand
in the story of birds painted like music
played at the window, minutes close to the day everyone
moving to dissolve whether under its tongue or beside the little it feeds on
in English, bottles to say nothing of salt in a glass, water on the floor
standing in the sound at the base of what he might have been
an instant cast by walls whose height, unknown, bends
to the edge of error—soon too much
with a glimpse of absence like days the very birds called summer
instead of sky the ceiling spent, though useless, asking
"speed to stand and wait," whose eyes above all
light the circle of no color in green
which talks in stone more than shade weaves between walls
hills, a book of matches across the vanishing floor
empty in the other roll of film until it stops at the woman
descending a staircase, phone's location moved in the dark of sleep, who wants
between the pages of the bed to be known, say *what I know* caught
in the light beside the words you wake to
another thing, something more
unequal to the pause I know to breathe, part margin, sphere
one thought of little at first remains.

43

Beginning in the light as heard, wheel on stone
were it ever at the gate between subjects
known as thought, arms and air mounted in the heat
a hand painted to divide into the transparent silence music leaves
two knots finished as one
breath, red mouth, mind you arrive at between your name and the window
the wind shut—how you answer sooner to the words
wanting the picture in the background, beyond it a pattern
of light and the shadow of figures
descending from a sign in the street to walls and diagonal roofs of houses
leading in reverse the plane of air backward, squares thought
sits up, mounds called as before to make red
redder and the floor
curve as if something acted at the end of less
this surface than names in the paper, missing perhaps, door locked
the ground in letters after the air closed
into glass, perhaps not
the first name in the house come to hear it
fall but a reading of stones
under the wheel, what leaf-silence and ear fades to tone
a form breathing in your hand like the visible beat of fragments
branches of the night divide, watching you sleep.

DONALD REVELL

Sirius

A vineleaf at the window
at night flattens
the world better
than Justinian.
A garden
is a species of policeman.

The cricket is a species of mole. When I think of loving someone new, I
feel blinded. I hear the jewels singing in the houses of my neighbors, in
the treetops and underground. We are all in hiding. The deportations did
not end with the war, continuing since the world began.

The loneliness
of a man's perversion
makes him an angel.
He finds himself
touching himself with a stylus,
hearing needle music
intently out of his skin.

The enthusiast does everything he can to postpone his pleasure. He takes
the lovely soprano to a bad cafeteria in a bad museum. She sings in spite
of all, something by Brecht, high and deadpan. When she leaves the
cafeteria, her hair bounces. Nothing can be postponed any longer. The
insect vaudeville of the trains runs faster.

If on Palm Sunday
not palms but panes of glass.
A man is not an animal.
The mandibles of desire
sting through walls.
In my shirt draped on the chair
a shadow-lyre
blackens windows with its sound.

If she were small enough, in the complete darkness, she could sleep between the strings. Music untitles the Jew of summer, a species of angel. The stylus reaches all the way across the alley. Sleeping there, the perfect soprano wears every surface of her body to bed. The starlight also reaches her, no one to say otherwise.

ED ROBERSON

from *The Aerialist Narratives*, Chapter Three

I.

A widow suckling
    the master's field
        bent over the rows,
the oddly backward

    trajectory of the bolls
        of milk
she runs with her hands,
    the cotton spilt

        from one breast on the ground
she fingers each drop
    into the sack plumping beneath
        her other.

Up on black mountain
    a child will spit in your face.

II.

bomb
bullet

            trajectory is only a line
someone has to draw it

or pull it out
and into the papery fibers

of skin, the responsive
skin where the slightest
initial mark,

the silvery slip of a kiss, the trail
writ of a stick, a whip, the ink
dip,

        sets up the conditions
of the art

living the line
drawing,   dowsing a delineation of
the human

so I thought the
silver lining was the inside
of a cloud
that flashed like that

little leg she shows when she sits down
her robe opens   across the plains of the bed

it is the outlining
of light

around the edge of that dark
cloud between her legs instead

and the inside of a cloud

that slicks with mist the divination
tools of beings mostly water
briefly written

III. On the Line

People die on the phone

Severe thunderstorms of guns

Snubnosed   silverplated

the lining on the ground positioning
       the body

          the cloud   the written
          something about how to contain
          a cloud

          how to carry air without a wrapping
          of leaves   of houses torn
          from their foundations   loose papers

          the spring arrivals of smells
          gliding song
          birds

the city in a basket   the jewels
of its lights in plastic
bags used
to house any evidence

                         *

Lanes are contained within the yellow line

The yellow line of the sun   the broad daylight mark

Wave-length maps out the colors

A city that chases itself into traffic   death
       escaping a band

          of the spectrum
          a black body erased across the tarm someone
          with a ball of mason's chalk recalls

          into an outline on the night ground
          uncoiled, the breath drops its wrapping
          the target that was skin   the arrows

the flights
the beautiful
cloud

The potent balls
of his eyes   turned off,
the whites turned up,
are bagged.

*

Too sharp to look directly at   (not the brilliant lining out
            of cloud form against background   but
The line drawn through us   (a different
            marking off of   conclusion   We are looking at
Struck by lightning
            on hold   writhing in the news
waiting on the open connection with extinction   for news
      of help

      a call connected at the moment
      of birth
      in nonsense and over time

      what adheres to that screaming
      is language torn off
      a background   a neighborhood shot up

      our single mother
      a speaking color
      a cloud

of event wrappings
dropped into those plastics of form
that the moving line around   one holding the chalk
picks as evidence off the closed ground   of the other.

*

Rain

IV.

There were these
mistakes between   the steps'
walk continuum   and the reign

of the consequences
of absence bam a lack
lapping misstep   that break
the fall of

a man rising from
a crash
land or the skip   free

of the takeoff   Seemingly spontaneous
power to lift off
to change   is deep   as religious

transformation as off
the water
the stone   the moon
the bird of spirit

flashes   People
do suddenly lift into the sky suddenly open
Not in this state

*

Punishment was supposed
to teach society
(teach "them" society)
But the teacher taught only
punishment
And when the punished suddenly

had learned

The change here was not achieved
by punishment's
format, not by the teachers
or any agents of punishment, but by
the punished
themselves, by those supposed

lacking.

When what is professed to be lacking
was achieved,
when that responsibility,
that manhood, which rehabilitation
for once had actually achieved,
occurred,

state troopers were brought in and shot them.

*

There must be
space between the trajectories
of the rain

of police machine gun bullets
that could trace the shape of a man
escaped
into more than smoke

from these
attempts to stand for
some kind of decency in living

even if it is come to
within
the meditation upon mistake

some country
the citizens of attica
had learned to re-think for all of us
and expected

300

                    rather than the barrel
                    that the nation
                    stood around the rim of
                    shooting into

                            them

V.

        And O
When I fell down on the ground
When I opened my eyes
        standing over me
                the light of a long freight bearing down on me
                around his face   one of the gandy dancers
                hitting a lick of the horizon's flying rail
                organizing a whip into a riding   he opens
                a place in line for me
                lifted in the physics of that singing
                rail   I am
        looking down at me
I lay down
When I opened my eyes
        standing over me
                their floated forms burned to invisible
                black bodies hiding stars   they lie
                the ropes of phosphorescent nebulae
                around their necks   moving like tie
                beams slatting the black night
                sky into which   from earth I hang
        looking down at me
I lay down
When I opened my eyes
        standing over me
                that start star

                trail slicked with the bloody
                feet of stealing themselves

                            301

            a way
        looking down at me
    I lay down
    When I opened my eyes
        standing over me
            one of the road gang in
            chain seen or unseen
            each his hair a rocky ore that burns
            into iron that splits the stone
            that splits iron chain into fires of spark
            flying free   I am become
            not just one of them but that one
        looking down at me
    I lay down
    When I opened my eyes
        they were rock under my feet
            I lay down
            my road

                        *

when we made the middle passage didn't we
walk the waters didn't we
have the waters paved with the skulls
of our grief for each other didn't we make it
on ourselves.
when we crawled under the mason dixon
didn't we jump the fence over jordan
didn't the river re-bed behind us and
turned blood because the bloods wouldn't tell
didn't we make it to this one side on our other.
on ourselves didn't we
get put up when we went back down
home didn't we hide in each other   no hotels
that we stood   uppity   a chance of gettin
shot didn't we walk
on the shadow years later of emmett children who did
didn't it make your step
higher than just to walk.

didn't the westward push opening
the country turn middle passage trying to shut
us out panicked at the plow flat and hardness
of our feet having stood on each other
didn't we open the rock like our hearts
didn't it bleed too to yield too to eat

didn't it

didn't it didn't it rain
didn't it rain

VI. Handed the Rain

given to
look into   the bowl
of sky

for it to fill
with future
see it turned

upside down on the grass
see the ladle pass

hear the god underneath
calling his inside
the heavenly vault   eternal

how that bump
reminds me   how we saw it
once

from the underside of
Nut   a mother's belly

303

see dissolve
against her vast ground
the drowned cloud of black

lives   the solution's population
of rain crowding the city
in the belly

see it now as the sea extended
the drowned city   lit   in this sky

see our sky
the bone clouds casting
African

tomorrows   only
an arm   black balletic cloud
extends itself

dark nimbic
invertebrate squall

I am handed rain
by a portuguese man-o-war
These are

new skies
once we absorb the seas'
solution as the bodies lost

the sting
fire of lightning   flesh

the water
body
air

we drown together
in our living
to drink

from this
bone

VII.

the flock of black cormorants flying
    underwater   are these the songs returning
        the escaped   lifting down into the cloud
of current turning
    back out of the fields of coral bolls
        to the abyssal skies
the undercurrent home
    to this day
        noticed   off any shore
the pile post   the cormorants alight
    on   Legba's mark
        open their wings and point

the bodies shining in their feathers

VIII. Ask for "How High the Moon"
(for Nathaniel Mackey)

    a half moon at midday,
if you've seen
    the gelatinous medusa

you know how it looks
    like it leans
its jelly umbrella and melt off-fringes
    into the wave   and wind
            of sunlight

The organism's membranous
　　delicacy, a silk stinging
　　　　thing like beauty
carried above beauty　carried away
　　the sky its

　　　　pale parasol borealis
the bride a gauzed nubian shadow
　　　　moon holding　carried away
damask balloon torn in two
　　over itself.

　　　　Such as yourself,
　　　　　　say,
　　　living down to what

　　　　　　means
the melt pools in the market lot reflecting

　　　　　a sky
　　　the ended days of freeze
　　have glaciered liquid flawless

　　　　　can afford
　　　for looking up...
　　　　Leaving the store

I overheard somebody say
　　"Look,　the full moon,"
　　　　at only the half

carried away up.
　　　And down time after time,
　　　　how many migrations
has ice made home
　　　to water?　and winters, to this spring?

the light and shadow holding together.

　　　　　　*

306

If in
the very pool you're looking
down into to look up   at the moon
out of   out of
it is thrown at you   a stone
from the tire
of a car plowing through it
the turning

seasons' wheel Or
there appeared
on your forehead
this stone that backwards
threw down   into the water's trouble

of turning and tire   that arrow
of time which film reverses
stilling the waters Then
see the hard thought at the bottom
weighting the reflection of its moon
creation   loss
each distinguished from our ghosts

*

Sculpted out of the sun-polished snow,
the small david of a puddle

out of how stones can sling up at you
if you're looking   (arrowheads the moon

ignescent associations between things:
the cold star struck from the broad day.   Light.

When Ailey set it
to music Billie got knocked down to

what a little moonlight can do
the white stuff of cost

307

danced   to music ask
for How High The Moon   and you want

Ella to sing it   bring it down
like the time she admits   carried away in time

she can't remember the words to this
but what she does in time

is
greater song the rest us

jus mostly cries out
no forward no back

                              *

hit in the head by the moon
no one can take the stone of that light

out of your human skull
no one can tell

where the bone and the sight
actually separate
                    now
the lost sight of all gap
opening on that

nothing they put in   their bones

                              *

the light at midway up
      out of the darkness
            orpheus

all you persephones you lazari
      christians and other
            resurrectionists

is that circle of listening
    decided
        to tear you apart

I mean this song
    this stone wants
        to dance with you

ELIZABETH ROBINSON

The New Language

I

Given the limitation of trees, what if each
season of leaves produces a bowl?

The machine of language has soft flesh;
a dirt portal has no room for roots but intends

that you speak gently.

And this bowl has hands of its own.

The hands claim that each flavor requires a name
and then that fragrance can manifest itself in juice and rind.

Any grove can promise this lexicon.

II

And given the discourse of seasons,
mouths are irrelevant.

The machine leaps up on the basis of what's foreign.

The fruit tends to forgive words;
it's an estrangement that turns
to mulch.

It's the shape of a body in a grove, everything sudden.

III

Inside the mouth, it's winter.
And no other cistern will convey

how a system has to release its own grammar
and fruit falls everywhere and a body should have to be
deft

and without trespass,

another form of the bowl rounding.

IV

The stem, the branch, the arc of the arm.
Say something now, under the awkwardness of law.

And dirt and skin combine.
It is impossible to see what was said before.
And blossoms issue from the tongue, but no memory.
And the newness of the phrase is obscured by its orchard.
And the stem is too tender.

Better than fecundity are lists.

V

What could marry the density of a seed to the explicit word
but hardness?

This clothes a bare arm while leaves fall and fall.

Mortar

Beholden or enlarged,
this mosaic,
its plaiting mid-entry
makes me follow

My uneven center, its mortar
comprehends the way, its pleasure
in the single tile

Enlarged and, now, unlettered
the pattern cannot redeem its
visceral spelling

Light enters the stomach,
reverting to the eyes whose
ceramic patterns

won't be burned
They can turn and expose

what passes for guidance, chip by chip

can illumine the fatigue
strewn in this path
of nourishment and flint

To prefer inadvertent knowledge, to recognize
nausea as something more than illness, its new circuitry

JANET RODNEY

from *Anywoman's Lyric*

Anywoman cannot *see* his dream, but they are so close on waking, same alignment, bodies lying north to south, feet pointing towards the coast where the south wind carries a sound of marimba across the lake & on waking, there is such a row at the door & T, it is Lear, don 't make a sound, old man talking to himself & to his prophets, bare feet scuffling on the porch, loud scolding & the curtains are drawn shut, so they can hear, but not see him lurch off, destination uncertain, rumpus & scandal of his 88 years. The night's stars like teeth, the gap-toothed sky covering over & soon it is raining, beats down on the corrugated roof of the *cofradía* where the xylophone fades & swells as electricity lights up a single bulb & leaves it vacant, candlelite leaping up, heating with incense, the rodents hanging from rafters, stuffed leaps across a sky of paper hangings & fruit, over the heads of dancers, some of whom are very drunk. Anywoman sways with another woman, hands clasped & held shoulder-high, bare feet & sandals raising mounds of pine-needles, back & forth across the room, crowd of starers-on, hats of woven palm, two men lurching beside them.

Anywoman looks out the door & a herd of deerboys races by, young antlers tied up with red ribbons, yellow, green, high-pitched cries and the whistle of jaguar among them & back they come in a wave, pause for a moment at the door of the *cofradía* swinging round once more in the courtyard before entry, pelts wet from the rain & antlers catching the paper sky, hook right, hook left, whirl round to the music, kneel suddenly & cross themselves four times to the East, South, West and North, pelts are discarded & placed on a table & one more round is danced, deer & jaguar in men's clothing now, sandals, platform shoes, faces shiny with sweat & rain.

Bottle & shot glass are passed along, old firewater, drink of moon raised to Anywoman's lips, goes down, eyes watering & they dance, women with women, men with men, her head and T's brushing the sky. Almost at midnite, they close the door & a daft-looking man who has been sobering up for the past hour, darting upward looks, is helped to his feet, gets up from the bench, leaves East for South, where he kneels in front of the altar, talking to Saint John, talking to the bundle & candles are handed round to everyone, lighted, he gets up, goes back to the altar, the bundle is opened, he puts on an old shirt, patterns of faded flame, or tiger stripes. Anywoman can't tell, pants rolled up and the exact sequence fades from her mind. He is dancing under great weight, eyes are almost closed, the room has lifted into the sky with many stars around, held by women & men. He dances around the world carrying this great weight, right hand cupping a cross, comes to rest by a table in the east & leans there, arms spread out in crucified position, head lolls on one shoulder & one by one men & women approach him, kiss the right hand, then the left, kiss the belly & kiss the feet.

It rains off the roof, ground soaking up, & in the fields, corn arms lift, corn heads look straight up, bean legs twine round. They close the door so the winds won't get out, so the rains won't flood. He dances high in the sky, a lamb-shaped cloud by his side, then kneeling again, changes into an older, even more faded & heavier shirt, tattered on one side, same shuffle, lamb close by, same end, head lolling, same kisses, small stars approaching in the night kiss the blood of his sacrifice, young sun fed by stars & holding her candle Anywoman grabs a dreamline, tendrils reaching out. Soft net of desire: deer & jaguar fight, jaguar gets deer & carries him into the house. Deer is sacrificed & offered up. A chorus of high-pitches, suckernose, penis pointing from each corner
of the building, covering cardinal directions, a bad dream
in the night,

        a premonition that he is burning mortal strength
snapping nerves too fast, dust licks her cheek, cat's tongue,
dust from the road, cat's paw of heat upon her shoulder,
thru an open window, a hole in the wall at the end of a
corridor: gallery of cantilevered arches, at the end of which,

        let a day run rough *you* somewhere, set down the time-burden,
yawns in her ear, do you think I should let the man out, the
other one living inside me, the man I was for the better part
of life & gave up being, is it possible that T only surfaces
for a brief moment, then falls silent, now retreating like a crab
into the whole he crawled out of? The ontological coil of the
question winds about her, a cobra of suggestion, for Anywoman
to answer, or let it squeeze the night around them, he must
not break his blood, must not run down these or any other stairs,
she opens her mouth to speak & a buzzing fills the air.

~

Everywhere she walks, a sound of hoes hitting, a human
sound inside the earth's stillness, stone bells flicked aside
& ridges build up, long where the field is wide, short where
the field is narrow. They are combing the earth, Anywoman
thinks, after the dry season when all is dust, the first
thing they do is comb her out in damp lines, damp from the
rain each afternoon, warm from the morning sun (clouds gathering
on the mountain pass) & the grains are separated in the patios,
those to be eaten & those for planting & after the beans
have pushed thru the top of the ridge, corn kernels are dropped,
two are three at a time, into a hole, have you buried the
little ones yet? Each kernel
                              a tiny skull
        Something
                    indescribable happening underneath, in this seed
and that, sprouting thru eyes & mouth, the earth & all its dead
bestowing cornflesh with its double meaning, a baby's wailing,
fat cheeks, among the shadows, too,
rising out of dark & heavy earth, a sliver of green,
                    a light, a life!
A spider
        has left a bag on the sill, earwig trussed & dressed
for storage & for days scorpions crawl across the planks, tails
hooking, fleeing the rains. T kills them with mixture of fear
& remorse, watching the walls at night. In the furrows, corn
pricks up, first shoots of green, soft as down.
        For three days, dawn to dusk, the farmer stands at the edge
of his field, long whip cracking at grackles that swoop down
on the cornshoots, for three days he stands in gladiatorial
combat with black wings, trumpeting beaks, until the shoots are
high enough to be covered with little mounds of earth, cradle-tombs.

~

        For a long time Anywoman sits crosslegged on her landing,
rooster-crow in compound up the path & doves in the avocado tree
cururu-u-u-u (like the girls when they make love) somewhere,
listens to the birds & the voices keep on talking. . .

315

closes eyelids,
opens again, if only you remember that the earth, the whole earth
is a *body* with head just like you, eyes, nose, ears, mouth to eat
& gets hungry & thirsty, arms, legs, feet, every living—as well
as inanimate—thing on it, even a cup of coffee or a box of
matches has a body, it all comes alive & makes sense, it all holds
together (in a minute relation of, invisible unless you know,
breathings, murmurs, caresses, swellings but don't forget for
a moment the sting, paralysis of poison, surprise of knife-wound,
shadow of something watching you all the time, Time) I put my
hand (contains also the seed of death & regeneration)
                                                on the ribs
of the house & there, Anywoman thinks, if she's very still, she will
feel it breathing.

                              ~

Anywoman lies
wrapped in a blanket waiting for rain, the windows rattle
as thunder prowls across the lake. Lightning makes a neon candle,
for the moment a darkened city's spires rise above the waves
where a lone canoe darts between & small rainbullets zing
on his plastic cloak, the boatman, home late from the fields,
his corn-rows other side of the bay, arms driving the oar,
tilling the water.

The procession moves slowly out of town with frequent stops
for moonshine & an off-tune from the sacristan's violin, a woman
beats her breast, leans from side to side on shoulders
that all but carry her up the path, they're carrying a box,
bare feet & sandals over stones & dirt, short of breath, under
a brother's weight, tired, and why did the sun come back so soon
(they thought), crops under water (that the world was coming
to an end), must be, Anywoman listens to rain hitting hitting
leaves outside, must be the cat
rubbing against the door,
"feed me, feed me, Sister Life."

DAVID ROSENBERG

from *Job Speaks*

Chapter 3

Rip up the day I was born
and the night that furnished a bed
with people to make me

the pillow from every night I lived
smother that day   cover its light
so God can forget it

let death's shadow
hold the ether mask there
clouds obliterate it

a total eclipse
blackout
swallow it a tiny pill

and that sweat that night beginning me
black oil absorb it
a hole drilled deep in calendars

shrivel that night in the hand of history
let it soften in impotence
turn off its little shouts of pleasure

every science unsex it
genetic biology   advanced psychology
nuclear bomb

no next morning shine on it
through the afterglow
singeing the eyelids of dawn

because it didn't shut the door
of the womb on me
to hide my eyes from pain

why couldn't I have been
a lucky abortion
where were there two knees

waiting for me
two breasts to suck
without them I could have stayed asleep

I could have melted away
like spilled semen
in transparent air

wrapped up in quiet dust
with gods of power and influence
and the emptiness of their palaces

with rich families their money
paper houses
for plastic children

with criminals who can't break loose
there they rest with tired workers
no more hell from bosses or jailers

who all fall down
under one blanket
not the simplest machine to serve them

why should someone have to live
locked in a miserable spotlight
bitter inside

waiting for death far off
they search for it restlessly
like the final person in a late-night bar

318

they can't wait to see the iron gate unlock
and the little grave plot
comforts them

why should someone have to walk around
blinded by the daylight
he can't wave off

that God throws on him
waiting at every exit
in front of me

a table of sighs to eat
and moaning
poured out like water

every horror I imagined
walks right up to me
no privacy no solitude

and my pain
with my mind
pushes rest aside.

Chapter 13

My eye has seen it
my ear heard and grasped
the vision

I know what you know
nothing less
than you

so I'd speak to God
to the one
whose reason is all

you are all plasterers
you think you are doctors
but it's only broken walls before you

you smear them over
with a whiteness of lies
a color you take for truth itself

you should shut up before them
and your silence become
a road to wisdom

stop then on your way
here on these lips
is a little plea

you speak for God
and in that acting
you can only be false

you have a case amorphous as air
the court is only a conceit
behind your forehead

what can you say
when you catch him
in a lie or contradiction

will you make him squirm
can you make him speechless
in his witness?

his words will unmask you
your conceit crack and fade
like a painted smile of piety

you will crack in the sun
of his majesty and fall
to pieces before him

your heavy talk in the dust
of ashes
with the clean little homilies

the niceties broken like clay
lay there then in your dumbness
so I may speak

opening to whatever
becomes
of me

my flesh may become
the one last meal
in my mouth

my breath become
the one last drink
in my hand

though he slay me
yet these words stand
to speak up

to his face
they are my voice itself
no false witness

could find these words
you see I'm not cut off
stand back   listen

to the voice of poetry
that is making my case
and may be lasting justice itself!

who else is there
to argue with this song
cut the air out of my life

321

then I'd rest content with silence
death sentence
but still two things more

I ask of you
to allow me to open
myself in your eyes

remove the hand that falls
leaden on me
like a heavy depression

except that I move   falls
like silent terror
except that I speak

and lighten my fear
I want to walk out of the dark
to meet your fierce stare

call me and I'll be there
just as right now I'm speaking
for you to answer here

how many crimes and untold lies
am I unconscious of
how can I see them

with your face hidden
veiled in silence
what enemy is in me

that you squeeze in a vise
but at such distance
infinite space

am I a leaf spun away
in a burst of wind
impossible to see

what power in that leaf
blindly
to feel terror

this numb piece of paper
you squeeze my feelings on
held in this painful air:

bitter words
you have written down
against me

a list I inherit
from the unspoken lies
of my past

my feet are also locked
as if you would hold me
ready for punishment

in that vise
some crime some slight
some monstrous pinprick

forced you to look
narrowly at me
narrowing my path

noting each unique footprint
brand of a slave
a voice singing out through the bars.

Chapter 14

Man swims out of a woman
for a few days of restless living
full of anxieties

a flower springing up
under the passing cut
of the share's thrust

a shadow fading out
of time
gone

disintegrating
like an old wineskin
an old coat

eaten away
by moths
drained

and this is the creature
you open your eyes on
take time to judge

as if pure earth can be extracted
out of lust-spattered hair
by a man himself

however young or innocent
he dies
in a dusty coat of experience

because our days are numbered
so we can count them ourselves!
approximate the whole

short story
you give us
with its "The End"

look the other way   turn your eyes away
why don't you
just let us be here

ignorant slaves
enjoying our work
enjoying our sleep

till we finish this simple story
and get a little rest . . .
even a tree cut down

has some hope
it can spring to life
old roots

start up tenderly
even if its body stump
dies in the dust

soon as it whiffs some water
it starts
growing like a new plant

but a man just disappears
one last breath
and where is he

lakes have completely evaporated
rivers shrunk away
and men laid down to rest

never to rise
or materialize
the sun can die

galaxy collapse
space evaporate
universe shrink to a ball

and we will not hear it
nothing will shake us
awake in our beds

if only you could hide me
beyond existence
outside of space and time

in a darkness
a secret
beyond the known

until your famous anger passes
and then you remember me
waiting for the book to close

waiting for an appointment!
is it just possible
a man dies and lives again?

I'd bear any day   every day
heavy as it is
waiting

for your call
and I would answer
you want to hear me again

this creature you made with care
to speak
to you

but now you number each step I take
note so slight a false movement
I can't even see it

as if my guilt is sealed
under a coat of whitewash
faded from my eyes but there

as a mountain
that will finally fall
a rock that will be moved

a rain wearing away the stone
a storm a flood
washing the earth away

as you wash away
the hopes of a man
we are lost at sea

our faces go blank
unrecognizable
painted out forever

sunk out of your sight
we swam a little
and we drowned

our families rise in the world
we don't know them
or they fall

or they disgrace themselves
sink into despair
we don't think of them

we only feel our own flesh
rotting   only hear
the echo of our body:

the pains of its dying,
the mourning
of its self.

Anywhere Out of the World

translated from the French of Charles Baudelaire

In the hospital of life
the patients are all mad with desire
for a change of bed

this man wants to suffer next to radiator
this imagines getting better
under the window

wherever I don't happen to be
feels good to me
my soul and I have a running discussion on that

what do you think my pale shivering
of living in sunny Lisbon
warm and alive as a lizard

they say it's built with marble
people there hate plants so much
they uproot all the trees

and it's on the seacoast
made completely of light and mineral
and water to reflect them

but my soul is not responding

well since you're so glued to peace and quiet
as long as something is moving to watch
why don't we go live in Holland

a place you think of often in art galleries
stoned by the mast-forests of Rotterdam
great ships anchored beside the houses

total silence is all that comes from this soul
say how about Batavia
where the European spirit mates with a tropical beauty

nothing—could my soul be dead already?
so down you enjoy suffering?
then let's go to some really dead places!

we'll pack our trunks for Torneo
or even farther—extreme end of the Baltic
farther—we could set up house at lifeless North Pole!

where the sun barely skims through the world
and the bare-minimum strobe of light and dark
nicely frames the monotony

which is half of the picture itself.
And we can take long baths of darkness.
For entertainment the Aurora Borealis

sometimes will color our pages
like reflections of a fireworks display
in Hell—suddenly my soul is shrieking

in its wisdom: Anywhere!
I don't care—as long as it's out
of this world!

STEPHEN SARTARELLI

An Early Spring

1.

Muted season evanescent
in the clay's soft footing,
wordless call of day.

A gleam of dry rock
mosslike on the earth-bark
flashes airless from the latening,
no metal for flint.

Cradle-bound and vertical
the green evades the gravity of water,
brushes lightly counterwind
anteceding fire
in a looming breath of sun.

2.

Pale wood browning
in a void of labor
blind to crescent moons
concealed by daylight,
a hundred-year trunk
skin of no animal
plumbs the minutes
that ever remain.

A fallow stillness
time-wild, clockless
in a field eluding
torsion of the plow,
deliquesces airborne
ahead of any wind
of blackbirds
sombering afar.

3.

Light-riven, stalwart
in the profligate soil,
plane trees mar the inviolate sun,
the uncut branches burgeoning
in countless little germs of shadow.

Day teems protean inside and out
the boundary stones, tentacular
revision of the work of wind and hands.

Should an unexpected tremor of still other life
invert the bedrock under hills of pine
unwintered on a winter afternoon,
perhaps old seasons would reblossom nevergreen,
inward, earthward to some core of time,
some godhead buried in the wasted matter.

A momentary sky of azure spans the day untroubled,
though, as if to laugh an instant of eternity
upon the slow and imperceptible corruption
of a temporary birth, myriad and necessary.

Phantasmatikon

for Simon Carr

From black against the nothing
hued upon the minutes
falling formless by the side,
beyond the choice of sight

the body and the field
momentary histrion
flexion of the ulna
rise toward the acid cast:

woman's breast or parry-thrust,
mirror-spawn, monster
of the act itself
the fight against the whiteness

freeze as if to be
an eye about to see below
the field of black and blank
the body come *ex nihilo*

That Land (3)

Anything beyond
the nothing when,
time-hum on a wing,
stillness troubled all
as one unique:

off the tender edge
tiding down, footloose
at a single point,
place of the fallow,
we rise away—

and there it went,
shuttling without,
around the earthen
mould of air, shade
of anything alone

where falling limbers up
the stasis of our birth

utters clouds upon a leaf

That Land (4)

Whatever else the turning
of a matter in a measure
over and over, seasonless along
the way beside the time without,

semblance, fugitive array of air
about a teeming vessel
lights upon the darkened hull
and there resides apart—

what other movement out again
in breathless space and privy
to the blood may carry light
beyond the gesture made and seen,

appearance less and more the time
still fret away the offspring
of the act:
            passing on alone
and back, sightless, it proceeds—

enfolded in its precipice
augmenting, now receding

LESLIE SCALAPINO

from *Crowd and not evening or light*

roll

the men — in the new bar — with the new
wave clothes — that are just outfitting them —
young — which are modest —
producing — that — but from them
— as really — something

      their — who're — not
      wealth — like — as
      grueling, deprivation — of that place — but
      of the really — modest —
      small means — from that — new wave clothing

as their — who're
muscular — fragile — though employed at
some — low — or modest unexciting type of
work — not of the power, wealth — and
producing — which isn't abroad

      people vacillating — though an
      overall stillness — butt, of the corpse, but not that as the
      matter — in this — and as a really passive
      thing, but which fleeces or with — their — hard — constant
      work

the dog coming trotting down to the bank — off from
which — we were in the boat — people bathing off the
steps — where a — greenish corpse has floated
— there for burial — to the bank — the dog beginning to eat flesh from
the buttocks of the body — but not as — our — from the outside
— the flesh being very soft coming off easily

335

the people — not mocking — from the boat rowing by — the
people bathing, off the
steps — who're filming, from the boat
— appearing such — not as — our — from the outside
— from the soft flesh of the — corpse — that had
been washed, up to the bank — but the innocent-looking
bathers, who're concentrating — facing, we were in

seeing a movie — of it — before — but having seen that — of
the corpse floating in the river — before — now — and
actually seeing again — close — to people
filming, this time — as not having to do with that — from
the soft flesh — or — their, who're bathers

the buttocks — of — the corpse — so facing
us, the boats — though submerged, with the soft
flesh of the butt — to the dog — who ate easily — the
bathers in the water — off the steps — close
who're inside — not noticing — I would think

a boy — we were in a busy street — kicking
a dog hard, who's done nothing to produce
that, another boy, responding by a joke
of kicking — the dog — again — between the two
children, or adolescents — having nothing — to do — with the corpse's
soft flesh, after

sales people — who're insistent — whether
they're not bothered — or fully saturated
— with — the sight of the bathers, the corpse — before —
floating, there for burial — to the bank
— commonly — so as — not having produced

336

weeping, having been a
long time since doing that — not from
— the sight — of the corpse, soft flesh — or
the dog — from being outside — which is
irrelevant — a funny thing

someone having been abusive — of
that type of thing — and to have gone ahead
and do that — with people — with no thought
— as transposed — our — which is
funny — stupid thing

just kicking it out — with some been —
not — a reference — to — the dog — or
boys — with it — the corpse, soft flesh — up
to the bank, having floated, there for burial — being
irrelevant to it

someone, before — having, so what
been abusive — as irrelevant — so when
there isn't anything there — the dog —
regardless — with it — euphoric — not
from having it there — as it not a repressed thing

that — there wouldn't
be any change, as irrelevant — in anything,
what occurs — over decades, not fleecing — or if it
does — as not viewed as having a function — whether
that is a — fragile — living in that phase

the inverting — of someone — not floating on
the water, which isn't a reference — to the corpse, bathing
— but not in submissiveness — as a reaction
or euphoria, which would continue — as
far as his ability to

tears — on someone's
part — as an odd — reaction
— when there's no reason
for what had produced that or
conceiving of it — which had occurred

as the fragile — muscular
— who're young — of the men in the new
wave clothing — as to — being —
the grueling, deprivation — city — which is
the really — modest means — they have

not mattering — that — they have
those means, which aren't wealth — or
which they aren't — abroad
— fragile — though muscular men who
were there — in that situation

a driver — going back — behind — taking a piss
before that — after, another driver, going in the middle
of the night — people sleeping on the sidewalk who are
innocent-looking — are — in that situation
constantly — not — like — that

not mattering — whether or not it does — of — their
grueling, deprivation — that appearing
as the substance — with it, and with
there not being — any — irrelevance in
to that situation

to have simply lived in the — lack of resources — that's entire
and to have trashed things — working hard — or some
getting past having access to it — that — isn't known
to the graceful men — not from being obtuse — and
as the same — work

338

— so irrelevant — to everyone in
— that setting — as up to — open —
believing the ridiculous — our florid
though which is outside — and — so doesn't
matter — that that is — what

the grueling, deprivation — of
everyone — with it, not a matter of it — so
that it's up to — as many people — as there are
as that as the continual run for the entire — din
— but feeling — so that it is the matter of it

a death of someone, a relative
— occurring
with — the writing — not
produced — by it — but expressed or
seen — before it

the relation — as the
representation — of people, not them being
— here — not coming from
it — but it seems to be

— setting —
and people sleeping on
the street innocent-looking
not have changed — with just
anything — being there

my grandmother dying in an accident — with
my imagining or seeing the scene, but as it
happens expressing a man's
situation whom I knew projecting my self as or in him
— becomes — real — which I knew after — in her
dying

can't imagine — what — someone's
protesting — or writhing — they — not with
change being relevant — or not — that kind of event — at
any time — and as grueling, deprivation
not existing — or that

ANDREW SCHELLING

Run My Hand Under

*Does Nature remember, think you
that they were men, or not rather that
they are bones?* —H. D. Thoreau

In a redwood grove, on a low hill facing east, I bent over a shovel and
buried my dog. Sun pierces a tree, the far ridge, a fresh growth already
laces the turned-over sod. St. John's wort in the shade. Where dirt's most
disturbed poison oak. Oneself, to end up, on a coastal North American
hill, somewhere, hell realm or bardo, beyond whatever—a comfort to
consider those bones—

Or run my hand over elastic frail ribcage, the woman I love, her pulse of
desire. What store of affection inside the bonehouse? Tilt of the chin, and
how her denim skirt falls to her shoes. The things a man loves. Her face
could be face of a dog. Face of ash. Ash and a trickle of bone.

It's an old Buddhist trick, got out of Mongolia, some Paleolithic recess up
north. Dress up in fur. Take off the fur. See your companion a scatter of
bone. Two ossuaries just a membrane between you. Remove it like
clothes.

Now love her like that. Take off her fur.

Taste a nipple, go for rough skin but find rib. Thigh against thigh, seem-
ing so fierce, it's only a femur, good for a flute. Try to be delicate, back on
your passion, tangle of nerve and wet tissue, all those veins at the crotch.
Find pelvis—hollow and dry. I came through that? Hard cartilage. Now
try her mouth and touch teeth.

Knucklebone, bone of the ankle, down past the kneecap. Run my hand
under, beneath beneath. Where does it come from? How did it get here?

Yet it's heaped on the bed. Next to a window. Imagine the aftermath.
Hipbone on hip.

September 1986

Isha Upanishad

A Note on the Translation:

Isha Upanishad is a poem—firstly a poem.

Once when I wanted to read it with some students I discovered all existing translations inadequate. Each tried to render it in the translator's cautious prose. Not one approached it directly as poetry—an insistent poetry, mysterious as some pilgrim's stave, founded upon tricky metrical changes, fragments of old prayer, and invocatory chant.

The translations, I found, had all been doomed by one thing, an inability to dwell in the uncertain. "An irritable reaching after fact" distorted the various efforts into English. Even the formidable Indian commentators, when they read *Isha*, largely did so with sectarian minds, unable to withstand the powerful—I think purposeful—contrariness of the thing. *Isha Upanishad* is poetry, not a book of catechism.

For my translation I must acknowledge the guidance of someone long dead—Professor Bhuwan Lal Joshi, friend, teacher, intricate thinker—one of those infrequently met scholars who is a poet of the classroom. Himalayan by birth and upbringing, Tantric by temperament, he led me step by step through these stanzas. How much his own insight was fed by the sadhus and holy men who wander his native Kathmandu Valley I did not have the foresight to ask. He took to *Isha* as primal song—as though the contours of its utterance were in no way separate from the mountains he'd grown up among. Yet he taught me to read it as territory native to myself.

For those who are interested, the verses of *Isha* ("The Great One") lie among the oldest strata of the *Upanishads*. They certainly date back 2500 years. A few may be rooted incalculably deeper, snatches of song from some very distant yogin. Where the astute rhymes and troubling phrases all come from is anybody's guess—the carefully torqued dialectic, the cryptic glimpses into the limits of work and learning, the nearly strangled cry for vision that finds itself echoed a hundred dynasties later in *Bhagavad-Gita*. Then finally, the eloquent crematory verses that close it. Who or what mind drew a thread, and strung these stanzas together? It is all very scary, and very nourishing stuff....

A poem is a mind that holds contraries.

342

1.

The Great One dwells
in all this, and in all
that moves in this mobile universe.
Enjoy things by
giving them up, not by craving
some other man's
substance.

2.

Engaged in works
hope to live
here for a hundred years—
it's what you receive,
nothing else.
There is no one for karma
to cling to.

3.

There are worlds
they call sunless,
turbulent,
covered with gloom—
those who
violate spirit
depart after death
into them—

4.

     The Immobile One's
swifter than thought,
not even a god
can approach it.
Stands, yet outflanks what runs;
holds the waters
the Hidden Female let forth.

5.

     Moves,
and does not move.
Is distant,
is near.
It inhabits all this,
stays outside of it all.

6.

     Who sees
all breathing creatures
as self, self
in everything breathing,
no longer shrinks
from encounter.

7.

When the spectator
of this unity
regards all creatures as Self,
who can suffer,
who be misled?

8.

It is out traveling—
bright, bodiless, pure,
unflawed,
unpierced by evil.
All objects
have in their self-nature
been arranged precisely about us
by that presence—
poet, and thinker.

9.

They enter a turbulent
darkness, who
cultivate ignorance—
a yet thicker darkness
who are addicted to
knowledge.

10.

   It is different
from knowledge—different also
from what you do not know—
this we heard
from the steadfast ones
who opened our eyes.

11.

   Who is cunning
towards knowledge and ignorance,
with ignorance
moves across death,
with knowledge reaches
the deathless—

12.

   They enter a turbulent
darkness, who
cultivate unmanifest worlds—
a yet thicker darkness
who are addicted
to empirical worlds.

13.

Different
from what you can see—
different also
from what goes unseen—
this we heard
from the steadfast ones
who opened our eyes.

14.

Who is cunning
towards loss and creation,
with loss
crosses death,
with creation reaches
the deathless—

15.

A golden solar disc
hides the gateway
into the Real—
remove it O Nourisher,
so I can see
the Unwavering.

16.

O Nourisher, sole Seer,
judge of the dead,
O sun, offspring of the Father of Creatures,
fan out your rays,
draw up luster—
    that most
splendrous form, yours—
I would see—that is—
the I am

17.

Animate breath
    is undying
but the body ends in ashes—
Om—
    oh volition, remember,
remember that which was done,
remember
that which was
done—

18.

O Fire,
knower of every
    creature's breath,
take us along the good road,
far from deviant evil—
we offer you
    precious verse.

LEONARD SCHWARTZ

Monuments to the Not Yet Lived

The streets I walk down are an incorporating of English into proscriptions of disturbance, a rupturing of thought by contingency after contingency, an insurrection of the actual. The lamp in the shadow, the screen in the sky, a cave as the Real's source: all of these part of the simple plane over which one steps, intertwined in two places at once. Aftereffects of a dream sensation, apparitions in a sun shower, translating into vocal music, into a harmony of street noise where *street* means **event**. Verbalizing daylight, swelling as the phrases transfer across. Only so much has reinstated itself through my authorship during the course of one year that I can divine for you no more than a fictive awareness of any place I am. This is Siberia, the sleepwalkers after a long march through bitter cold and snow are reconnecting with their beds. William XYZ was taken out of himself, if only to enter the underworld. I bend backwards like a bow to shoot forward towards all that I love, and that tautness is the future power of the past's repositories. And so on, down a finite number of invisible avenues spilling into the visible. So the well-nourished microcosm with its compliment of fillibrations shows itself willing to hazard a reasonable guess, and externalize a soft and tattooed macrocosm in the distance of night. Over and over the future is reconfigured in this way, but the future too is finite and bears its freedom grudgingly.

On a point in technical procedure all the muses fall into vast disagreement, their voices demonstrating that widespread beliefs can combine into new kinds of complexes that sap the psyche because not believed firsthand evidence, only hearsay and intuition. Like a surgical operation in which the artificial organ is rejected, this way of thinking, although the organ is left in anyhow and *something* continues to function. Aren't we all suffocating for the lack of some object capable of moving us out? The body is left without tools to understand where its voices emanate from. Experiment finds itself in a new incarnation whose attributes cannot flourish. A friend says that it was a dialogue that will bring them back, that we are already outside ourselves but that it is too lonely there to know it. Good and bad, then, that the bodily ailments retain everything. That the scanty trance-like mood that holds you down when you can do nothing finally erupts into vision. That a voice for thoughts relocates the wound. *One is always stopped just as one starts finding out where it is that the messages are written.*

How cruel that this wing with all its prison cells always seems to alter to meet the present's needs, that the psychological function makes the living pass through so much trouble, distorting even the derivation of that wing of cells. Imprisonment is more than a metaphor, it is a way of being. I always imagine myself next to something that is really very far away, feel myself perpetually on the approach, although it is for another time, the satisfaction, if at all. The awareness of confinement spills over into the allied acts of planning out a campaign of frustration and feeling the brunt of that planning in distanced form. . . . So much is battle, the fields littered with dead mammals and burning skin, and all so that key messages might eventually experience interruption. The will is felt behind awareness, preparing its own demise in the wills of others. . . . Out of a human consultation erupts a dreaded image of the fallen body, a derangement in nocturnal garb, a black language on colorless tablets, stones huddled around an inscription in rags. And all from impatience, from the fear of immobility, from the chaffings of a confinement whose terms escape definition but whose culmination is a false relief that is only a further proof of the enormity of the exclusion that each being extends to each. In the end, it is euphoria that has been sabotaged.

It's strange that so much of who one is remains the same. Because there is pain in so much seeing. As hopes are ground down, ever more naive certitudes arise, their hovering routes connecting one perspective to the next. And just as a certain fragile mass of contingencies are the only thoughts, islets of desire gradually plait into monuments to the not yet lived. This is the time of day for a militant openness concerning spiritual acts, but this is also the time of day that refuses to open to anything. Refer us instead to some sort of law, to a procession of sanctions, to all sorts of deposit information that ought not to have been purchased—or even produced—in the first place. Pick up what one has been given, work it, better it, yes. But one can never be sure whose suitcase is whose. There is an effort made to keep track, but everything is so coextensive with everything else that one's bearings start to sag as under the weight of a drink, or as if we had uncovered an inexplicable weakness in our characters, the whole fractious nuclear jumble careening into view like a station wagon, the identity of space with the mind, and of the mind with its

350

earliest memories, reducing us to the most passive of numerals, the numeral one. We **are** number one, always thought we were, always think we will be, however infantile it is to think so. Which explains why we cannot move, why at the heart of the cheer awaits a lengthening silence, a silence that can never be entered. And so the space we can move through becomes ever less.

The totality of thought hurtles past, at the most filmy remove from the immediate. The eye is that film. Totality escapes it. We kill what we see.

As experience stands to reflection, so to the silence an absurd variety of upheavals. The more unlikely they are, the more passionate the trouble. Sometimes I fortify myself against them and retreat abroad, in a manner of speaking, simply dismissing the new by not being there, by releasing the mind's ethers. Or like the shreds of evidence some authors build into sweeping truths about life, no doubt as a matter of doing their job, I allow myself to inflate to fantastic proportions. Such declarations ache as they swallow reality, not exactly digesting all of it. This is a partial listing of how they ache: a partial listing too of how they deliver. Waiting for a phrase to open up to a series of phrases, and for a series of phrases to forget themselves as they become the actual. A question, then, of what value one assigns to that moment of forgetfulness. But I cannot stop to think now about any but the most immediate of truths, and those are that I have no mind, no body. *You must measure with your gaze the abolitions your gaze contains, point more explicitly to your quarrel with the world. You are an apprehension of all that is not and you must never withdraw from that, the sciences of the body more than willing to convert you to their object. Theirs is a stern standpoint without contact with things themselves; they will always insist that you pay attention to their own awkward forms. But you will not. You will want to, mean to, but what you have forgotten will be stronger still, and nothing will be able to distract you from the act of futile recollection, no one will be able to prevent you from failing to remember all that is.*

The unsettledness of any strip of earth, investigators piercing beneath its bedrock, tracing a new line into all that tonnage. Returning to the surface, this interrogation makes contact with itself in an immediate nothingness of dark colors, listens, listens for an approximation of the total situation despite having just added something new, then lowers its head again, sinks its teeth down into the crust, like a thoughtful animal pawing into the vast body of a mineral wealth it cannot understand the purpose for. And although nothing here can be understood, the torso of the visible, the shifting truth, bring language to fulfillment. The nascent state misleads the dreamer, however long his history. A questionnaire half filled out, comments half abandoned to the other's gaze, modulate into a less distant obscurity, restively extending itself over fundamental solidities that fade in turn. Slowly the exterior turns to look at itself as if it were some unkempt rustic type deposited abruptly in a vast metropolis. Spiny intersections overwhelm the eye, and mammoth spigots; even the table-tops inside a pancake house come informed by their own particular allure. Each street noise carries an imaginary rebuke, one to which one is more than willing to listen. These are the allures desired, the voices of impera-tive. They never last, but there are many sensitive points on the ear, some of which retain the memory in a form that at any moment can sing from the actual.

The shorthand must be disentangled from its expediency, the whole of perception calling to it. Offices rapidly closing down like lights on the mainland, until you are alone at sea, the raw air on your face assuming the feel of necessity. Or taking a risk, wandering in Central Park well after nightfall, a strange white light glowing in the sky to the East Side. Do you know that in all my wanderings in Central Park after nightfall I have yet to meet a single soul? On the outskirts they walk their dogs, but at the heart of a thing there is nothing but what your eyes chance to see and your heart happens to feel. So much darkness goes by so quickly it is impossible to turn it into light. Then more walkers, more dogs. Taking a risk: the grounds are wet, the moisture will soon freeze. But to bring this over into language requires another turn in the obscurity, a further preparation of the grounds. Even at the heart of a thing there is nothing but what your eyes chance to see and your heart happens to feel, there is this total vacancy. The burly trees offer no assistance, slumbering in their metaphors. The lamps glow whitely, weakly, on the ragged fields. My love, you were confident and full of lofts, and from here, where you are not, where you appear to be invisible to yourself, I imagine I can see all of you. So many girders fly past, so much glass, it is impossible not to tremble from it, not to reel from the power of what is made. At the sight of such a creation, finite but extreme, the mind grows extreme, seeks the extremity of the finite, but finding nothing, stops. The extreme of beauty must be outside creation. Then more walkers, more dogs.

Everything that the people in the room have seen collects along a single line to which no one in the room has access. But outside the room the line appears a vertical figure.

Exiles: Ends

It adds itself to the list of other places
as if a hand leaving its signature upon the earth—

    A place
among the other places
that situates the rest.
An avenue of sounds multiplied
five-thousand times.
Walking for blocks,
the heart growing hoarse.
Facetious facial twitch,
an exposed woman's shoulder,
an exposed white strap.

Given the facts of solitude and of death,
what can matter more than a despair
capable of suddenly flaming into rapture?

Walking out of the way to buy
the milk of my mother back.
Other wants, tugging away.
Running out of time on this earth,
always, always.
The illusion of permanence
a permanent illusion.
The partial vision of the living.
All projects of the word,
illusions of the word.
Welfare hotels, construction teams:
a dried-up scale
falling from the eye.
It should and it shouldn't
happen this way, and it does.
Fumes of our loudest fears,
skull seared by the pressing heat:
fruit markets, funeral homes.

Thinking nothing, walking for blocks.
Central Park West, Columbus Avenue,
the sun a kind of windfall profit
trickling down. Thought is inseparable
from my nature, thought Descartes:
it really is a saving grace,
the sun, an object above
sustaining the shadows below.
When did things grow so solid?
At the joust: sensation's lance
shattered on a shield,
leaving only finite perception,
perceiver and perceived,
the writer, the reader,
in uneasy complicity.

And the loser is feeling, always feeling.
Erasing sadness and too extreme joy.
Adding and subtracting parts of a book.
Revising, revisiting, reforming the past.
Résumé-writing, writers of "ought".
Looking at a duck in the pond in the park,
panicking, then lurching away.
Drinking coffee like a duck eats bread.
Caffeine in the aquarium's tanks
unnerving the fish. Feeding my frenzy.
Falling in Canada, acid rains freeze.

The music contains desire
in negative form. Condensation
of love into despair.
She waited at the train-station,
glowing with warmth.
Arrival at night, laughter at first:
then frantic illusions, lingering cares,
three-dimensional flesh, caressing her hair.
Desire as such, rapture at odds.
Love-making bodies, baking like bread.

Entwining intent, bodies at rest:
saddening hold and light of slow ferment.
The cynical self, fermenting
inside the foment of lives.
Discord of pleasure,
hand on her thighs.

Cast-iron cots in the soup kitchen/shelters.
"Almost like India by now," he added, "the sheer number
of them, all begging for change":
editor of a Marxist journal who knows only Newport,
issue on Latin America coming out next.
The hemorrhage of another scream,
the impossible questions the homeless are posed.
Human brows crashing against the stone,
newspaper account: the cardboard is comfortable.
Cities' center, the eye of the exile.
A whole fever of rednesses,
one disfigured sky. The word: a lie
that never tires, that reads till the end.

Rage on the sleeves, but the sleeves never real.
Tripping on truth, retying one's shoes,
stooping to use tools one's never thought useful.
Meeting someone new, thirty years my elder
who as I undress demands to be called "mother".
The frenzy for Freud. The disappointment,
hers: no semen forthcoming. Brief spoken words,
hasty departures, though the idea appeals
for a brief sparkling instant in another man's brain.

Swirl of identity, nothing the same.
Invalid experience, frantic tries elsewhere.
Cars in the dark, driving or parked,
hoods glistening with rain.
The light that passes
with the passing of an hour.
The light a day contained.

Each instant counts, each instant counting.
Self-from-which-all-poetry-stems.
Insisting on the impersonal "who" that I am.
Slick streets of night,
streets cobbled with bone.
Facing the wall, eyeing the phone:
cement in the thighs, exhaustion as such.

Memory of other cities, ducks resting
silently on East Berlin waters.
Soot of the war still on the streets.
Elegiac feeling in the aftermath
of nightfall, elation of discovery:
Kristallnacht temple, crystal-clear night.
Exciting source, this fallen synagogue,
covered with boards, exodus still-born.
Returning to the ruin, again and again,
booking the gloom in memory,
promising it more time, shivering cold.
Dry lactate of stars, suckle of sorrow,
blistering loneliness crouched in the stone.
Night — exile — elixir — exodus —
Seizing the heart, nothingness foaming.

The Lake

We give you the lake,
we give you moonlight on the lake.

We want you to have this,
this belongs to you.

We give you the window,
and outside the window

you have the lake.
We take your breath and place it

on the windowpane,
and we give you the shapes formed by the mist,

and as they fade there is the moon,
and beneath the moon the lake.

We give you the path
and at the end of the path

the boathouse and the mud
and your feet sinking into the mud

as you walk to the lake.
You hear the boats sway in the dark shed,

you hear wings flapping,
and you want this.

We say loons fly above the frosted lake
through moonlight,

and you hear *looms*,
and this too is yours.

This belongs to you.

The Spread

Who goes beyond appearance
is a searcher after.
Head through adamantine vault,
darkness without bottom,
living theater perfect spell
perpetrated upon an exquisite
harmony of contradictions.

Revelation challenge to accept
intercourse that hid itself
under an image of the sacred
warning and promise
whose answer is to veil both terror
and fascination, to bind the world
to something previously divided.

There stands judgment,
just like two knobs formulated
in triumphant paradox.
Partners in a dialogue,
pairs of concepts defining
a division brought to life
by each experience.

To cut something in two
is the mark of a ritual passing
from one state to another.
Because it is so fateful
we cannot help noticing
the space cut off from the roots
we used to worship.

A process like a voyage
appears somehow to grapple
with a statement of purpose
that suddenly becomes inadequate.
One moment it's all there
while the next embraces shadows
we can hardly imagine.

Something said against a story
moves uneasily between extremes
of high-pitched voices and
faces on a wall made contemporary
by aspects of a positive negative
presented in a series
of unacknowledged events.

Endless products illustrate
what happens when this problem
becomes more direct. Looking
outward at a world we never made
creates a window of tyranny.
How we feel about the damage
pushes in two directions at once.

DAVID SHAPIRO

After

There is the gate or the copy of a gate
Blood outlines the gate, like a nude
A pink flower like a tree emits sparks
They gather into a yellow blue fragmentary flower
In the other space, formed by flowers torn apart
It bites the ground, like a blackened moon
Blood outlines a few jagged petals
Where does this flower emerge if not from history
The night-flower beside it is not dark enough with
Turmoil of strokes, with labor of **having been there**
The night-flower explodes, is blue less
Relentless, should there be nothing but shadow
The twentieth century falls off below and fragility
And the kitsch of flowers above, finesse of heaven
No one can enter here, and there is nothing but hope

Sentences

It is raining in my heart, but I don't believe that it is raining.
It is raining softly on the town, but I don't believe the town exists.
It is raining softly on the tip of my tongue, but not now.
You say it is a sentence, but there is some possibility it is not a sentence.
It is a sentence, but it is very difficult to explain why it is a sentence.

My love is on the phone, but it is not now that my love is on the phone.
I am moved, but I do not know that I have moved.
I am in a position to assert the summer has ended, but I don't believe it.
A raven screamed at one in the parking lot, but it was not a raven; it was
      a prisoner.
My love is a double agent, and I hesitantly believe she is not.

Time is brutal, but I do not believe time is brutal.
Fact: Time is a brutal fact, but it is not certain time is a brutal fact.
Fact: Time is a social animal, but it may be that time is not a social
      animal.
Time satisfies all these conditions, but time does not satisfy all.
Time depends on future sentences: What I find hard to believe.

The book contains your barest preface, but I do not think it is a book.
The table of contents is unhelpful, but I do not think it is the contents.
Worst of all there is a key, but I believe there is no key.
The reader loses his way richly, but it is not certain that the reader loses.
Nevertheless, you found your way about, though I do not know you.

House (Blown Apart)

I can see the traces of old work
Embedded in this page, like your bed
Within a bed. My old desire to live!
My new desire to understand material, raw
Material as if you were a house without windows
A red stain. Gold becomes cardboard.
The earth grows rare and cheap as a street.
Higher up a bird of prey affectionate in bright gray
    travels without purpose.
I beg you to speak with a recognizable accent
As the roof bashed in for acoustics
Already moans. What is not a model
Is blown to bits in this mature breeze.
If students visit for signs
Or signatures we would discuss traces.
    We would examine each other for doubts.
Old work we might parody as an homage
Losing after all the very idea of parody.
Traces of this morning's work are embedded in this page.

A Book of Glass

On the table, a book of glass.
In the book only a few pages with no words
But scratched in a diamond-point pencil to pieces in diagonal
Spirals, light triangles; and a French curve fracture lines to elisions.

The last pages are simplest. They can be read backwards and thoroughly.
Each page bends a bit like ludicrous plastic.
He who wrote it was very ambitious, fed up, and finished.
He had been teaching the insides and outsides of things

To children, teaching the art of Rembrandt to them.
His two wives were beautiful and Death begins
As a beggar beside them. What is an abstract *persona*?
A painter visits but he prefers to look at perfume in vials.

And I see a book in glass—the words go off
In wild loops without words. I should
Wake and render them! In bed, Mother says each child
Will receive the book of etchings, but the book will be incomplete, after
    all.

But I will make the book of glass.

Archaic Torsos

after a dream

You must change your life fourteen times.
Change your way of living like writing.
You must change your method and your mind. You
Have to transform life fourteen times. Change life.
It has become necessary to change your life.
You need this change. We need to change your life.
And now you'd better change it: you, yourself.
It's up to you to exchange your life. Change, change!
Alter your life, patch and reshape your life.
"A change come o'er the spirit of your change."
You might shuffle the cards spin wheels change wheels.
You must convert resolve revolutionize your dissolves.
You might change life itself. And you might change.
You must change. You must not outlive your life.

To an Idea

I wanted to start *Ex Nihilo*
I mean as a review of sorts.
It's too much of a burst for some,
Too unanalyzably simple for others,
As one called perspective that vicious
Doctrine, but is it: to know nothing,
To taste something, dazzled by absence,
By your chair, by the chair of Salome?
Or yet another familiar dedication:
To an idea, writ in water,
To wild flesh, on the surface alone.
To you who carried me like mail
From one house to another.
Now the cars go past the lake, as if copying could exist.
The signs shine, through the Venetian blinds.

Lateness

The nerves are foolish invisibility induces offers
Tears streaming as if attached to some creed
Are mildly antiseptic due to salt content
Tears secret and stainless
Precursors for the sound of your voice

People burst themselves open and are released and release themselves
Easily picked up in that wind
At the lower and rounded end of the "heart"
No man ever saw those forests of fern but I see you in your bed
As you floundered in a stream of air and light

Blue and brown and black and hazel
The eye divested of tears like insignias with a blow
The lachrymal apparatus remains and the bright room
We are separate now and move rapidly like tears
The legs from the knees are missing

And the arms are joined awkwardly to the body
A lion tears your hair fallen low at the back
The whole world would have been the pediment
The lion's mane has successive rows of flames
In your missing hand you would have held the lion

My face, the "epigram" is carved in large red letters
Above are holes
Feet of the deceased
And traces are preserved of the wise and excellent doctor Aeneas
Doubt is represented and traces of blue wine with nine carved petals

Leaves are falling in schematic folds
The tongue of a conquered hero protrudes slightly
The face is long with a battered surface
Inscriptions we engraved on our thighs
A leaf falls from your lips and I am in love with my lot

Only the upper world is intoxicated
Colour would have covered you
The scene itself comes from some original
The child extends his hand in an eager manner toward his mother
In his hand a puppet doll of the deceased

In the hole in her right breast
Would be wedged the spear of the victorious warrior
Only her head is preserved
It turns back in agony
Thus drowns back into the depth of the shrine

It is the work of a good sculptor
It is difficult to distinguish between the living and the dead
The deceased plays the piano
In the airy plains of the ocean, a rich throne which shows
The need to heroise this woman, unjustly dead

Eros touches her lightly
With the palm of his left hand
The little refugee can scarcely stand on his feet
A young woman is leaning on her arm which, stretched vertically,
Closes the composition

Taking a Look

Nobody doubts
that it is snowing now

Rounding out their interpretation of the month

February, here is our
formal sketch

Everyone concedes a certainty to this snow

The upshot of which is NOT thrown projection

Well, or definitely not "disclosedness"

Again and again, February

This winter irretrievably put aside

Taking a look
It shows we have clung to idle talk *all right*

"I'm going to write a little thing
About Nothingness"
"Go ahead dearie"

And curiosity *would* be giving out summer information

The cars confine themselves
to the lot
Which is also the foundation for our feet
Now being covered up
In the sense of flakes
The driver weakened
And the certainty of being covered up

AARON SHURIN

Agora

The jar is where the month is unclear. by stamping, by inscription, assertion marks the head. angular shapes easier than cursive forms, *though I am here.*
      seems to have been
two different hands, at this period gives
himself the jar, a thief
in hard clay, rounded.
property for the first time, both sigma and omega

A large hunting requires appalled or delighted subscript (*soot of the city is ink to dry, fly*). gift requires otherwise unknown inside and out.
two
gods in one shrine.

the dedication
requires muses
omitted.
      of the victories, a large disc cut from the wall,
some
kind of game

a mood seems beautiful in this tender scene, depends on the uncertain illustration of this text and gender, a fragment name. As goes high the cranes escape their wing, streaming to the ocean no ordinary bloodshed. The elaborate decoration is no ordinary lines glaze. *presence not of the wing enacts distance.*
A fragment
preserves part of
unfortunately a scene
too lightly. It may well be
work of an artist

So he picked up a handy
message passing
by *would intrude right*
now, parody
of the splendid amphoras. slurred over in ordinary pronunciations may not know how to return it to status in his other capacity. A dispatched boy borrowed his shape by means of a passing grandmother.
The inscription is written
(has the early
form) in
coarse
household
water

371

From the public market everyday objects beginning soon. Casual alphabet, scratching of a name. virtue giving no thought the searching eye of triviality, intent on history reveal and so on. Public objects come private everyday pots.

A writer, a god, a friend to complicated messages, achieve
intent. *This too will be your irony ration.* a kind
of giving pure
and period. evidence
shapes values, thousands
scratching shapes. Beginning soon after, increasing era

Over-daring to suggest that this is the difference? Might be drawn any-where, door-jamb, shops. significance is divine now we call logo. exuber-ance of empire and material after empire. saw in a lamp a resemblance to a word and drew the parallel.

plain marble on which to hang
speeches

Tempting to suggest the figure is anatomically indifferent, emotionally contemporary. Who to tell is hiding? Voter behind another tree, exile *in history, bound* to such a role
his growing
power might fear. Apparently
words was worth a picture.

Presiding
a vase is a ballot
cast to risk
diagnosis. Quite a different
context drawing this case.
interpretation
means
perhaps

I am a master making
deception without
deceiving. This is
that thing.
             Depended on the number
that began with letters. A list names
men and women side by side with shapes. Range from their owners,
vessels; particular household, club, shop or office. marked
challenges employs
speculation. function
proclaims origin

Coffee, water, wine will ease this message. *All my dreaming* have been selected with care *by someone.* So that in addition to writing a surface provides a means of attachment.
of the recipient measuring or urgent capacity.
a pitcher holds owner's filled mentions.
serve for use.
a girl who has not stopped to put on her shoes.

a portrait in common, pressure to cut through the glaze, out of the mouth the represented nature of contents. incising a unit of ordinary consumption, stages the life of sound.
attested production recording owner's something.
the letter
on this large
word here
played by
century end.
　　　　　numerous
inscriptions
thereof

Temptation

The stairs of sleeping climbed against the first night with real gods. Communicates with him an imperious air of ambiguous sex. And of his body softness, heavy eyes, vague lips, lifted its head and suspended vials of personages in relief. He sighed, secret insects of his breath hung in the illuminated air, warm, purple, and turned toward him with shining eyes.

His hand spread the contagion of a golden chain — look down as he was, attracting to yourself the sculptor of clay. In a melodious voice of insidious pleasure escaping a greater master.

If you wish, keep your remembering; the second air insinuating vast proportions hung down over his thigh. His hurrying skin representing figures to lose themselves in yours. Recognize that perfumed beauty in another being, you forget your dubious disadvantages.

This one said "procure everything!" Seems to hold their fascination as of voice — huskiness washed with echo — and the seductive trumpet of those pipes reverberated the unbridled air.

A laugh went rolling, bore the indecent names. A certain person drinking his fury somewhere. Still musky with pleasure he lifted his eyes, looking for actual men. In truth I am awake, begging them to forgive me.

Continuous Thunder

There exist rebels, strange possession joined a conspiracy and in question were arrested. Worthy men consult death — his favorite player — he was a lover of morals — the fine arts of enemy have won him a historian. Write anything for pleasure, one forms a vast stage for his monster forms.

Suddenly one of his most famous roles probed deeper: "condemned to die." When people are using an expression they can still distinguish the actor, the day arrived. He walked and saw a singular beauty in the impersonalization of the possible real. To me, believing in the idealization as alive, a fury blended my eyes for you around his head that irrefutable way, trembles has never left me, beams invisible while I look for words but visible to me. And the abyss, on the edge of paradise, does not see the whole audience.

Everyone gave himself up to the voluptuous pleasures of the grave. The noise joined him without a qualm of mourning. Did he feel in his forecasts the striking justifications flouted in his face as I watched the pallor compressed and applauded his fire? At a certain moment his lips flashed across his face, he left.

A few minutes later a hiss awakened; the theater of his mouth fell backward. There is ground for the last time — sweet and large — but none has been able to rise. They say he was almost one of the friends, a discontented attraction; those like myself staggered forward a step. No punishment remained.

Very Days

They give what she has, and wind up here for the future. How many refugees between birth and death, wrapped in white paper as its name works, she inserts between teeth. The hard peach, the sour gray bread, the small pears in their skin.

In the evening we stroll off the long day, setting across her bed. Air by the river beaten down with the heat; spotless blue keeps her troubles neatly within. The children in their eye, wide mouth, cascade ear; the hillsides — poplars — with the shadows and hues of tapestries. Everyone is singing the praises of goose fat and bacon.

Where I was born in a grocer's cellar made me think of women wide at the hip. Over there his sleepy eyes this way of blue, eyelashes going wisp of smoke, to the fields with melting sugar as he folds his lips . . . fresh, penetrating pine . . . his path with dangling arms, furry under dew, murmuring up against pebbles into the rhythm of water and dry leaves.

Meaning and sonority descend the slope. The golden weight of attention. His two hands altered the sound of his voice, swooping the air one clenches. The wind can snap them up this exhalation.

We lie on the grass in the grass, our ears spread passage. Covers us and ignores us, thinned with sunlight and heat. Pass between the leaves enunciated sky, between our whirlwind heads, shutterless. Under the swallows, turning empty air. . . .

MARY MARGARET SLOAN

Eccentricity of the Middle Ground

covering
a given distance, a countryside, is an open conveyance to the
starting point, through the city's edge

to astronomical indices with
a memory only for moods, curved, carving

boundless surface
zero volume

a character with the gift of disappearance begins a
journey on the available road, occasional slopes and curves,
sonic tones in forest tones, trees breeding branches

a mark was not upon the air
coruscating anonym

cartographic graze of continent swimming in horizon line,
a populace flees downhill   trailing   lives negotiate   views,
rivulets amid skylines

one voice sub-vocalizing stood for
the absolute value of singing

time warms
accumulating
midday
warms light
stands still sonic
word blind

infancy held at edge of many storeys oversight of
fruitful coalition, perception nestles in coverts misplaces mean-
ing shaken from tectrices

when wing hits air

feeling as
from a former time, to calculate the distance conveyed above the
surface, beyond gravity's reach, the distance covered and
the distance sustaining apparent reality as in a foreign country
one stops for the night
situated at a coast, assembled
characters brush together in notions of rationality foreign to
a place; alarm incites a moment requiring gravity: make
travel arrangements from the sea

sub-vocalizing
circular research
obedient vaccilation's
tailspin
parallel to life

"these people"
were all that remains of shelter leave a wake as in water

if only a strange sound
would come along
the path of fortuity:
substitute, prevaricate, suffice

as thought disappears within itself, sequence covers itself,
as layers of the water clear, flinch, shiver

predicate seizure scaling the form, geological final aspect

on that flight
door opened
in came a crowd

invents repose
advancing into the picture plane intimacy of lesser velocity,
ocean slowed to a standstill

call, summon, shout
ten storeys down
catenary curve

falls as one for a while
before dismantling
a species of disarray

modes of transport,

at first a
scene wanted something: early summer or a character with
the gift of anonymity makes a time from the past sound promising:
face value — shuttered light, facades, vacant square, the ocean
itself, peaks shift, lit

cursive
as a ratio, nest of exchange, breeding transfer

what was seen then
was never seen again
to annul or revive
a presiding aura

a treeline bows from across a field:
beyond eddies of leaves graze attend reach in

a destination

alarm spread assimilation
of laws, of news; from midnight to midnight invasion stands
by the sea. Bring self-possession landward. A first hint of a
time out of the past: will it be more, will it be warm, has it been?

pursues too closely, arbitrarily fast transformation, uses, misus-
es, overuses a foreign body

now please see the sea as it's
left in the past, a road developing a name, the Via Anon, a
lapse rate gradient from the bliss of incomprehension

in long sentences
from another century the characters trail; sensation of easy travel,
loss of a "whole world", a change of scene. Refugees through
vacated outlying areas, some trees, a sequence overlaps, preset
as if in antiquity, a feeling abridged

branches abroad
a memory only
for moods
fail to recognize
a difference
nothing also
has a face

the front in its infancy, at the window, in the air, in the
light, as gestures' emotional refrain, synalepha

a road renamed all it travelled through; from an elevated pas-
sage, houses amid trees left standing; a dwelling with walls
stripped away, artifacts of possession arranged to express the
personality of departure

travelling en masse
is vivacious, off the road, wandering in dust; yellow leaves
light anfractuous landscape, fractious character

populace diffused across a continent, rivers,

rivulets, aerial views delve to the center, time in which to
complete the story runs to ground in the foreground; illustrat-
ed artifact

                              sees the whole curve blue, land
masses swimming, dwelling equal to travellers, marks upon the path
from a cardinally neutral point a destination is conveyed,
characters curve from the map; a list of substances carved
from another century, enigmatic categories, bliss and others

                                        its circular research
                              landward, seaward
                                        routines of darkness
                              light, fly between latitudes
                                        incite signing
                              of treaties

                                        in an agitated
state, a thousand miles away obscured from view the sea

                                        gives way
to a schedule of minor torment, an air of refrain, a refrain
of covert rebellious impulses; within the house characters accumu-
late atmosphere of denouement

                                        distance transposed
                              imaginary synonyms

                              scrutiny
                              of lost thought

                              rotation without a sphere
                              world blind

emotional heterosphere marks instability mixing
suppressed rules of the given from rules of invention, transfer
of momentum through much deep layers
                       of   to

                                 place characters with the
gift of unanimity breaking forth as a flood to a foreign
border amid city streets; a clandestine crossing

of early summer evening through streets from a former time or a
less elaborate place

                                 lost in a center
                                 begin at the ends

                                       a dry river bed
is the Via Unanima, yellow walls smeared with dust, gallery
of sandy windows

                         peering through instruments' slow
transpositions modeled on an imagined present, public
spaces assigned to depletion, structures stripped of facades took
positions
noiselessly

         measures
         never where it is but where it was
         "misgivings fall to the purpose"

                                 by these tactics
see them less completely predicated, diagrammatic orders of moods
intersecting   in the wake of emotional reverses

                         water spilt glass
                         smooths light on
                         stochastic surface

the one part repels the others eastward, westward
southward, northward, inward

sees through this thought: a crisis
washed away in its residential aura

when sounds
exchange
conjecture
it's a cloudy science
unanimity resists
resistance

forms possession analogy — form from consonance sound branches
— few form recognizable — most from inherited primitive lost
types — of all or most but went on in the road renamed but lost,
wanders as in a separate language, no conveyances in the
streets, route learns itself through erratic breaches to a cross-
over point, a changing room, where characters mass and tend,
tend to move in the direction in which they are embedded
through structures as old as natural features

behaving as though
concentrated at one point foreign to a place, trees find eccen-
tric positions, middle of the road proliferation of disorder,
public squares misguide relation to branch routes inversely propor-
tional to spare the distance between them

a body of water concealed: rectangular but limitless, surface tamed
except by the sky, reflecting pools, immerses its uses
known to the populace unknown to authorities
given over to
index of possession proprietary of the broadest sense, any-
where along its lateral extent it meets

a purpose beginning to develop, contradicts
inadmissible returns
a dialect fractured

until in places a wall was leaving, driving sea strewn for miles

384

the Via Anomie ends in a glassy surface, swimmers' shining bodies

eustatic reflection
purpose falls to misgivings

circulations world-
wide morning to
morning pacing
faraway seeks
an ampler space
a light touch
letters put to flight
to sing
the sea quietly withdraws
a crowd
distance exceeding any
ordinary tempo slows

lazy, nearly, water falls from glass, arena falls from sand

falls as a gift with the character of any dimension

this way to a sea, this sea away
guiding through hills of grass
taciturn windward refrain

"and the wind carries it" by analogy or guess no matter how
farfetched: stones at the bottom of the sea were heated by the moon

GUSTAF SOBIN

Notes on
Sound, Speech, Speech-Crystals and
the Celestial Echo

For Jim Clifford

1
The Conch

sound   secreted the form,
   blew

through the water   its undulant fibers,
breathing the green volutions   and the ivory
of the spiralling vortex.

spoke it! made it, its allegro! twisted the creature
out of the luminous clay   of its tremor!

2

sound the progenitor, by continuing to ring through its creation, its
forms, begets speech.

speech both the resonance and celebration of sound.

speech, that's never pronounced, but *cast, diffused, exuded.*

that communicates with nothing except its own ebullience.

that varies with the depth and contour, the vibratory shell of each form.

the iris emitting a different speech than the dragonfly.

form being instrument (as the body on the octaves of its pulsate sensations).

to imagine the fruit as oboe, and the wind as bassoon! blood-harp!

sensations are the fibers of speech. are its quills of flowing crystals that, myriad, determine its volume, its intensity, its 'voice.'

speech radiates *outward*, and aureoles its own energy.

an agony, exuded inwards, submitted, is an inverted speech. a convulsed exhilaration.

of all things spoken, excepting death, love, in its tremor of lust, is the most spacious. and the ultimate motivation of all speech.

space being the efflorescence of speech. its circumference.

~

what is *said* is only the glowing residue of what is spoken: the silage of the ecstatic presence.

language that originates in speech, being reduced to a system of semblances, symbolic equivalents that can only obscure—and no longer instigate, assume—its existence.

constant and successive repressions having pillaged the original magic of language, and neutralized the immense power of its crystals.

having cleaved the light, and isolated the voice from its colossal drama.

imposing a communication, an anti-speech, that conveys everything but its own reality.

language remains speech, remains power (springing translucent out of its source) only when uttered with a *total intent*. when it's the flesh that proffers it.

387

when the breath commits itself to the crystals that it breathes.

as sometimes with the whisper, the green sigh, the jagged shriek.

or whenever the ode is a rich, glittering secretion.

where the word-crystals rise in a charged and radiant energy-cluster. a blossoming ellipse.

where they generate the exact substance they invoke.

each thing defining itself not by its form, but by its resonant discharge, the spacious aura it exudes, its dynamic circumference.

where as speech, in reaching the ring of this circumference, its diaphanous membrane, it luminously *resounds*. where speech, itself, *replies*.

for the imperative of speech is to hear itself: hear itself *realized*.

as the red concerto, stunned in the shower of its magnificence.

where, reverberant, the creature is englobed in its own magnitude: the element of both its origin and its most spacious impulsions.

~

psalms of the leopard and the phosphorescing mosses! flesh in the wisdom of its crystals! what if heaven (its vast dilapidated structure) were never more than the resonant colossus of each creature? of each ion? as the opulent sphere that envelops the earth, the earth's speech, in the skin of a celestial echo.

Violet City: Aspects of the Transitive

saw the glass towers
slip,
     liquid, through the louvered
venetians; the light, in thin
strips, quiver
shut.

. . . .
call: call shapes, faces. . . . each
'heart'
has its
number (its specific
fo-

liations). even
here, as your

room
rises blanched, amnestic, an
     island, already, in its piled,
pulsate florescence: speak,
ring shimmers. from
your

sibilants, shake
mass.

~

. . . falls, you'd
say, of
itself,
that
virtue,

                 breath-
tipped, that unbundled
fire . . . .
. . . .

                          here, even
here, contours table, chairs;
runs —in
pinched ripples— to the linen's
slack
re-

lapsing
edges. (even
here —at this
distance, these late
stations— that script-vestigial . . .).

                     ∼

vine, out of
what
voices?   fumes, buds, annunciates of
what
dead injunction?

                          puzzles your
wrist, now, the
tips
of your fingers. . . .   you,
in whom its movement, moment-
          arily, courses: its channeled
pro-
traction . . . .
. . . .

would bring, to the
dark
mouth, its dark
syllables. being
transitive, 'take, as object,' its
least creases. into that
re-

cessive, still-indeterminate
image, the fixed
interval's,
enter.

~

. . . .
. . . floated bronze, once, in your
spread
fingers. fanned damp,
expansive, a ponderous sponge,
in a
dull

shudder of reflections.

                (the projected, at
last, depleted; the image
brought, taut, to that
burning con-
vergence).

~

. . . speak, even
here. ring
voices. for the word's
ad-

dressed: a flame
trained to its trellis.   from your
tongue,
now, tease
ash. . . . here, even

here, in this
city

of surfaces (Manhattan gone
violet, glossy, now, in its watery
up-
rights) ex-
tract measure, elicit
sound.

                        '. . . fumes, buds,' but
out of
what
scuttled work?   on which
extinct frequencies, those psalms?
a
breath's

lapping breath, limbs
limbs, that
that ray
shot, into its dark alveole, quaver.

What the Music Wants

In Memory of George Oppen

what the music
wants is
pod and tentacle (the thing
wiggling,
wild

as washed
hair, spread).   is our-
selves, in-

serted.   within
our
own rhythms: wrapt, voluted,
that miracle
of
measure-

ascendant. *to*
stand, that there's some-
where to

stand.   marble
over

moorings, the
scaffolds, now, as if
vanished, and the steps, the
floors: spoken
forth.   *to*
stand, stand there, with-

in
sound alone,
that

miracle!

                    is what the
waters comb, and the
bells,
beating,
count (faint, now, over the

waves, in a
garland
of
bells). *is*

somewhere, and
wrapt

in the bulb
of its
voices, are buoyant among.

On the Nature of the Iconic

what bursts in the very moment of bursting is image.

its bunched chimera.

even though, immediately after, she'd as if begun gathering together her every gesture; as if collecting —once again— the scattered, grey blades of her gaze.

accumulating —as you'd put it— diaphanous.

just there, where the curtains ripple, each time, through the draft of their own deafness.

neither this side, nor that.

(of what, indeed, knew no end, no depth, no dimensions whatsoever, but —being verbless— existed in an underworld entirely its own).

a well of shadows —you might have written— surrounded by a garland of splashing leaves.

by the gloss of so much apparent matter.

while she —steadily— as if thinned into focus.

(fixed rays of her earrings; what she'd just fastened, sapphire).

muscled, luminous.

as if such signs (in an uninterrupted emission of signs) might only have erupted out of the disarticulated. its depths.

cast in so much counterpart.

she, as if reconstituting that white memory to which you'd otherwise have had no access.

miming its exact outlines, its deepest cleavages.

toying, thus, with those immemorial losses, thoroughly unaware, in so doing, of the very magnitude of her provocations.

the tips of her fingers, that instant, running nimble over her glowing cheeks; adjusting here, there, the slightest wires of that all-too-perfect dissemblance.

like notes, struck vibrant, off some dismantled instrument.

yes, just then, as her each feature converged. grew limpid.

the circumstantial, absolute.

oh, all the meanings, values, irrefutable definitions we'd given ourselves.

the alphabets. the blown letters of how many driven alphabets.

(within which, notwithstanding, had adored).

as she stood there, now, her name changing with the light, the shadows, the time of day: pure replica of the otherwise obliterated.

as if the door alone might be altar. our very last.

and the moment itself, sacrificial.

Premises

as if all language were rooted in the silent grammar of an implication.

deriving from, and —inseparably— referring to.

as if, indeed, there were two languages: our own, which is perfectly audible, articulate, appreciable, and another —uninterruptedly mute— which is never more than the taut, vibratory surface of the implicated.

but the *frappe* of so much white letter.

what our own words aspire, reach towards, as if to imbue themselves with the sonorous luster of their own origins.

. . . in, say, a sheer coincidence of mass . . .

what we can only qualify (bound as we are to analogy, metaphor, conceit) as their confiscated mirror.

as, in sort, an etymology abandoned in the exact same instant as its formulation.

for words, by their very nature, fall into the shadow of their facetted parts; by their very agreements, undergo eclipse.

the breath catching on its own viscosity.

sublunar, subliminal, nothing's written, in effect, that's not underwritten: no world, in effect, that's not —ultimately— underworld.

within which —dense nexus— alluded.

having gutted the heart of every humor but its strange, abstract efful-gence: its counter-trope.

whereby, on certain days, certain creatures, beautiful in the bulk of their luminous particles: in so much pure, undifferentiated mass.

whereby less, even lesser, as it flexes with magnitude.

stripped, finally, of all gods, scriptures, all myth but the living mineral of the eyes as they vanish, now, beneath the roll of their own lashes.

whereby the word: the word-wordless: what would enter, now, the sheer immediacy of the remote.

wedging, as it did, that vaporous expanse: what had been, until then, meticulously withheld.

. . . the null, at last, as if invested . . .

in the rhyme of those matched annunciates, rendered palpable.

———————

. . . there, just there, where the
mouth rounds to
its
scuttled rose, even the silence,
suddenly, would have
grown

re-
verberant.

Towards the Blanched Alphabets

. . . like so much weather
out of the west, sound arrives with its
scooped
hollows, the caves it makes in the
very midst of

mass. wrapt, now, in the
blanched
half

of antiphon, you're carried in its
quick, irresonant folds, its
mute
repliques. saying only
what you can't, haunting only
what isn't, you drift now, through the

intervals. there, in those
late
landscapes, that
vaporous ground: grammar's

ultimate retreat. really yours, these
fingers? this breath
dismembered
for the sake of some final reprieve?
spoke, you

wrote, where speech couldn't, spelling
'hand' free
from hand, 'moon'

from its florid marshes. were
what's left, the
air's
least outlines: mask
that's creasing the folds of the face, just

there, where the face
had
vanished.

JOHN TAGGART

Twenty One Times

1

Napalm: the word suspended by a thread
the word grows as salt crystallizes
I will grow cells of the word in your mouth.

2

Napalm: leaping as if wrought in the sea
leaping as if pursued by the horse and his rider
a young hart a young heart comes out leaping.

3

Napalm: rub the new-born child with salt
"the fault is that we have no salt"
if the master's word is taken the salt is love.

4

Napalm: soap will not wash the word out
the word breaks through partitions and outer walls
breakthrough of cells of the word in the mouth.

5

Napalm: the heart rubbed and smeared with soap
the young heart is soiled with fire
soap cannot cleanse the soiling of the fire.

6

Napalm: why the child caught on fire
the itching as of creatures for possession of words
glitter for self and nation.

7

Napalm: the word leaves an acrid taste
the word a thorn in the mouth
the cells of the word connected by thorny sticks.

8

Napalm: edges points of acid edges points of fire
edges and points tear the young heart
tear the heart from doors of the neighborhood.

9

Napalm: the child born again as son of the fire
like and unlike resolved by fire
sunlight on word-hoards dazzling eyes of the nation.

10

Napalm: footsteps ring in a tunnel of the word
tunnel of jacks without a ball
there are four tunnels within each cell of the word.

11

Napalm: ring around the young heart
driven in and driven inward by the hunter's fire
not one door open to the heart.

12

Napalm: child and son wear six corroded rings
no divine light no peace no contentment
no memory no understanding no love for the unloveable.

13

Napalm: a stumbling in chains in the word
a kind of a dance or march not just for ladies' night
footsteps in the dark in the cells of the word.

14

Napalm: fiery chains around the young heart
chain-chain-ch-a—e—a—e—a—e—ain
the heart driven into dark and resonating tunnels.

15

Napalm: if a carpenter's saw cannot be found
if a carpenter cannot be found
child and son become rings become chains of fire.

16

Napalm: the word lives on like a coal through frost
jelly stays on the mind word in the mouth
cells of the word cells of the burning crystal.

17

Napalm: jellied gasoline turns one thing into another
fool of the fire into heart of the crystal
the young heart becomes the pulse of the crystal.

18

Napalm: it's too late to take the child's hands
it's too late to take the hand of the son into your own
the master says pain is privation.

19

Napalm: the word severed from its thread
the word glows with each breath
I have grown cells of the word in your mouth.

20

Napalm: the glowing crystal records one word
a record of one word plays and plays in your mouth
you will have to know it by heart.

21

Napalm: speak and the word glows and plays
speak and suffer torment for love
because of you no one will have to write the word down.

GEORGE TYSH

Genitalia

whose genitalia are these anyway
so sweet and lovely

is there no need to apologize
for spreading them lightly on a table

her silk panties swollen testicles
malady of youth

this penis in the desert
tied up by police

imagine how they feel
drifting slowly in your heels

displayed on two levels
the absence of any mark

belonging to one of the sexes
you said shave me closer in my folds

subjectivity
not essence

breaks into its wrapper
how much can you let

the excitement of a whole hand
in a mirror behind your back

the success of my face
and rubber skirt

let you suck me off slowly
so to rip it off

to have only calculated the expense
of absence which results

how a hard-on
if tightened

will not taste good
in a prophylactic

first you feign love
that at a certain point

one must stop looking
ellipses taken off

then you genuinely
show love the dildo

there should be time for worship
as a binary opposition the man

before you and the woman
beware of ceremony

pancreas spine breasts
in descending order

our shopping list
the scarf or choker of skins

and as you are not permitted to be
in love in good earnest

your face again registers
screw by screw

prick by prick
the sham

circles
that her meaning

a pretense of love plunging
is in conflict

she hated it
and kept it under a hat

the scent of herself
as apparatus

love until sore
through which to pee

the more differentiated
the more abstract they become

rectangular lights
a bending gentle over sign

internal storm
the black cincher of woman

nothing but the playstuff
in your underthings

and the comfort in my mouth
of swallowing

as the pictograph suggests bondage
within disguise of

everydayness
transparent

beadlets and droplets
sprays like creams and devices

unlikely genitalia
that once posture of salesgirl

suggested to vibrate
from suede

let's get something straight
for women in disguise

wringing and wrapping
her frantic material

to have held the shorter
theory of face to face

back to belly
brow to blow

the g-string projected
as a style grown out of bounds

inlaid lips
in shadow and its shadow

of currency between states
hardening

and lubrication
invasion

and abandon
paint with light

contains it
small decisions

paint with light

ANNE WALDMAN

Evangelle

She has not imbibed LSD in many years until today. She's a guest of Merry
Pranksters, the next generation. A farm in Oregon. An August day with rain
and fragrant breeze. Someone was on a tractor. Someone was singing. A com-
pany of strangers. Someone back home, he she changed a life for (I love him) she
thinks (perhaps erroneously) has betrayed her with an adverse wife. She must
rescue him from Mrs. Difficultness. Or so she thinks. She wants him with her.
She is manic in her mind with this. She makes magic on this. She despises his
weakness to make a clean break. She puts a spell on him to make him love her
with insatiable hunger. She gives his ticket away to a comradress, true daughter
of like-poetic lineage. They go off. Who will catch this poet's imagination, her
eye? She has eyes for no man. But room for a confidant. Skyline, a meadow, a
bower, the Magic Bus, the way the hay looked stacked there, many oddments in
the house, a musty room with musty beds. Broadside of Rilke in the bathroom.
Mementos of a dead son. The Native storyman who repeats himself like Gertrude
Stein. An old dog beneath a child's legs. Pies in the oven. The gutsy singing of
Rosalie. Ramblin' Jack shows up. Deadheads out there in the meadow, in the
"audience," on blankets, weary with getting there to pitch a tent, feed a child, but
cheerful nonetheless, waiting for nightfall for the magic show. Show of strength.
She is featured with Robert Hunter, maker of songs, tender intellect who has a
mind of poetry, in his Hawaiian shirt, cigarette holder held in emphatic gesture.
She's been reading and singing out from gut on stage, and falls into the aura of
X, daughter of Y, who proffers the Owl's brew. And she hooks up with a Saint
who is making a movie, he downs it too. And everyone is mad at him, Gus the
Director: his Dutch lover, his little dog, the crew. She watches the face of her dis-
tant lover superimposed on the Haida shaman backdrop. Where is he tonight?
Her voyage is not revenge, (melt o melt this revenge) but strip down to under-
stand her great new love, its place in the cosmos, duty to herself & others. Duty
to the poem, its song, vows (this poem) on the page.

ol

  d

er

                              plan

to make a spectacle —

illusion's mad song & apron of a stage
because we mask this one always always
& need the illusion
puppets at the screen

kliegs
Clytemnestra

I say
would
a woman
be
to love you

                                        (put   on   a
jkt/cold

cellular shiver
frisson
 outside)
her mask on stage?
powered by......
I say powdered

closet   a mirror

edit

me down
or mea dow

(placed)

I'll take these notes

to save
my skin

ground down

the ego it takes
to write this down

grind down
 grrrrr
el cid
a cid

tween
cars who got the people here
a farm's

a lot to travel to

of people need to come together in large open spaces
(writ that again)
of peoplein need

comerainorshine

out of the cities

talking
to

(train of
self
taut
toughen

control to get what's
tangible
fleeted alike

fleeced down

thought)rough.

I am a stranger here.....

stub

  that thought stubbed
or stumped
the maid

I am feeling I must come back in my next life Clara Barton or Ms. Nightingale
to save these folk out here in the meadow in drizzling cold, gnawing on meat
& alcohol. I wake thru bodies, steamy, rheumy, I wake I walk thru them. I
wake I walk in between the bodies & someone calls out to offer something. I
wake to smile. I wake to see in the midst of the them in all of them. If there are
no words? Their mist their breath. I walk I walk thru them.

If there are no words?
  their dicey looks
if there are no words?
serving up a meal
no words?
"horns of a dilemma"

Ho! I am alone.

a megalomaniac

  an *evangelle*

But in the kitchen
later

a deity of the house stokes the fire
behind
a broom
Hearth-Lady
who prays

who is holy
I recognize her out of this cock'd eye

clouded tho it be
with love decidedly acid

I made with my brother Osiris as end to the eating of men
I revealed mysteries to men
I broke down governments
I made an end to murders
I decreed mercy to suppliants
I am Queen of the rivers & winds & sea
No one is held in honor without my knowing it
I am the Queen of war
I am Queen of the thunderbolt
I sit up the sea & I calm it down again
I am the rays of the sun
Whatever I please, this too shall come to an end
With me everything is reasonable
I created walls of cities
I am called Thesmophorour
I brought islands up out of depths into light
I am she-lord of the rainstorms
I overcome fate
Fate sticks to me, harkens to me
Hail, O Egypt, that nourished me

goddess of a thousand names

My nod governs the the shining heights of Heaven
the wholesome sea breezes
the lamentable silences of the underworld

The primeval Phrygians call me Pessinuntica, Mother of the Gods
the Athenians, sprung from their own soil call me Cecropian Artemis
for the islanders of Cyprus I am Paphian Aphrodite
for the archers of Crete I am Dyctynna
for the tri-lingual Sicilians I am Stygian Proserpine
& for the Elusinians, their ancient Mother of the Corn

413

Some know me as Juno
some as Bellana of the Battles
others know me as Hecate
others as Rhamnubia
but both races of Aethiopians whose lands the morning sun first shines
upon
& the Egyptians, who excel in ancient learning & worship me with
proper ceremony
to my godhead
call me by my true name Queen Isis
I come in pity of your plight
I come to favor & aid you
Weep no more
lament no longer
the hour of deliverance is at hand
(Apuleius, The Golden Ass)

(tears running down his hairy face)

*But what caught & held my eye more than anything else was the deep black
lustre of her mantle. She wore it slung across her body from the right hip to the
left shoulder, where it caught in a knot resembling the boss of a shield; but part
of it hung in innumerable folds, tasselled fringe quivering. It was embroidered
with glittering stars on the hem and everywhere else, and in the middle beamed
a full & fiery moon.*

and she was in her acid dream deity again, but also
like insect, she was sliding in the dirt, slithery
gleaming but also slithery
she was wanting to be under the others like servant, like slave,
like snake, undercover, under grass, slithery

rambunctious in the daylight, following the communal course
with "tribe" with "group" with "sanctuary"
in an innate language only we
may understand
wired into our psychotropic brains

Homo habilis,
a tool-making people
with developed larynx
>   I/she was sliding again

she wanted to be a nurse
she wanted to sound the emergency siren
she wanted to be with them when they were in pain
& she saw the whole world dancing in front of her eyes now
& it was, verily, in pain, the whole world

(thirsty now,
"water," "water" she says to no one in particular)

(Rebecca on the horizon, Rebecca smiling now on the horizon
Rebecca wife to Isaac, mother to Jacob & Esau
sister of the Rebbe
on the plains of Abraham, on the plains of Abraham...
Rebecca out of my vision now, she's "real")

In her right hand she holds a bronze rattle, the sort used to frighten
away the God of the Sirocco; its narrow rim curved like a sword-belt
and three little rods, which sing shrilly when she shakes the handle,
pass horizontally through it. A boat-shaped gold dish hangs from her
left hand, and along the upper surface of the handle writhes an asp with
puffed throat and head raised ready to strike. On her divine feet: slip-
pers of palm leaves, the emblem of victory.

& the emblems of victory are
>   key, voice, olive branch, crown, radarless sword, F-16s, dead bodies
all around

consortless gods on the new day, without women
or with them

Mrs. Difficultness, my new path

>   confront & love

confront /or/ destroy

415

waves of tenderness

scratch out her eyes &

then blame the man

the man, man, man

andros

O sister, what love hath we?
that it come to this great rage?
a terrible thing
that we could be but clan
(in the dream She-who-rages-slams-doors-weeps needs help ascending the
smoke-hole, the ladder in our collective sky
I'm above & tug at her long blond hair
come up, come up, we will be fine!)

=clan life was reincarnation=

=clan life held us, held her - a place to be=

=it was wide like a river can be & currenting=

="currenty", the runny child said...=

=clan life was being a beaver in the mushroom gulch place=

=clan life was exciting, it was the only life=

=because we were together, we were clan=

=not brother not sister but all of that too but clan=

=clan like normal propensity=

=what could last some might say=

=or inbred-ness of it=

=clan blind=

=bristle of clan in morning everyone hungry=

[dear Mom,

You are the annoyingist person. You think everyone likes poetry! The
world's in love with it! And you are the Queen of this world, O Mom!

Love, Ambrose]

=I sweep my hand away to show you the rest=

=beaver clan, bring back the industry of beaver=

I touch the earth

this is witness-mudra

bow, scrape then write this down again,

again

listen, listen

how the lord spread out his net to enfold her,
The Evil Wind, which followed behind, he let loose in her face.
When Tiamat opened her mouth to consume him,
He drove in the Evil Wind that she close not her lips.
As the fierce wind charged her belly
Her body was distended & her mouth was wide open
He released the arrow, it tore her belly,
It cut through her insides, splitting the heart.
Having thus subdued her, he extinguished her life,
He cast down her carcass to stand upon it.

(I go inside to warm myself) (I want my lover to love me, love me)

The lord trod on the legs of Tiamat,
With his unsparing mace he crushed her skull.
When the arteries of her blood he had severed,
The North Wind bore it to places undisclosed.
On seeing this, his fathers were joyful & jubilant,
They brought gifts of homage to him.
Then the lord paused to view her dead body,
That he might divide the monster & do artful works,
He split her life a shellfish into two parts:
Half of her he set up & ceiled it as the sky

the other half of Tiamat's lifeless body became earth (Enuma Elish)

He heaped up a mountain over Tiamat's head
pierced her eyes to form the sources of the Tigris & Euphrates,
and heaped more mountains over her dugs,
which he pierced to make the rivers
from the eastern mountains that flow into the Tigris
Her tail he bent up into the sky to make the Milky Way,
and her crotch he used to support the sky

we're near the end of Sumero-Babylonian civilization
(now see ever increasing emphasis on war & conquest)

born of brutality, rape, conquering, born of the heaped
  mass upon mass of female
suffering

(to trip
a fall
in narc
issus pond
& wedge mys
elf upon all body pain)
    Yap! Yelp!
                    . . . mass upon mass of female . . .

rotator cuff is located below the chin & to your side
look there....

I'd had the great wine, performed the great reading where I sing to/of
John Cage,
  and we're back on the farm on the bus
highest heels not for a climb like this one to be on the bus,
tight skirt not for a night on this town, this bus, high rise, and laughing
& getting inside the mind of Hunter
this bus is a museum, not moving
but I am moving laughing to fall off into a frog pond
Rebecca catches me in her arms

& sleep in the room with many bodies, musty
bodies snoring on the floor

remember?
but earlier

I see the stripe the pattern
 of the cloth
now clearly
& outside it was a calligraphy
a calligraphy of us, me & Gus Van Sant as at the sky &

we (me & Gus) walked to the barn
& we spoke (I tried to speak it was hard)

to see a man clothed up as Shaman
He was also the Boss Kesey
He was running the show
He was paying

He had the edge on lights
& color

And the crew wanted to throw the basketball (at us?
 with us?
 with Gus?)
and she will throw a key
or some small object
through the hoop
and she will be calm
some kind of show-off calm

to show she is not stoned
she is cool
thinking of her son
& how he will hook the show
& she will survive to meet him at hoop & dare
what am I doing here?

some kind of warehouse garage
& the Boss in elaborate robes,
accountrements of magic & dare
fur & feather
it is the sham in shaman
who rehearses this circle out

all the molecules spitting at
molecules
hoop a ring of fire (to think of her lover)

it is a lovely story of a tender seal
Gus's eyeballs are big
he is lithe
& nervous
I start to speak but
he hides behind a bush
to watch his own movie
before it's shot

at this point
the multifarious
names
of all I ever knew named
flood in of

of
light —
no —
of semantic referent

same coin
a trace
modified echoes come down to me

wilt worship me
"little master" who is Satan
half made for me
crowded with hair

crowded with fear

a sign of a cross
in vain
I am a devil now
in my pride, in my fancy

more powerful than that *other* goddess
I spell for better harvest on this farm
I would not heed
more cattle?
erudition not bridge the abyss
    feel in heart
the soil, and curse her heart

go down upon this earth
out now
out out
pull me out now

victim of interrogation
inquisitors

      I thought "a witch, a fool, dancing
      on my own grave"
      I thought "where is my cortege of
      ecstatic women?"

a word of dead
gone back under to
people-on-blankets-in-drizzle
making a humble party
having a time
on the margin of this day
got qualified: old drug day

making a bed for a child
pity for her runny eye...

making a song for children:
    pity her runny eye

        battle for the fertility of this field
    a show tonight, there will be a party
    inside the farmhouse to make the land grow

inside the soil of imagination
imagined house
imagined lover
a river bed

then later I caught Gus
we parted
I, to the parking lot
wandered off
in my head hiding
behind a bush
"directing" his movie
I thought
"the meadows of the underworld"
I thought
"a dense fabric"
I thought
"what is my power"
and
"flank my temples"
I thought
"a film is a lighted house"
head's afire
I thought
"the proper ceremonies"
 & the report of the "mistress of the good game"
had two stones around her eyes, one on each side,
that open & close at her wish
"She had a black
band around her head with patches before
her ears & eyes
so she could not

see or hear
anything"
as confirmed by Caterina della Libra of Carano
for "everything she hears & sees she makes hers"
I thought of a mission for life
O to be a hunter

if she could
see everything
she could do
great harm to the world

or
 she could help what she sees

make a choice
bend not sinister

whirrrr

          (I miss my love)

Hunter is close
hear his gentle code
& caution in the world

how many people to touch to touch
with a verse
a song

(hold back?
push on)

these small notes not a story
I try to track a trip that's all

Words of visionary precision
I thought
"I've been handed down by the fourteenth century"

I thought
"Impure people:
I turn into a bird"
I thought
"Shall I duel with my lover
to show him who carries the most
passion?
Shall I strangle his wife
in my head?"
I thought
"I am in my catalepsy"
& seeing the beginning & end of time
curses of those
who catch the myth
something about the unquenchable
thirst of the dead

Billia la Castagna had given all the participants
a repulsive looking liquid:
those who drank it
were incapable of leaving the sect
It was said the liquid had been made
from the excrement of a large toad which Billia
kept under her bed
feeding it meat, bread & cheese..
Another woman, Alasia de Garzo
had been accused of mixing to the potion
the ashes of hair & public hair

to have done with the judgement of God...

Please be gentle for him I snapped
sentient beings deserve to "have a life"

you'll end up in her poetry
not as embarrassing as Nin diary
j'espère

perhaps as fraught as

she had an ambassadorial intent
what conveyed her here
launched a chain of command

& Oregon a kind of sideshow
what she did learn of external maps
was restituted inside the
climate
inside
the wood
inside the
nail
inside the
shelter-charnel-ground

inside the daylight's gentle plan
a trickster resides here
　& she is his guest

but she used them
the demons
o yes she did she did

LEWIS WARSH

Precious Mettle

One ends in ignominy because one begins mistakenly
virtue is angelic & vice makes us meek
we haven't drawn the lines around our hearts so clearly
it's impossible to tell where one begins & one ends
& it's hard to say "no" to love, or anything,
easy to imitate nature but what part of nature should
        we choose
the face of the passing stranger who runs her fingers
        along your sleeve
I think I'd like a drink but I don't have any money
the perversity of a tree whose leaves forgot to bloom
should we imitate the sky or go to our room
where the stars painted on the ceiling revolve in time to
        the music
which imitates our fears of feeling too much without
        knowing
if it's love of ourselves which makes us feel weak,
a person fainting at dawn on the street,
the scars of the person beside you in bed,
I trace your face with my fingers & you awaken
to the touch, pornographically speaking I love you less
or too much, deformed by wickedness like all of life
if you can define wickedness as the way other people
        think
& who can remember the night in December
we walked hand in hand through the empty street
struck dumb by the snow as it fell on our faces
this wasn't hell, but the outer traces
you paid your tab at the grocery on 6th
I bought a pack of smokes for the journey

426

JOHN YAU

A Different Cereal

The moon shrinks behind a row of shriveled trees.
An empty parking lot, a man reading a newspaper
        inside an illuminated box.
After reaching into the cupboard, her hand closed
its five fingers around a leatherbound volume.
Later, the aspirin would not dissolve in a spoon of water.

An empty parking lot sinks behind a man
reading a leatherbound volume of fingernails.
Reaches for an illuminated cereal box, teeth closing.
Later, behind a row of trivial shrieks, the car would not start.
Inside the envelope were three blue stars, the dead general's
        photograph.

After relieving the television of its promises,
she reaches for her illuminated fingernails,
while he sinks the rest of his teeth
into the leatherbound cereal box.
Beside the orange, an envelope
with three blue spoons painted on its flap.

The general quickly dissolved into a shriveled cereal,
his fingers scratching an empty box of illuminated shrieks.
Later, beneath the rows of parking stars, a man
grinds an aspirin into the cement.
When the wind ripped the leaves from the trees,
it was as if murder slid out of the swamp.

After licking rows of stamps
she stood behind a tree.
He wanted to know why his car would not relieve him
of the headaches of television.
Eventually, the moon is replaced by a picture of trees,
each ripped from the leaves of a leatherbound volume.

The dead general wrote to his mother
asking her to send a different cereal.
The doctor's ashes were spooned into an envelope
and mailed to a woman who reads newspapers in a car.

Smiles broke the ice that formed along
the rows of fingernails illuminated by the moon.
A box of shrieks was delivered to a television station.
After circling the tree four times, the general's dog
placed the envelope inside the cereal box.

She watched the cars inching back and forth
            across her television.
Stands behind a smile, a handshake, a newspaper.
Eventually, the swamp will reach the gates of the parking lot,
where the shadows of the living mix with the dust of the dead.

After carefully opening each letter,
she placed the shrieks in a leatherbound volume.
She liked the way they illuminated the parking lot
when the wind ripped her sighs to shreds.

Gloves removed the hands
and placed them beside
the newspaper.

Turned to the smile that worked best beneath the moon.
Crack of a whip, wrack of a crib.
Enough that inside the envelope
            was the cereal
the children have been shrieking for.

We Are All Vultures

The man in the next bed died just after eating lunch. You were staring at his daughter, and wondering what she looked like in a silver nightgown. She had just finished telling you about a dream she had had the night before: You had fallen out of bed, but the traction pin held you upside down, as if you were an animal waiting to be slaughtered. She was running to save you, but kept tripping over her nightgown.

Of course, the dream was about her father and not you. Still, you were staring at her and wondering if you would ask the obvious: Why didn't you take off your nightgown.

You didn't. She would have been embarrassed about taking off her clothes in front of strangers. And you were equally uneasy about asking her why she didn't.

That was twelve years ago, and you never saw her again.

The nurses drew the curtain, wheeled him out, emptied his locker, and sponged down the mattress. All you could do was listen.

What is terrible (and beautiful) about the past is its remoteness. There are things that happen to you long before you are born. Sometimes, they are smoothly in place when your moment comes around.

Somebody leaves. Whatever is left behind will soon be gone, devoured by words.

Edificio Sayonara

It is time to say good-bye, adios, sayonara. He heard the words and then wrote them down. He knew what they meant but he was not sure what he meant by them. Yes, it is time to say good-bye, adios, sayonara, but he was not sure to who or what he was saying or thinking them. It may be that these words are departing, are turning and looking back before they vanish through the door separating him from the earth.

He wondered how long he had lived above the earth, above the room he saw himself in, walking across its wooden floor to pick up a green and white book, riffle its pale pages until he found the illustration he was looking for. He wondered if the one he was looking at was him or someone that looked like him, someone who ate at the same table with someone who knew his name, the name he called himself by when he went took the bag of dirty clothes to the laundry or ordered a blender from a catalogue.

He asked her what she was doing. I am masturbating. I am lying in the dark, listening to your voice and masturbating. But I have given you a different face and body, the face and body of a lion though now that I have told you that I will change your face and body into something else, something that will bring me back to the muddy field where I first met you, where we first made love, before you ever looked up from behind your desk and saw me looking back.

He heard the words and decided to write them down. The voice was his though he was not speaking. He wondered how long it had been talking and why he had not heard it before. Someday I will learn to speak, someday I will have assembled all the words I need in order to say what it is I need to say but until that time comes I will sit here and listen. A slight murmur, like that of distant traffic on a rainy night. moved in the distance.

Each summer his father went to Las Vegas and gambled on the shape of the future, while his mother stayed home and told him stories about her childhood—the bright colors of its passing—in a country she had no desire to return to. He thought he would someday be able to find the space between his father's schemes to control the future and his mother's memories of the past.

I would like to get married; have a child; leave the city; go on some kind of assistance so we can have more time to be with each other. But before doing that I would like to sleep with this man I met the other night, he does not look like you so that is good. We might all be together one day, but I would not want to be the center of attention. I want something else but not right now or maybe now but not the now we are in but the one we are about to be in, the one that is coming towards us. Right now, I need some stability. I need to see you sitting there. I need to know you will be alone in that chair when I come back from the store.

His parents had traveled a long distance to come to America. They once lived in different parts of a city that no longer existed, its name assigned to either the cold pages of history books or the yellowed pages of novels in which passion tore the characters into tiny pieces for others to scoop up while they walked toward the temple in the mountains.

He used to tie me to the bed before he went out. Sometimes he would be gone all afternoon. He once told me he had murdered a man and buried him in the field near our house. He said no one missed him and no one would ever find him. He said that he loved me. He said that I had to learn that this was how it was done.

I have to count all the windows. I will only live in a house that has an odd number of windows, thirteen or seventeen, say. I only wear brown or green. Blue reminds me of the sky or the ocean. I will not wear blue. I will not eat off blue dishes or drink out of blue cups. I will not allow my body to merge with anything but the earth.

He had been masturbating in front of a mirror, seeing if he could change his face into someone else's when he heard a door open and a voice he did not know call out his name.

He had a thought. It was not his. He put it out of his mind, onto the table, next to the blue vase containing yellow flowers. The thought returned to its cage and sang. He listened to its melody. In a few months or years he would learn the meaning of its song.

431

Angel Atrapado VIII

Where will this voice go once it leaves me, leaves the mouth kissing pockets of air as if one of us has left the room? Someone said these words, someone running behind the one who is silent, the one elected to speak by the ones whose language does not fit their tongues. Someone said: It will dissolve in the shadows pressing themselves against us, it will run down the walls of sunlight filling the room you lease when you are in the company of others. Someone said these words, someone floating face down in a bathtub full of food.

I wanted to see you swimming between the pages of a book, all the words in profile. I wanted to hear you talk about the oracular menaces infiltrating the daily rust.

It was the hour of the day when the flames thicken, and smoke climbs its ladders and blocks out the sun. You told me you wanted to see if I could find you, who was burning one of your faces off beside the library of stolen books.

You were paid to throw oranges at a man old enough to be your uncle. Not your father's age, but your uncle's, this was the distinction. An uncle was someone you threw oranges at, someone who smiled at the juice running down his chest.

I tried stealing what was mine, you whispered. I tried stealing the body I once slept in and wore, the one that looks like something is missing from the air it breathes, the one I had been using as a ramp.

This time it will be different, you tell yourself. This time you won't swallow the nails you carry inside your mouth. This time you won't impale your tongue on a knitting needle, offer it to those whose tails have been severed from the rugs heaped in front of the fireplace.

This honey will inhibit thirst.

This word was used to fill the space between one thing and another.

This shadow was once attached to its base.

This photograph will make it impossible for you to remember me.

Escape, he told me, was unacceptable. You cannot escape from your life into mine. You must do something else. You must reach me without leaving, must reach me who is looking through the place where you are standing. Yes, I am inside the mirror, and I am watching you.

GERRIT LANSING

The Gold in the Mud

    legendary darkness in the dayshine,
    how it works to be,
    sleeping on the floor,
    how bodies love.
        shrewdness of it,
        of being in time,
      what it takes to know
      what gnosis is,
      that our knowledge
          exceeds our having minds,
          newspapers of fate,
not madness but logic of the rites of whatever seasons come to be.

    (A scribble,
        as might a shepherd say,
    whose sheep are human sheep.

WILL ALEXANDER

Alchemy as Poetic Kindling

". . . poetry has no other mission than to transmute history.
And therefore the only true revolutionary poetry is apocalyptic
poetry."

—Octavio Paz

It exists, as a cycadaceous spur, as ceaseless motion towards gold. Its
fire is brewed in concentrated spirals reflected in the poet as genetic
nettling water. Poetry being the language of concentration through destiny.

One commences the poetic quest with a thirst for illuminate language,
as if one had been branded in the womb, with the anti-linear condensed
in the image. And I am not speaking of an affected, self-appointed heroics,
condoned by escapist grammar, but conviction, burning like a phantom
mesmerism, always calling one home to the fruit of one's bones.

Conviction, like an intuitive vulcanism, does exist, like a singular body
of sound. And this sound pre-exists the composition of intense parables
or poems. It pre-exists the maturation of multi-lineal ideals. It is a
condition in the way that one reflexively exists. Whether it exists in the
way one holds a cup, or the way one pursues a suicidal interest in iguana
or stars. One breaks the pattern, one severs the quotidian mode. Like a
torrential truth pouring out invisible vibrations, the community is alerted
to a ghost at hand. Not a ghost mind you, in the despicable popular sense,
but nevertheless a ghost, who feeds on transparencies from birth. These
psychic regions exist, are born and become alert through the power of
poetic nigredo. And when fully ripened they explode with a-sequential
pyroclastic, leaping the lower boundaries, existing in an ignescently
transmuted reality. One surmounts each imaginary crippling by means of
an in-judicious language. One expands the realm of speech, one takes in
odours, in foliage, in contra-band. One speaks in alchemical atonality, in
constant mercurial voltage.

So the alchemical poets find themselves genetically ensconced in the
aforementioned nigredo. The proto-fires, the pre-emotive hurtling of
language, the tenacious image foci seedlings.

So when the first implantation of signs occurs, one feels a great mark in the right direction. An instantaneous antidote against bad civic magic, against the rays from bureaucratic reason.

We know about viridian meadowlarks being forced from the voice, about operant pinnacles obscured by the deadly haze of analysis. So how to destroy the great arthritic claw, that great arthritic burden that engulfs the mind with sequential hazard? With the intensity of the image, alive with its maturation by anger, by exhaustive whirling and craving, like a vampire after blood, in the pen-ultimate clockwork before dawn. This is what Philip Lamantia calls the "Red phase" of the "Great Work," when the linguistic voltage shatters the flank of despotism, of the transfixed form which masquerades as rigour.

Alchemical language is a passage through stages; and if we could see the visage of Hölderlin quickly flickering on a visual reel, we would readily sense the alchemical shadings, not through the force of our obvious optical appendage, but through our sense of interior weathers, moving back and forth through linguistic turbulence. Ultimately, an elevated life atop "eternal mountains." And Hölderlin sees this elevation as a struggle, as he posits the difference between "the warm life" within, and "the icy history of common day."

An imagination, pre-cluded against contamination, where one could imagine a slaughter house producing arisen angelics, or imagine a gryphon atop boulders staring out into a magically crafted dawn of magenta.

In the alchemical poet images arise from a high state of risk, from advanced flotational scarlet. I am not speaking of a secondary utterance conditioned by rigid laryngeal suture, but a vital deafening electrics, filled with incalculable summas. And this power is conditioned by development, each stage of the inner expression linked with the outer peril through which one passes, seasoned by melancholia, and darkness.

As the poet traverses the covert domains, we witness the outer ironics, the flaws, the disasters, the handcuffs, the boundaries. One day composing in a lion coloured villa, or another, destitute, scrounging, choking on liters of spittle. The contradictions inherent in the chemistry of risk, cradling torment in one's singing feathers, so as to magically rise from densely riddled charcoal lagoons.

And it is in this rising when mesmerism becomes synecdoche and spillage, where the words take on a butane colour, in constant orphic transmutation. The eel, the fiery hull, the red and glistening princess, become elaborate, and take on the sonar of Herons. Then one gives the words the power to fly through the eye of the skull. The poem transfixes without modelling, entrances without deciphering. Therefore, the ambiguity thrills, and opens up the reader to constant illuminant spiralling throughout a duration of simultaneous transparencies. The image then becomes a crystalline manna, a sun exchanging its forces with water.

Like Shelley or Artaud, the alchemical poet, by magically ingesting demons, is able to enunciate prophetic enigmas, is able to take as riddle a fount, which pours forth tenacious wanderings from an essentially rebellious interior. A gust of eternity from the voice, not as mechanical paradigm, but as a beatific holocaust of monsters. A "nocturnal wolf at high noon," "standing in fields of fresh "blood," "laying down its entire chromosian hand," its image, glowing from the leaps of an oven, carving with its knives an inconsolable mercury, so as to hew out the void, with an odour of "immaculate" frenzy.

And if there is one thing the poet requires it is heat. It is the multiple and enduring friction which honours its lashing out and bewitchment. And from each quotidian annihilation comes a fruit of a higher and greater energy, of a fire of fertile and surreptitious turquoise. The poet in this era of exploration and methane has had to surmount the power of tyrants and magicians and has had to take on the authority of a phantom Egret ruling from a transparent throne of sound. Rimbaud and Campana can be deftly described in glossolalia and iguana, Artaud as fishing from a darkened deck of veins, with Pessoa flinging his findings into absinthe and hamlets.

These poets have committed war against the rational, and are right in keeping with Borduas and his seminal statement on "Global Refusal," with its resistance, to "public opinion," to "ridiculous justice," to "general disapproval." In the works of these men there is always a copious frying, a schema of splintered stratification and absurdity. And whether it be in situ, or on the open road, a restless anger always prevails. An exploded salt, a seasoned mercury. And this anger is a gift which springs from the angle of the work—the dialectics of the study hall and the brothel. It is a work which swallows discredit and venom, which takes on opprobrium, weaving from its hollows magical bells and glass. Over the past two-and-one-half centuries it is the itinerant who has possessed us, who has inscribed the language of ecstatic delirium. Conversely, it is the scribes, the official pamphleters that we vilify, that we seek to re-inter in oblivion. So when Césaire demands a sincere and internal African wholeness, he is rebuffed by communist ideology and told to burn his own solutions, to stuff his crows' nests with candles counted by machine and bureaucracy. He disembarks and walks away from the ramparts, knowing full well that the bastion is the glow from within.

When discussing this level of energy, words like maniacal, absolute, seem to balance themselves on equators of terror. One does not self-serve, or superficially deflect, the maze, and the contradictory tediums of the moment. When Paz resigns his ambassador's bureaucracy because of student "blood" in the sacrificial "Plaza," he unloads himself of "bile," and takes on water, restoring a level of dignity. He underlines defiance as honour, which throttles neurosis, which upends deception. Therefore, the alchemical poet exists as a dangerous vagrant, chattering in elusive cobalt, walking in a personal zodiac garden, trailed by "Raw Sienna" moons glowing on the backs of Zebra.

And I'll always remember my first encounter with Bob Kaufman, at an angle on a street in North Beach, wordless in his phantom movements, like the silence of an alchemical crucible. The nutrients inside his skull like interior flashing muscles, his seismically arched back beneath fables of sonar. His lines, evolved from a beautiful alabaster titling, from a blank zodiacal craving, continuing to send their signals with "secret Medici keys," with original "glacial" octave, farming grains with splinters from the sun. Kaufman churns at the core of the alembic smuggling salts through his poetic ventricles. Seeing Kaufman in high relief, one can poetically graph "the symbolic meaning of the various alchemical operations," of "calcination," of putrefaction, of "solution," of "distillation," which becomes "the coincidenta oppositorum," the union of the primary principles, the male and the female, the consciousness and the unconsciousness. Images of a "face" . . . "like a living emotional relief map," or "the cry of an amethyst heron," ascending from a magic germinal grave.

This is poetry as "precipitate of pure time," where the wheel stops, where fiestas boil. By its very nature poetry blinds us and takes us levels and levels beyond abnegation. It thrives on linguistic rebellion and is an enemy of exchange and common monetary retrieval. The life of commerce it assassinates and purges, speaking with the force of "irreducible" intensity. In its essential register it is not clannish or ideological, it creates its own pattern with a relentless meteoritics. From the word, the phrase takes life as the arch movement of language; and in this arch movement there exists the poetic flower speaking in clairaudient ramblings of chance. In this feverish metropolis of energy, there exists the sweltering electrodes, of image, line, poem, breaking onto a fertile glycerin shore, where totems of fire stare amidst solvents of glass, into the motionless inter-action of eternity. This is the realia of linguistic nobility, the height from which all cerulean evolves.

One could say that the poem is like a bird drifting off from a lightning tower of language, gliding through the miraculous circulation of infinity. A language of power which overcomes opinion and seasonal reaction. The best plays of 1944, the infected spinning of a popular romance chronicle. Instead, the poem is in league with a more enduring passion, not inclined towards rewards, or instantaneous outcome. As García Lorca attests, "I know that he is wrong who shouts 'Now! Now! Right now!' with his eyes fixed" on immediate recompense and profit.

We live in a land where the popular expression has been imprisoned and engineered for the use of illusion and debasement. It is the mental equivalent of physical cholesterol and poison. And this is how the masses consume their weight in readily available cultural fat. The attention span stiffens, the absorption rate contracts, to a few feeble jabs of the memory. Any relatedness to a deeper strata of feeling is annulled, and if allowed to momentarily surface, is insidiously tainted with a pejorative metaphysics. Therefore, a more refined perception takes on the status of debility, of an ably endowed fraud, of a weirdly empowered anaemia. With the commercial tenet at hand the artist loses the mark of maturation, and the poetic combat with the invisible. How can the commonly hailed image cope with suffering and transmutation? How can it seethe with the letters of the dream? As rejoinder, there is spareness, a sculpting according to fickle tastes and momentary tenets. Nothing but straw, turned into a false and tufted cashmere. An impaired and ungracious linguistic capacity.

On the other hand in Bali, when the witch-queen Rangda appears, the visible and the invisible instantaneously exist. Rangda, with her "curved white fangs," with "her yard-long . . . tongue" with her "goat hair wig," carries power from the visible to the invisible, returning again to affect the visible. This, of course, reflects a society with refined psychic circulation. A sensitive astral theater. This is the point where Artaud lost his public in the West. He sought a thrilling catharsis of existence for both performer and audience as one unbroken flow. He desired an inhabited theater, an impalpable poetic theater. Instead, what he confronted was theater as a fort for legal entertainment, to be forgotten upon entering the boulevard. What Artaud called for was a poetics of thirst, a striving for greater existence.

And we see this same carnivorous thirst in another country, in an earlier time, when Lopez Velarde enters Mexico City, discovering his language through doubt, who, like Artaud, was able to chart his "anguish," always challenging the drama of parochial assumption. In "The Malefic Return" or in "Ants" or in "I Honour You In Dread," there is the bitten inch of the nail and the percolation of wine in a coffin. Like Artaud, his writings take on an alchemical bravado, speaking with previous imponderables. Not a poetry of duplication, or a sum of emotional forgeries, Lopez Velarde has stated that he longed "to eject every syllable that is not born of the combustion of my bones."

Therefore, poetry seems fed by aggravation and danger, by opprobrium and fatigue, like the current pulsing through ignescent waters. Bewilderment and perfection by bewilderment. Superficially ambiguous yes, but in terms of its deeper archery, poetry is able to open its target congealed in lightning. It carries the power to illumine, to exemplify transformative purity and stamina, which pre-dates Homer, which survives the blast of Armageddon.

CLARK COOLIDGE

from *The Crystal Text*

Who were they out there through instruments
in the light? I didn't know and don't.
Perhaps I didn't wonder so much but now I do.
But then I do not realize who *I* am either.
Present time makes the stranger of yourself, whom
you do not have the charm of watching walk away.
How do I think of myself, having long had the practice
of never. A mirror? False view, always
behind the shine of one's own hands. To write
a long book of nothing "but looking deeply into oneself."
I feel this sentence turn on the flinch of a laugh.
A scorn, not for oneself probably but for the
possibility of a self view. Does it wait out there
in the black shine of spateless corridor world.

Large books are not for oval minds.
Handwriting is not a frame for the self.
A shocking caliber of words that would hoof
one off one's own best known path.
The prime abstraction of "one" seems necessary
to hold the self in the frame. And A life
of sentences in rooms one holds no plan to.
I dived at you, self, but you rubbed me blank
in all my own mirrors. Scorn. No one owns,
can possess, a mirror, the reflecting surface.
If I walk in the hallways I will first see
the light before I can identify what precisely
rejects it. This is not knowledge, but then
what is it?
I can see the largeness of the world in a
stone ledge I could then place in my pocket
for all the world's care. How many hunches,
that might prove out, there?
The crystal attains toward a transparency
my mirror approaches, face or no face.

EDWARD FOSTER

Poetry and Joy

for Gene

"My mirror image needs no mirror of its own."
—William Bronk, "Obliquity"

"Given the facts of solitude and of death,
what can matter more than a despair
capable of suddenly flaming into rapture?"
—Leonard Schwartz, "Exiles: Ends"

I. Jason

As Moreau painted him, Jason is a youth with brilliant silk to hide his loins; within the picture that we see, the silk becomes those loins, and hence our source of joy. The silk is colored gold or yellow, like a flame, as if this Jason were a god.

Within this work, the gnostic flare proves once again its source in whatever we conceive as true. Embrace the man called Jason, and you will find a sweetness in his languid arm. We feel the broken sword, the beast with rapture in its eye and broken wing. All this Medea thought she knew, and yet she could not see into his mind, so did not know how ruthless he'd become. Nor would he change if he were someone else: the only thing he wants is joy.

II. Moreau

First this: our darkened room and paradoxical assent, knowing nothing is agreed. All rooms, all crevices, even these charmed webs along the wall, are formulations in the mind.

In great disdain of all we've made and said, we once more loose ourselves into some loathing of the self, and nothing much outside the present touch is known. Plundered of intent, the darkened world allows us to descend and leaves us quietly within. Nothing can release the color or the shape until we know there's nothing to be seen or named.

Oh, Gene, affection's nothing but the consolation of this magic ring and weakens those who only wish and care. And yet, we still must love. Resolve this paradox, and nothing more is done.

So you are there, and are you still as weak as I? Or will you leave? Will I?

Holding you as if you were the elemental he, I try to reach not consolation but that bleak despair that is our ecstacy and can transform us both. For in this way, the syllables and colors will emerge, and in their destitution we at last are free. As if within that silken flame, we are taken willfully.

And in this spirit, air begins to rise wherever we can see. I think of you and act. The present prospect is your breath, or mine. And thus it is that I, as well as you, now find the words or roots and rocks on which we both agree.

FANNY HOWE

Weil Over Void

"Before there were any creatures, God was not 'God', but he was what he was . . . So let us pray to God that we may be free of 'God'." —Master Eckhart

"As we cannot eliminate language all at once, we should at least leave nothing undone that might contribute to its falling into disrepute. To bore one hole after another in it, until what lurks behind it—be it something or nothing— begins to seep through . . . It will perhaps become possible to feel a whisper of that final music or that silence that underlies All." —Samuel Beckett

"We must continually suspend the work of the imagination filling the void within ourselves." —Simone Weil

---

Silence is only what you don't yourself utter; otherwise there is none, unless you are deaf. Beckett wanted to give silence time. He admired the silence of painting, the use of silence in music, and the given silence of geometry. He was sorry that literature had such a hard time boring holes in words and letting the silence out. "To accept a void in ourselves is supernatural," Weil wrote, explaining the difficulty.

The pursuit of silence runs contrary to the pursuit of literary expression; it was also considered a heresy in the Middle Ages, when gangs of individuals, all over Europe, practiced Quietism, a gnostic religious cult with its discipline in poverty and silence. For the Quietist, desire and the renunciation of desire were equally vain, and a person could do either, or neither, and it would only ruffle the surface of that person's psyche. The Quietists would have fared fine in India, but their fate as Europeans led them to be excommunicated, if not destroyed, as the Cathars were.

The Quietists had a practice of lying utterly still and waiting to discover what words rose from the void into their consciousness, without an exertion of will. Like those who speak in tongues, they experienced ravings and messages from the deep. They were mystics and anarchists. And in some cases they were poets. If they had belonged to an order of Discalced Carmelites, they might have been all right, too; because once you were lodged inside walls of the Holy See, you could be a poet, a mystic, and an anarchist.

The Quietists were heretics because of their refusal to adhere to any of the outer forms of the Church. And the Church, like literature, is structured to contain and organize "divine madness," not to follow it. Weil, who was repelled by the tyrannical efforts of both Rome and Israel on the human side, saw such mystics as Quietists, Cathars, Albigensians (all, in a sense, gnostic) as being the only hope for union with God (the void) through their ability to desire without an object.

The austerity of her own style was a choice she made against the power of illusion and beauty. ("The beautiful is that which we desire without wishing to eat it. We desire that it should be.") A practiced austerity: the quotidian reduced to its most categorical, geometric operative—the intermediary of thing to word to the void.

(On great work in our times—the twentieth century—"It can only be solitary, obscure and without an echo . . . but without an echo, no art." She might have been describing her life.) She was not an artist, but was called a heretic, a Martian, mad, and many other unflattering (as well as loving) names. She carried thought as far as it could go—given her chosen direction, eternity, and she died when she couldn't carry her thoughts further. By that time she wasn't eating anything at all.

Words used by Mystics to describe annihilation of the sensible faculties:

rapture flight of the spirit negation transforming union soul loses herself dazzled blinded incomprehensible alienation infused contemplation pierced by a blaze hypertrophy of attention spiritual marriage natural somnambulism deep & profound sweetness rapt absorbed plunged in divine water swooning levitation mounting soul elevates & dilates all

447

knowledge conveyed undifferentiated state Blessed Be He The Unnameable.

"God" scares me, and that's a fact. It also scares me to imagine that I might be seduced by the tones, turns and musics of a poetic tongue which is arranged to create a false idol, an illusion. Babble, excited showing-off, the prettiness of the reports coming in from a poetry which is the equivalent of an IQ test. Silence is the only effective and terminal antidote. Before that, it may be the case that the prose line is the least apt to succumb to falsehood. Much of my writing has been an effort to rearrange, rewrite the word "God" by filling up pages with other names. I don't like the name "God" because of its Roman weight. But when I write, I rewrite that name, and then what I write, if it is written well, becomes not a new "God" but a new person, a human face. If a face does not gaze back at me from the page, there is only paper and wood, the static object empty of divine spark. The human face in repose and in silence is the face I see, when what I have written approximates the unspeakable.

And I lay there dying
For my asylum

Was myself.

When I first discovered the writings of Simone Weil, I was at once aware that she had hit the wall of silence. She had carried her thought as far as it could go. There was no way I could address her thought, in speech, therefore, because I would always be trailing my subject. There is such a thing as experience that precedes speech. I would have to convey my experience of her thought without speaking about it. I would keep banging into the wall of silence—a reality as solid as stone. But I would persist, because she had fulfilled her thoughts, and she had managed to gather into them, as evidence, responses to history, both past and in the making. She was political. I wonder what happened to her to make her know as much as she knew, since her life was quite short and solitary. No one can learn from nothing. She had learned somewhere and somehow

448

what she would later describe in an unembellished prose and in abstractions that sting. She had been wounded by love, she had been nurtured by it too. She had felt what it is to work long hours for the absurdity of cash exchange. She had been oppressed. Perhaps she had experienced all these in relatively minor ways, but the intensity of her response and her intelligence had generated the genius of her generalizations. I was sure I could go no further (if as far!) in the direction of thought I wanted to take, too. So she was my teacher.

Sometimes it is clear that filaments of light infiltrate the bloodstream, just as surely as they do the shoots of greenery on the brick walls. This light resonates as ecstasy. It produces print, the handwriting that is a mirror of the face behind the sweating mask, just as it produces all work that burns up against silence. The face of a human that lives from light, and is open to silence, is usually the face of someone poor. Poverty is not always a condition. It is a way of treating the material world. It is non-dominating. The poor in spirit are those who are—regardless of their condition, up to a point—non-acquisitive, and non-transgressive. Non is close to silence.

And few are agreed on the way to pronounce WEIL:

vay veil vale vial vile weel wail wile

as if her name itself was outside captivity, non-speakable.

ROBERT KELLY

Spirit/Vanguard Art

In the *Pedagogical Sketchbook* he compiled for his Bauhaus course, Paul Klee wants to tell us about an energy that finds us in the *point*—tip of a line moving along. The energy wants us. As soon as pen touches paper, this energy—a point is energy—moves [us along]. The consequent line gets our attention, and explicates the current or passage of which it is the wake.

What is there to pay attention to when we're paying attention?
  A. Where the line has been.
  B. What the mind wants to do with what it is seeing.
  C. What my attention is itself up to.

History is (A), and I have nothing to say.

For it is in the closeness, but antarctic otherness, of (B) and (C) that there's something useful for us, a joining that I've found instructive, even a pressure to renew.

It is the help that *spirit*, which is (C) in operation, brings to avant-art, which is (B) in extension.

At this moment I'm thinking of art as: the anxiety and ceaseless producing elicited from the ground of our being in the world by raptly attending to the question: "What's next?" I'm thinking too that it is the natural outpouring, not always conscious, of the—should it be previous?—question: "Who's asking?"

If you keep asking "Who's asking?" you won't get distracted by imaginary projects and propositions about the world. You keep intent on regarding as your business the very process of asking, bit by bit, line by line, word by word. A line, a word, again.

This is how we have been discovering the glad abyss of the minimal. (It is the source too of the insistent, if austere, personhood of the postmodern.) The minimal in art is that which never lets itself (or the observer) forget that it is art. This is its special glory, and its limitation. It breaks beyond itself when it forgets itself, succumbs to the excitements of the image, the lure of proposition, demonstration, *narrative*. That is, those

450

domains where the characteristic question of the artist is "What to do now?"

And all along the characteristic question of the person of spirit is still, "Who's asking?"

One name given to that very question is meditation.

Early Buddhist statuary from Gaulish times (the so-called "Meditator of Roquepertuse" for instance) shows an early Western presence of that way. Pythagoras was *listening*, hence all the talk about him and music, and his method was all about listening.

Listening to the endless speakable and unspeakable answers to that question.

All faces are the Buddha's face—inescapable rule of portraiture.

All beings are your mother.

The meditator suspends in quiet lucency the imputation of words, all words. (Consider the old name for enlightenment: "the repose of named things.") In this way, in "mental strife," a machete is laid to the social underpinnings of language and the linguistic underpinnings of society, both at once. The way is similar to, and (for the meditator) perhaps more effacious than, the project of de-referencing language announced so powerfully, even epochally, years ago by Steve McCaffrey in "The Politics of the Referent," and usefully lately by Bruce Andrews's "Poetry as Explanation, Poetry as Praxis" (*Paper Air*, Vol. IV, No. 3, 1990).

Power of poetry: to employ propositional language not to make assertions, but to make, for a moment, lush gardens where one is free from assertions, exalted in the fragrance of presentness.

Such deconditioned delights, subtle, struggling free from associations yet enduring with pleasure all the temporary ecstasies of them as they slip off, may indeed give the reader of contemporary poetry a taste for such unconditions, dis-situation. And you may wind up trying to live free of the obligation of attending to your own habitual intentions.

February 1991/Encinitas

LESLIE SCALAPINO

from an interview*

EF: In *The Return of Painting, The Pearl, and Orion: A Trilogy†*, you write, "The Comic Book is the self," and that seems the basic assumption or aesthetic throughout the book, but particularly in *Orion*. Could you summarize what you mean by that and how it effects the writing?

LS: I am trying to use the writing to be an examination of the mind in the process of whatever it's creating; and to have there be a distinction, or there not be a distinction, between that and actually being in present time: to have the writing be that. Some parts of the book were being written when something was occurring, such as going on a trip to the Middle East, being in the Sudan, writing in a plane over the Red Sea, or writing when I was travelling in Boston and having whatever was occurring going into that writing—although at times also remembering things and putting that in but always a sense of the writing being a mode.

The comic book is actually done where the lines are each a paragraph, and sometimes the paragraphs are only one line, are the frames of the comic book and are what are being seen and are being created by the reader in that you are producing actions and motions like running or like perceptions. A location is created in which the perceiver is the center. It's the self in that you're inside of that perception, and you're creating it by reading it. It's watching what the mind is doing and trying to collapse the distinctions, all kinds of distinctions: like the distinction of what's the child's mind and what is the adult mind, so that you are trying to find what is in a sense the original mind. And to use that as a self-conscious form is merely a convention. You would be seeing your way of seeing is a convention, sense of time is a convention, sense of parts of the mind and parts of development which are a sense of progression from childhood to adult. I was trying to get the writing to be passages that are juxtaposed against each other so that you're collapsing these distinctions while looking at them. I think one question or one aspect of that is to make this kind of innocent surface that is the comic book, which is just this really obvious form. And then you exist in that simply, in there.

*with Edward Foster, first published in *Talisman* 8 (Spring 1992) and reprinted in *Postmodern Poetry*, ed. Foster (Hoboken, NJ: Talisman House, Publishers, 1994).
†*The Return of Painting, The Pearl, and Orion: A Trilogy* (San Francisco: North Point Press, 1991).

EF: But the comic book is a set of discrete panels, and experience doesn't have that kind of division. It's continuous, however it's represented or understood.

LS: Well, I'm trying to do the sense that one has of making discrete experiences. That you're doing that artificially which is normally. You're making progression. And so I'm trying to do both what one tends to do with the mind in establishing order, so that you can arrange things but to realize that that's a fabrication.

It also has something to do with a crossover between prose and poetry. Sometimes when a paragraph is just one line it's a poem that just gets pushed out of shape in a sheet of such lines which continue like a scroll. Observations occur individually within that extension of one-line paragraphs.

Actually the sense that I have was that the three parts of the *Trilogy* are one thing, although they're discrete. In reading the whole text from beginning to end, what I wanted to do was to have something that would be empty in the center and be still and calm in the center even though there is a lot of commotion, things happening at every point, and that one would get to the end and wouldn't have a sense of where the center was because the center would be at every point. You wouldn't know where the context, being empty, had taken place, but you would have a feeling that it had. It's discrete actions or precise actions in that you're always in that center because it's always trying to be in present time; so that you'd be only concentrating in the place where you are. It's usually done as locations in the sense that you're exactly there.

EF: So are you suggesting there is no interiority, no internal self?

LS: You're creating the illusion that there is. That the moment you are within that center, wherever that center is, in that precise spot, you're believing that and seeing it—seeing that as your interiority, and yourself as possessing that. In a way, I wanted the writing to be ahead of itself. I guess the comic book is a genre where you have to complete the motion of the story, but the story is irrelevant, the plot is irrelevant, and it has merely the locomotion that a dream has. It is created inside, and it fulfills the terms of itself. In a way it has a kind of motion, and there is something about the unfolding of that that occurs back inside oneself—particularly in *The Pearl*, I think. And it appears to be either out ahead of oneself or behind oneself in terms of where one is apprehending something. It is either before or behind or moving alongside of something. So it's always

453

a question of choosing a form and trying to create where that center is. But the center is that empty place that has nothing to do with plot.

EF: So would you say the self is itself the seeing, the act of seeing?

LS: Yes, it is the act of seeing, but you believe that you're seeing something which you take to be real, and you're seeing it in that moment but don't know when that took place later. The only thing that the self is then is the seeing of it, and you're empty because you're only seeing a thing that's outside of yourself or the illusion that you are.

EF: But then what decides the form of the individual panels in this comic strip that is the seeing?

LS: It's having the sense of being in actual locations and that the location is something that is created by the writing so it is the form the writing is, the phenomenon that that is. The location is that.

EF: According to the trilogy, "An event is not in the person." Could you elaborate on what you mean there?

LS: I think the point particularly where I said that, was having someone describe something that occurred, a person described being beat up by the Ku Klux Klan; this had actually occurred. It is taking something that is very real and then observing the fact that one is no longer that person in describing it. The whole attempt is to be in present time, and yet you're there. As writing it's a fabricated event even though it's real.

EF: This brings to mind all sorts of interesting questions about time, the nature of events, and the way they're represented, if that's the word, in language. You say at one point, "No events occur. Because these are in the past. They don't exist." But you suggest there is such a thing as present time and memory also, and so it would seem to me that there must be events before there is memory—it's just that since their present can't be reached, they can't be understood in themselves.

LS: One is kind of struggling with the fact that the entire fabric of what one is seeing and writing is illusory, but it is very focused in an attempt to understand the thing that you're observing. There's a point in *Orion* where I'm trying to concentrate on seeing so that one is being aware that the viewer is nonexistent and what is being seen is nonexistent... It's on page 222. It says, "looking and not see the observer and so there isn't it / (isn't it which is looked at)." And then footnote 18, "either clear dazzling pan that is person or what is seen." I think that this writing has everything to do with that in terms of the surfaces that are held up against each other. They are both the person seeing, and that is the same thing as the so-called "clear dazzling pan" is the object that you're looking at. And it's trying to reach that kind of state where it's as if you would be seeing through the lens that you're writing.

EF: So if I understand, what you're suggesting is a tension between two realities—on the one hand, the outside world, which is presumed to be there but can't be authenticated, and another which is always in some sense self-generating. And this second reality is trying to move into or possess whatever is outside. So the energy of the work involves that movement toward the outside, which remains unknowable.

LS: One's observation of mind is like an experiment to see what you are going to come up with. There is not going to be any objective observation of something. There is only going to be more mind stuff that you're coming up with whether it is emotion or it's something you're describing as analytical observation. There's no real distinction between those things. It's related to the issues of an essay that I wrote called "How Phenomena Appear to Unfold," where I was talking about Philip Whalen's process and Meredith Monk's work "Quarry." You don't know where something's coming from. It appears to be coming from outside you or from inside yourself, but what you appear to be creating is actually occurring out there seen as if under your control. You want to disturb that control. It is the unfolding of events which actually occur, but you don't know where they are or from what focal point they're emanating.

GUSTAF SOBIN

A Few Stray Comments on the Cultivation of the Lyric
(in answer to a young poet who asked for them)

: a poem, from the outset —from its very first syllable, vocable, breath cluster— should pull, draw, attract the reader (and remember that the very first reader is oneself), implicating her/him in its movement that's already movement —in motion— before the poem has even begun.

: begun, then, *in medias res*: the 'running start.'

: that the very first line contain —innate, covert, undivulged— the entire poem in its yet-unraveled trajectory: i.e., not only its 'message,' but both the direction of its thrust and the rate of its movement, its meter: everything it shall deploy for the sake of its own *dépassement*.

: always draw the next line out of the hidden implications of the previous, the past line.

: don't write a poem: grow it. it's a shoot (the breath-in-sprig) that we'd train onto a trellis: draw —sonorous— over its taut, overhead cross-pieces.

: the poem grows out of the poem, not out of one's own, particular intellect. the intellect is merely a guide, a gardener to those shoots, those roots: to that deeper set of imperatives which are first of all organic.

: first of all, so much psychic flora, sprouting —in the very instant of their articulation— into so many measured bars of sound.

: arising as they do from the preconscious: from one's own, particular prehistory: from the deeply embedded —deeply invisible— inscriptions of the exhalation-to-come.

: the poem, then, seen as the lyric cultivation of one's own shadows, one's own dark: those deep, vegetal secrets we've kept from ourselves (so jealously harbored against our own disclosures).

: the poem, then, unearths a mirror of sorts. is a mirror, unearthed.

: it brings its dark, still inarticulate light into the yet irresonant world of the manifest: illuminates that world from within. bathes it, at last, in sound.

: the 'outer world' of the manifest (palpable, perceptible) and the 'inner world' of one's 'inner breath' simultaneously fuse, unite, coalesce: even their categories are absolved for the duration of the poem, as the breath —articulated— shoots forth, refutes the cleavage between 'outer' and 'inner,' rises in a crooked vine: the green lightning-bolt of its own utterance.

: reaching either way as it rises, oscillates upward, drawing as it goes on its echoing opposites, its facing pairs, its *ying* and *yang*: pure androgyny caught in a single voice: the poem in its spiralling, irrepressible ascension.

~

: always draw images from the immediate, the exact, the closely observed. no distance is too small, no detail too obscure.

: if an image has sufficient meaning to oneself, it shall inevitably have meaning to others. use it: turn it into verbal currency.

: (remember that the 'other' is the ideal, the ultimate, the perfect reader, towards whom the words of the poem are aimed. is why the lyric doesn't linger, but precipitates).

: (if this 'other' is first of all oneself, as writer-recipient, it becomes —at the completion of the poem— the projected other, the eventual other, the dart blown into the heart of the still-invisible).

: beware of observing/describing from a uniform distance: the eye doesn't, so why should the voice? move in (the eye within the chalice of a tulip), move back (the eye crossing the far pinnacles) and continuously so as the poem works itself forward.

457

: poetry is as kinetic as cinema. its movement should be irrepressible as breath, restless as white water, volatile as piled cirrus on the first morning of mistral.

: the poem is alive for as long as it moves, develops, deploys: for as long, that is, as it leads out of its own inception and —allying, fusing, then separating as it goes— creates (with as few words as possible) the sudden drama of a lyric sequence.

: to move too quickly foreshortens, truncates that sequence, fractures its wave: the bone and fiber and breath of that wave.

: whereas to move too slowly creates stagnation, stasis, checks passage (the poem in its *élan*, its anticipation).

: (it's as if the so-called 'drama' of the poem were determined, in part, by the cadence at which it's disclosed: by the rate or speed at which its 'materials' are revealed).

: ('movement' and 'material,' in this instance, being syncretic).

: as the poem moves forward, *towards*, in a ceaseless gesture of transmission, distribution.

: each word adding, incremental, to those that preceded it, powered by a dynamic that's simultaneously thrust and oscillation, vector and vibration, as the poem attempts to satisfy the dual nature of its complements, opposites, in its continuous zig-zag forwards.

: beware, at all points, of making small compromises, of not striking —with each word— *le mot juste.* an approximation, a slight divergence in either sound or sense (the lyric gemini) increases with each succeeding line: the 'error' gets progressively compounded. one veers, goes astray gradually, then massively from some very minor point of divergence. when this occurs, work backwards to exactly that point, that instance. then rectify, retrain, rewrap the vine about the invisible iron of its upright.

: the poem is verbal, rather than nounal. it's not so much the expression of its transit as the transit itself. as its own interlude-in-uninterrupted-movement.

: its verbs should be vigorous, active, *transitive* as possible. should carry (rather than merely convey) the entire syntactical weight of each phrase, each "nounal accumulation."

: "there are no nouns in nature," Fenellosa. But there are, alas, nouns in language. make them both light and evocative, and where the only possible noun happens to be an exhausted one, spike it with a vivifying adjective. verbalize it.

: no taboos on adjectives, and even less on adverbs. but beware of participles: they're apt to spin haplessly in place, and move nothing forward.

: between the verb and its adverb, the noun and its adjective, within *all* grammatic relationships, stretch usage, expand on given linguistic habit. a poem's *élan* is both in its spring, its elasticity, and in its projection (as it is, indeed, with bow and arrow). the more spring a poem possesses, the more vibrant —vivacious— the expression. this 'springing' is brought about by stretching the potential distance between words to an absolute maximum without, of course, breaking, snapping that tension —that sprung wire— by excess.

: over and over, all words adjusted to an exact measure, *le juste milieu.*

: and, as with meaning, so too with resonance: stretch usage to a full range of sonorous possibilities: let words hiss with wind, crackle with pages, rasp with each of the heart's contradictions.

: the words are sprung, stretched, because the poem is *aimed.* the analogy with the bow (and before the bow, for charming game, the lyre) cannot be too stressed.

: the poem, then, is aimed, but at what? towards whom?

459

: towards its own totality that can only be assured, accomplished, completed within the hearing of its ever-projected 'other.'

: therefore, be spare. never give more than just enough. imply, suggest, hint, infer: the poem is a set of cues for that still-invisible reader. it's the heart's shorthand, and the spirit's. just enough, no more (for the 'more' belongs to the other, whereby she/he might surmise, interpolate, complete the poem in the poem's full intentionality).

: the 'other,' then, not as a passive recipient, but as a participating creator: the very creature for whom the words have risen, spiralled, and hang now from the treillage of her/his own inner hearing. within whom at last the lust of the root —and the root's trajectory— comes to ripeness.

ANNE WALDMAN

Both, Both: An Introduction*

Today I write in the context of 4 white walls. I woke to overcast sky. I stayed up late last night. The night was still. I could think clearly again extracting myself from the child's voice: demand & interruption. & yet I had the notes of his contribution to the long poem which he had sung out in the car outside Telluride. It was a list for the guardianship of plutonium, all the coverings to encase it: "one of every single stone in the world, pennies, quarters, everything" or "playdough—dried & dead peoples' bones, & then there's plain dead people with nothing on them."

Last night I had nibbled at the psychotropic mushrooms & was lying in the grass in the yard waiting for the near-full moon to rise. I was counting the "fathers" I had known in consideration of the long poem which among other things male, celebrates them. How many of them were dead now? How many of them had become stars in the sky? In any sky? I invented a list of questions for my father about World War II. What were the names of all the towns in Germany he passed through? Had he met any women in those travels? What had he told me years before O tell me again about the dead arms reaching to heavens near the Maginot Line! "Imagine O" I heard then & now. I experienced the dread of the act of making this poem for seven years & of all the men dead & alive going into it & saw them beckon to me to speak of my relationship to them in a language perhaps only I could understand. & I heard lovers, grandfathers, brothers, father-in-law, students, husbands, son, and the friends of my son, boys, speaking to me. And a persistent sound too was the sound of a bigger vatic voice inside any myth, classic archetype, any ritual sacrifice.

Then I tried to imagine my great-great-grandfather Thomas Hand, a sea captain, shipwrecked—no—lost at sea between Cape May & Liverpool delivering the south Jersey oak & pine they craved abroad. Who was he? What was the vocabulary of that boat & occupation & what tempest rocked him dead?

I feel myself always an open system (woman) available to any words or sounds I'm informed by. A name. Images of war. Other languages to which the ear attunes. What you said in your letter about the praying

*introduction to Anne Waldman, *IOVIS: All Is Full of Love* (Minneapolis: Coffee House Press, 1993)

mantis: "I brought it right up to my face and opened my mouth and it wasn't afraid" or what words go on between the nouns & verbs you choose. What phoneme exists there.

I get up & dance the poem when it sweeps into litany. I gambol with the shaman & the deer. It is a *body poetics*. I am in the context of those before me who worship a goddess whose eyes were mirrors. One eye reflected the "inside," the other the gorgeous & dark phenomenal world. Take your pick. Both, both. She, the muse, puts an invisible protection cord around my neck to protect me from ego. She exceeds my aspiration to disappear.

I write with the disappearing coral reef in mind & the total extinction of the dusky sparrow.

I exist in a community of my own choosing & making which is attentive to language & poetry before language. It harbors the secret wishes of all my tears and predilections. Community is "voice." It strides the blast. So many have heard these words in earlier form, recrudescent though they be, and felt the heat and Zeus's juice. They asked this book to be. I thanked them.

In the dream of "Friedrich Hegel" later the same night, Hegel, a father, was 88 years old, with copious red hair & crisp spectacles. He was to perform his latest piece in a bright green meadow & he let it be known that all the women present were invited to fall in love with him. He was philosopher-patriarch, often irresistible. He could mouth the plan or structure of a stable, composite world but would he take it apart again?

"Iovis omnia plena" from which Iovis springs is a phrase from Virgil—*all is full of Jove.* & I wanted that sense of filling up: "plerosis." How that is both a celebration and a danger. And how complex is the relationship of this poet to the energy principle that does that. In Sanskrit the masculine energy principle is "upaya," skillful means. See it everywhere. How skillful is a war in the Middle East? But how sweet is the grandfather bidding his wife purchase a sweater-coat his size in 1908. All the life I want to make things happen. Stop explaining I have to say.

I honor & dance on the corpse of the poetry gone before me & especially here in a debt & challenge of epic masters Williams, Pound, Zukofsky & Olson. But with the narrative of H.D.'s *Helen in Egypt* in mind, and her play with "argument." I want to don armor of words as they do and fight

462

with liberated tongue & punctured heart. But unlike the men's, my history & myths are personal ones. I want & need the long poem. In one doctor's description I've "too many male hormones." Let them sprout & spurt off the page. But let it not be said she wanted to be a man. Point of view: both accommodation and scorn. And don't forget Wit, a dark fairy. She teaches balance, redress, how to face the end of the world with dignity: make a space for her entourage. Sisters of beauty & seduction with no truck in the male poems these past years. Come out of exile, something still a real person we hope, welcomes you in.

Each section in this poem is a "take" on the last: strands, leitmotifs come back around. One friend notes—as if to see the "questions" from many—not points of view—but on many scales, as in sizes/proportions. There is a structural constant how the sections evolve: cumulative, wave effect—each self-organizing as it proceeds, thick with sperm that binds them. Fragments built on other fragments, finally organizing, one hopes, each other toward some kind of cohesive landscape. The field of Mars. May I be so bold to say these things? Narrative tags at the beginning of each section track the poet's steps as they thread through a maze.

Words are used here with awe, dread, submission, humor, cheek, as if they were sacred creatures—pulsating, alive, mocking. As such they are little mirrors. For this poem I summoned male images, "voice," & histories as deities out of throat, heart, gut, correspondence & mind. Call them *dakas* as they set off, like seed syllables, into the sky. They are semi-wrathful messengers, protectors. They're the heroes, thought forms of the theistic father and the pagan shapeshifter or boy-child-trickster of the poem. Every epic requires them. And she who sits at desk under dark spell and dances out under hot moon names them to release them.

A.W.
Autumn Equinox 1989 — Winter Solstice 1992

"Here is the difference between the poet and the mystic, that the last nails a symbol to one sense, which was a true sense for a moment, but soon becomes old and false. For all symbols are fluxional; all language is vehicular and transitive, and is good, as ferries and horses are, for conveyance, not as farms and houses are, for homestead." —Ralph Waldo Emerson, "The Poet"

Contributors' Book Publications

Will Alexander (1948-): *Vertical Rainbow Climber* (1987), *Arcane Lavender Morals* (1994), *Asia & Haiti* (1995), *The Stratospheric Canticles* (1995)

Ivan Argüelles (1939-): *Instamatic Reconditioning, The Invention of Spain, Captive of the Vision of Paradise, The Tattooed Heart of the Drunken Sailor, Manicomio, Nailed to the Coffin of Life, What are they doing to my Animal?, The Structure of Hell, Pieces of the Bone-Text still there, Baudelaire's Brain, Looking for Mary Lou, "That" Goddess, Hapax legomenon*

Dodie Bellamy (1951-): *Feminine Hijinx* (1990), *Answer* (1992), (with Sam D'Allesandro) *Real: The Letters of Mina Harker and Sam D'Allesandro* (1994)

Ted Berrigan (1934-1983): *A Lily for My Love* (1959), *The Sonnets* (1964, 2nd ed. 1966, enlarged ed., 1982), (with Ron Padgett) *Seventeen* (1964), *Living with Chris* (1965), (with Ron Padgett) *Bean Spasms* (1967), *Many Happy Returns* (1969), (with Anselm Hollo) *Doubletalk* (1969), *In the Early Morning Rain* (1970), *Guillaume Apollinaire Ist Tot* (1971), (with Anne Waldman) *Memorial Day* (1971), *Train Ride* (1971); (with Tom Clark and Ron Padgett) *Back in Boston Again* (1972), *The Drunken Boat* (1974), *A Feeling for Leaving* (1975), *Red Wagon* (1976), *Clear the Range* (1977), (with Harris Schiff) *Yo-Yo's with Money* (1979), *So Going Around Cities: New and Selected Poems 1958-1979* (1980), *In a Blue River* (1981), *A Certain Slant of Sunlight* (1988), (Aram Saroyan, ed.) *Selected Poems* (1994), see also "Poems from 500 American Postcards" in *Talisman* 3 (Fall 1989)

Mei-mei Berssenbrugge (1947-): *Fish Souls* (1971), *Summits Move with the Tide* (1974), *Random Possession* (1979), *The Heat Bird* (1984), *Empathy* (1989), *Sphericity* (1993)

Charles Borkhuis (1947-): *Hypnogogic Sonnets* (1992), *Proximity (Stolen Arrows)* (1994)

William Bronk (1918-): *Light and Dark* (1956) *The World, the Worldless* (1964), *The Empty Hands* (1969), *That Tantalus* (1971), *To Praise the Music* (1972), *The New World* (1974), *A Partial Glossary: Two Essays* (1974), *Silence and Metaphor* (1975), *Finding Losses* (1976), *The Meantime* (1976), *My Father Photographed with Friends* (1976), *The Force of Desire* (1979), *The Brother in Elysium: Ideas of Friendship and Society in the United States* (1980), *Life Supports: New and Collected Poems* (1981), *Vectors and Smoothable Curves: Collected Essays* (1983), *Careless Love and Its Apostrophes* (1985), *Manifest; and Furthermore* (1987), *Death Is the Place* (1989), *Living Instead* (1991), *Some Words* (1992), *The Mild Day* (1993), *Our Selves* (1994), (ed. Henry Weinfield) *Selected Poems* (1995)

Lee Ann Brown (1963-): *Polyverse* (1996)

Joseph Ceravolo (1934-1988): *Fits of Dawn* (1965), *Wild Flowers out of Gas* (1967), *Spring in this World of Poor Mutts* (1968), *Transmigration Solo* (1979), *Inri* (1979), *Millenium Dust* (1982), (ed. Larry Fagin, Kenneth Koch, Charles North, Ron Padgett, David Shapiro, and Paul Violi) *The Green Lake Is Awake* (1994)

Norma Cole (1945-): *Mace Hill Remap* (1988), *Metamorphopsia* (1988), *My Bird Book* (1991), *Mars* (1994), *MOIRA* (1996), *Contrafact* (1996)

Peter Cole (1957-): *Rift* (1989), (trans.) *Selected Poems of Shmuel HaNagid*

Clark Coolidge (1939-): *Flag Flutter & U.S. Electric* (1966), *Clark Coolidge* (1967), *Ing* (1968), *Space* (1970), (with Tom Veitch) *To Obtain the Value of the Cake Measure from Zero: A Play in One Act* (1970), *The So* (1971), *The Clark Coolidge Issue* of *Big Sky* (3) (1972), *Oflengths* (1973), *Suite V* (1973), *The Maintains* (1974), *Polaroid* (1975), *Quartz Hearts* (1978), *Own Face* (1978), *Smithsonian Depositions/Subject to a Film* (1980), *A Geology* (1981), *American Ones* (1981), *Research* (1982), *Mine: The One That Enters the Stories* (1982), *The Crystal Text* (1986), *Solution Passage: Poems 1978—1981* (1986), *Melencolia* (1987), *At Egypt* (1988), *Mesh* (1988), *The Symphony* (1989), *Sound as Thought: Poems 1982-1984* (1990), *Odes of Roba* (1991), (with Philip Guston) *Baffling Means* (1991), *The Book of During* (1991), (with Michael Gizzi and John Yau) *Lowell Connector* (1993), *The ROVA Improvisations* (1994), *Registers (People In All)* (1994)

Diane di Prima (1934-): *This Kind of Bird Flies Backward* (1958), (ed.) *Various Fables from Various Places* (1960), *Dinners and Nightmares* (1961), *The New Handbook of Heaven* (1962), (trans.), *The Man Condemned to Death* (1963), *Poets' deville* (1964), *Seven Love Poems from the Middle Latin* (1965), *Haiku* (1966), *New Mexico Poem* (1967), *Earthsong* (1968), *Hotel Albert* (1968), (ed.) *War Poems* (1968), *Memoirs of a Beatnik* (1969), *L. A. Odyssey* (1969), *The Book of Hours* (1970), *Kerhonkson Journal* (1971), *Revolutionary Letters* (1971), *The Calculus of Variation* (1972), part I (1973), (ed.) *The Floating Bear: A Newsletter* (1973), *Freddiue Poems* (1974), *Selected Poems: 1956-1975* (1975), *Loba, Part II* (1976), *The Loba as Eve* (1977), *Loba: Parts I-VIII* (1988), *Wyoming Series* (1988), *The Mysteries of Vision* (1988), *Pieces of a Song: Selected Poems* (1990), *Seminary Poems* (1991), *The Mask Is the Path of the Star* (1993)

Joseph Donahue (1954-): *Before Creation* (1989), *Monitions of the Approach* (1991), *World Well Broken* (1995)

Stephen Ellis (1950-): *Site Drafts* (1995)

Norman Finkelstein (1954-): *The Objects in Your Life* (1977), *The Utopian Moment in Contemporary American Poetry* (1988), *Restless Messengers* (1992), *The Ritual of New Creation: Jewish Tradition and Contemporary Literature* (1992)

Edward Foster (1948-): *Catharine Maria Sedgwick* (1974), *The Civilized Wilderness: Backgrounds to American Romantic Literature, 1817-1860* (1975), *Josiah Gregg and Lewis Hector Garrard* (1977), *Susan and Anna Warner* (1978), *Richard Brautigan* (1983), *William Saroyan* (1984), *Jack Spicer* (1991), *William Saroyan: A Study of the Short Fiction* (1991), *Understanding the Beats* (1992), *The Space Between Her Bed and Clock* (1993), *Code of the West: A Memoir of Ted Berrigan* (1994), *The Understanding* (1994), *Understanding the Black Mountain Poets* (1995), *All Acts Are Simply Acts* (1995); editor (with Geoffrey Clark) *Hoboken* (1976), *Cummington Poems* (1982), (with Vadim Mesyats) *The New Freedoms: Contemporary Russian and American Poetry* (1994); *Postmodern Poetry* (1994)

467

Kathleen Fraser (1935-): *Change of Address* (1966), *Stilts, Somersaults and Headstands* (1968) (children's poems), *In Defiance of the Rains* (1969), *Little Notes to You from Lucas Street* (1972), *What I Want* (1974), *Magritte Series* (1977), *New Shoes* (1978), *Each Next, narratives* (1980), (ed.) *Feminist Poetics* (1983), *Something (even human voices) in the foreground, a lake* (1984), *Notes Preceding Trust* (1987), (with Sam Francis) *boundayr* (1988), (with Mary Ann Hayden) *from a text . . .* (1993), *When New Times Folds Up* (1993), *Wing* (1995), *Selected Poems 1964-1992* (forthcoming)

Forrest Gander (1956-): *Rush to the Lake* (1988), *Eggplants and Lotus Root* (1991), (ed.) *Mouth to Mouth: Poetry by 12 Contemporary Mexican Women* (1993), *Lynchburg* (1993), *Deeds of Utmost Kindness* (1994)

Drew Gardner (1968-): *The Stone Walk, The Cover*

John High (1957-): *Ceremonies* (1984), *Sometimes Survival* (1987), *the lives of thomas— episodes and prayers* (1991), (trans. with others) *Blue Vitriol* by Aleksei Parshchikov (1994), (trans.) *The Right to Err* by Nina Iskrenko (1995)

Anselm Hollo (1934-): *And It Is a Song* (1965), *Maya: Works, 1959-1969* (1970), *Sojourner Microcosms: New & Selected Poems (1959-1977)* (1978), *Finite Continued* (1979), *No Complaints* (1983), (trans.) *Pentti Saarikoski: Selected Poems 1959-1980* (1984), (trans.) *August Strinberg: A Biography* by Olof Lagercratz (1984), *Pick Up the House: New and Selected Poems* (1986), (trans.) *The Poems* by Egon Schiele (1988), (trans.) *Franz Werfel: The Story of a Life* by Peter Stephen Jungk (1990), *Outlying Districts* (1990), *Near Miss Haiku* (1990), *Space Baltic: the science fiction poems 1962-1987* (1991), (trans.) *Paavo Haavikko: Selected Poems 1949-1989* (1991), *Blue Ceiling* (1992), (trans.) *The Czar's Madman* by Jaan Kross (1993), *High Beam: 12 Poems* (1993), *West Is Left on the Map* (1993), *Survival Dancing* (1995), *Corvus: New Poems* (1995); Anselm Hollo is also the translator of novels by Jean Genet, Lennart Hagerfors, and Aleksandr Blok, screenplays by François Truffaut and Louis Malle, plays by Bertolt Brecht and Georg Büchner, and poetry by Gunnar Harding, Philippe Soupault, Sirkka Turkka, Andrei Voznesensky, and others.

Virginia Hooper (1955-): has published widely in such journals as *Sulfur, Pequod, New American Writing, Southwest Review,* and *Talisman.*

Fanny Howe (1940-): *Forty Whacks* (1969), *First Marriage* (1975), *Bronte Wilde* (1976), *The Amerindian Coastline Poem* (1976), *Holy Smoke* (1979), *The White Slave* (1980), *Eggs* (1980), *Poem from a Single Pallet* (1981), *The Blue Hills* (1981), *Yeah, But* (1982), *Alsace Lorraine* (1982), *Radio City* (1982), *In the Middle of Nowhere* (1984), *For Erato* (1984), *Taking Care* (1985), *Introduction to the World* (1985), *The Race of the Radical* (1985), *Robeson Street* (1985), *Lives of a Spirit* (1986), *The Deep North* (1988), *The Vineyard* (1988), *[Sic]* (1988), *Famous Questions* (1989), *The Quietist* (1992), *The End* (1992), *Saving History* (1992)

Susan Howe (1937-): *Hinge Picture* (1974), *The Western Borders* (1976), *Secret History of the Dividing Line* (1978), *Cabbage Gardens* (1979), *The Liberties* (1980), *Pythagorean Silence* (1982), *Defenestration of Prague* (1983), *My Emily Dickinson* (1985), *Articulation of Sound Forms in Time* (1987), *Federalist 10* (1987), *The Bibliography of the King's Book; or, Eikon Basilike* (1989), *The Captive Morphology* (1990), *The Europe of Trusts: Selected Poems* (1990), *Singularities* (1990), *The Birth-mark: unsettling the wilderness in American literary history* (1993), *The Nonconformist's Memorial* (1993)

468

Ronald Johnson (1935-): *A Line of Poetry, A Row of Trees* (1964), *Sports & Divertissments* (1965) (translations from Erik Satie), *Assorted Jungles: Rousseau* (1966), *Gorse/Goose/Rose* (1966), *Sun Flowers* (1966), *Io and the Ox-Eye Daisy* (1966), *The Book of the Green Man* (1967), *The Round Earth on Flat Paper* (1968), *Reading 1* (1968), *Reading 2* (1968), *Valley of the Many-Colored Glasses* (1969), *Balloons for Moonless Nights* (1969), *The Spirit Walks, The Rocks Will Talk* (1969) (translations from *Le Facteur Cheval* and Raymond Isidore), *Songs of the Earth* (1970), *Eyes & Objects* (1976), *RADIOS I-IV* (1977), *Ark: The Foundations: 1-33* (1980), *Ark 50: Spires 34-50* (1984)

Andrew Joron (1955-): *Force Fields* (1987), *Science Fiction* (1992), (with Robert Frazier) *Invisible Machines* (1994)

Robert Kelly (1935-): *Armed Descent* (1961), *Her Body Against Time* (1963), *Round Dances* (1964), *Enstasy* (1964), *Lunes* (1964), (ed.) *A Controversy of Poets* (1965) *Lectiones* (1965), *Words in Service* (1965), *Weeks* (1966), *The Scorpions* (1967), *Song XXIV* (1967), *Devotions* (1967), *Twenty Poems* (1967), *Axon Dendron Tree* (1967), *Crooked Bridge Love Society* (1967), *A Joining Songs I-XXX* (1968), *The Common Shore* (1969), *A California Journal* (1969), *Kali Yuga* (1970), *Cities* (1971), *In Time* (1971), *Flesh Dream Book* (1971), *Ralegh* (1972), *The Pastorals* (1972), *Reading Her Notes* (1972), *The Tears of Edmund Burke* (1973), *The Mill of Particulars* (1973), *A Line of Sight* (1974), *The Loom* (1975), *Sixteen Odeas* (1976), *The Lady Of* (1977), *The Convections* (1978), *Wheres* (1978), *The Book of Persephone* (1978), *The Cruise of Pnyx* (1979), *Kill the Messenger Who Brings Bad News* (1979), *Sentence* (1980), *Spiritual Exercises* (1981), *The Alchemist to Mercury* (1981), *Mulberry Women* (1982), *Under Words* (1983), *Thor's Thrush* (1984), *A Transparent Tree* (1985), *Not This Island Music* (1987), *Doctor of Silence* (1988), *Oahu* (1988), *Cat Scratch Fever* (1990), *Ariadne* (1991), *A Strange Market* (1992), *Mont Blanc* (1994), *Queen of Terrors* (1994), *Red Action: Selected Poems 1960-1993* (1995)

Myung Mi Kim (1957-): *Under Flag, The Bounty* (1995), *DURA* (1996)

Gerrit Lansing (1928-): *The Heavenly Tree Grows Downward* (1966), *The Heavenly Tree Grows Downward* (1977), *Heavenly Tree / Soluble Forest* (1995)

Ann Lauterbach (1942-): *Vertical, Horizontal* (1971), *Book One* (1975), *Many Times, But Then* (1979), *Later That Evening* (1981), *Closing Hours* (1983), *Sacred Weather* (1984), (with Jan Groover and Bruce Boice) *Greeks* (1984), *Before Recollection* (1987), *Clamor* (1991), *And For Example* (1994)

Nathaniel Mackey (1947-): *Four for Trane* (1978), *Septet for the End of Time* (1983), *Eroding Witness* (1985), *Bedouin Handbook* (1986), *Outlandish* (1992), *Djbot Baghostus's Run* (1993), (ed. with Art Lange) *Moment's Notice: Jazz in Poetry and Prose* (1993), *School of Udhra* (1993), *Discrepant Engagement: Dissonance, Cross-Culturality, and Experimental Writing* (1993), *Song of the Andoumboulou: 18-22* (1994)

Kevin Magee (1957-): *Tedium Drum* (1994), *Recent Events* (1995)

Tom Mandel (1942-): *Ency* (1978), *Erat* (1982), *Ready to Go* (1982), *Central Europe* (1985), *Some Appearances* (1986), *Four Strange Books* (1990), *Realism* (1991), *Letters of the Law* (1994), *Prospect of Release* (1996)

Bernadette Mayer (1945-): *Story* (1968), *Moving* (1971), *Memory* (1975), *Ceremony Latin 1964* (1975), *Studying Hunger* (1976), *Poetry* (1976), *Eruditio ex Memoria* (1977), (with Anne Waldman) *The Basketball Article* (1978), *The Golden Book of Words* (1978), *Midwinter Day* (1982), *Utopia* (1983), *Mutual Aid* (1985), *Sonnets* (1989), *The Formal Kind of Kissing* (1990), *A Bernadette Mayer Reader* (1992), *The Desires of Mothers To Please Others in Letters* (1994), *Proper Name and Other Stories* (forthcoming)

Albert Mobilio (1955-): *Bendable Siege* (1991), *The Geographics* (1995)

Laura Moriarty (1952-): *True Cross Seizings, Persia, Duse, like roads* (1989), *Rondeaux* (1990), *L'Archiviste* (1991), *Symmetry* (1995)

Sheila Murphy (1951-): *With House Silence* (1987), *Sad Isn't the Color of the Dream* (1991), *Teth* (1991), *Pure Mental Breath* (1994), *A Clove of Gender* (1995)

Eileen Myles (1949-): *The Irony of the Leash* (1978), (with Anne Waldman) *Polar Ode* (1979), *A Fresh Young Voice from the Plains* (1981), *Sappho's Boat* (1982), *Bread & Water* (1987), *1969* (1989), *Not Me* (1991), *Chelsea Girls* (1994), *Maxfield Parrish: Early & New Poems* (1995)

Claire Needell (1965-): *Not a Balancing Act* (1993)

Alice Notley (1945-): *165 Meeting House Lane* (1971), *Phoebe Light* (1973), *Incidentals in the Day World* (1973), *For Frank O'Hara's Birthday* (1976), *Alice Ordered Me To Be Made* (1976), *A Diamond Necklace* (1977), *Songs for the Unborn Second Baby* (1979), *When I Was Alive* (1980), *How Spring Comes* (1981), *Waltzing Matilda* (1981), *Tell Me Again* (1982), *Sorrento* (1984), *Margaret & Dusty* (1985), *Parts of a Wedding* (1986), *At Night the States* (1988), *From a Work in Progress* (1988), *Homer's Art* (1990), (with Douglas Oliver) *The Scarlet Cabinet* (1992), *To Say You* (1993), *Selected Poems* (1993), *Close to me & Closer (The Language of Heaven)* and *Désamère* (1995)

Geoffrey O'Brien (1948-): *Hardboiled America* (1981), *Maciste in the Valley of the Pagans* (1983), *Dream Time: Chapters from the Sixties* (1988), *A Book of Maps* (1989), *The Phantom Empire* (1993), *The Hudson Mystery* (1994), *Floating City: Selected Poems 1978-1995* (1996)

Michael Palmer (1943-): *Plan of the City of O* (1971), *Blake's Newton* (1972), *C's Songs* (1973), *Six Poems* (1973), *The Circular Gates* (1974), *Without Music* (1977), *Transparency of the Mirror* (1980), *Alogon* (1980), *Notes for Echo Lake* (1981), (ed.) *Code of Signals: Recent Writings in Poetics* (1983), *First Figure* (1984), *Songs for Sarah* (1987), *Sun* (1988), *For a Reading* (1988), *An Alphabet Underground* (1993), *At Passages* (1995)

Simon Pettet (1953-): *Lyrical Poetry* (1987), *Conversations with Rudy Burckhardt About Everything* (1987), *Twenty One Love* (1990), *Talking Pictures: The Photography of Rudy Burckhardt* (1994), *Selected Poems* (1995)

Stephen Ratcliffe (1948-): *[where late the sweet] BIRDS SANG* (1989), *spaces in the light said to be where one/comes from* (1992), *Selected Letters* (1992), *Present Tense* (1995)

Donald Revell (1954-): *From the Abandoned Cities* (1983), *The Gaza of Winter* (1988), *New Dark Ages* (1990), *Erasures* (1992), *Beautiful Shirt* (1995)

Ed Roberson (1939-): *When Thy King Is a Boy* (1970), *Etai-Eken* (1975), *Lucid Interval as Integral Music* (1985), *Voices Cast Out to Talk Us In* (1995)

Elizabeth Robinson (1961-): *My Name Happens Also, Eight Etudes, In the Sequence of Falling Things, Bed of Lists, Nearings, String, Iemanje*

Janet Rodney (1941-): *Chameleon's Cadmium* (1978), *Crystals* (1979), *Orphydice* (1986), (with Nathaniel Tarn) *Ashka* (1989), The Book of Craving (1995)

David Rosenberg (1943-): among other titles, David Rosenberg is the author of the following books of what he calls transformations in poetry: *Paris and London* (1971) based upon Mallarmé and Valéry, *Leavin' America* (1972) based upon Rimbaud, *A Poet's Bible: Rediscovering the Voices of the Original Text* (1991), *The Lost Book of Paradise* (1993) restoring the Hebraic sources for Genesis and Song of Solomon; other books include *Blues of the Sky* (1976), *A Blazing Fountain* (1978), *Chosen Days* (1980)

Stephen Sartarelli (1954-): *Grievances and Other Poems* (1989), *Phanyasmatikon* (1992), (trans.) *The Devil in Love* by Jacques Cazotte, with a life of Cazotte by Gérard de Nerval (1993), (trans.) *Voyage Around My Room* by Xavier de Maistre (1993)

Leslie Scalapino (1947-): *O and Other Poems* (1976), *The Woman Who Could Read the Minds of Dogs* (1976), *Instead of an Animal* (1978), *This eating and walking is associated all right* (1979), *Considering how exaggerated music is* (1982), *that they were at the beach — aeolotropic series* (1985), *way* (1988), *The Return of Painting, The Pearl, and Orion / A Trilogy* (1991), *How Phenomena Appear to Unfold* (1991), *Crowd and not evening or light* (1992), *Objects in the Terrifying Tense / Longing from Taking Place* (1994), *Goya's L.A.* (1994), *Defoe* (1995), *The Front Matter, Dead Souls* (1996), *Selected Poems* (1996)

Andrew Schelling (1953-): *Claw Moraine* (1987), *Ktaadn's Lamp* (1991), *Dropping the Bow: Poems from Ancient India* (1991), *Moon Is a Piece of Tea* (1993), *For Love of the Dark One: Songs of Mirabai* (1993), *The India Book* (1993), *Two Immortals* (1994), (with Anne Waldman) *The Quenching of the Lamp* (1994), (ed. with Anne Waldman) *Disembodied Poetics: Annals of the Jack Kerouac School* (1994), *Old Growth: Selected Poems & Notebooks* (1995)

Leonard Schwartz (1963-): *Objects of Thought, Attempts at Speech* (1990), *Exiles: Ends and Other Poems* (1990), *Gnostic Blessing* (1992)

Barry Seiler (1946-): *The Algeria Poems* (1969), *Making Body Glue* (1972), *The Day* (1973), *Retaining Wall* (1979), *The Waters of Forgetting* (1994)

Spencer Selby (1945-): *Instar* (1989), *Barricade* (1990), *Stigma* (1990), *House of Before* (1991), *Sound Off* (1993), *Malleable Cast* (1995), *No Island* (1995)

David Shapiro (1947-): *January: A Book of Poems* (1965), *Poems from Deal* (1969), (ed. with Ron Padgett) *An Anthology of New York Poets* (1969), *A Man Holding an Acoustic Panel* (1971), *The Page-turner* (1973), *Lateness: A Book of Poems* (1977), *Introduction to John Ashbery's Poetry* (1979), (co-translator) *The Writings of Sonia and Robert Delaunay* (1979), *Pop Art* (1980), *Poetry and Painting* (1980), *Jim Dine* (1981), *Lateness* (1981), *To an Idea* (1984), *Jasper Johns* (1984), *House (Blown Apart): A Book of Poems* (1988), *Mondrian: Flowers* (1991), (co-translator) *The Selected Poems of Jacques Dupin* (1992), (co-translator) *The Eight Names of Picasso* (1992), *After a Lost Original* (1992)

Aaron Shurin (1947-): *Woman on Fire* (1975), *The Night Sun* (1976), *Toot Suite* (1978), *Giving Up the Ghost* (1980), *The Graces* (1983), *Elsewhere* (1988), *A's Dream* (1989), *Narrativity* (1990), *Into Distances* (1993)

Mary Margaret Sloan (1946-): *Infiltrations* (1989), *On Method* (1992), *The Said Lands, Islands and Premises* (1995)

Gustaf Sobin (1935-): *Telegrams* (1963), *Ascension* (1964), *The Tale of the Yellow Triangle* (1973), *Wind Chrysalid's Rattle* (1980), *Caesurae: Midsummer* (1981), *Celebration of the Sound Through* (1982), *Ten Sham Haikus* (1983), *The Earth as Air* (1984), *Ideograms in China* (1984) (trans. from Henri Michaux), *Carnets* (1984), *Nile* (1984), *Sicilian Miniatures* (1986), *Voyaging Portraits* (1988), *Venus Blue* (1991), *Dark Mirrors, A Novel of Provence* (1992), *Breaths' Burials* (1995), *By the Bias of Sound / Selected Poems: 1974-1994* (1995)

John Taggart (1942-): *To Construct a Clock* (1971), *The Pyramid Is a Pure Crystan* (1974), *Prism and the Pine Twig* (1977), *Dodeka* (1979), *Peace on Earth* (1981), *Dehiscence* (1983), *Le Poeme de la Chapelle Rothko* (1990), *Loop* (1991),*Prompted* (1991), *Aeschylus/Fragments* (1992), *Remaining in Light: Ant Meditations on a Painting by Edward Hopper* (1993), *Tauler Sentences* (1993), *Standing Wave* (1993), *Songs of Degrees: Essays on Contemporary Poetry & Poetics* (1994)

George Tysh (1942-): *Sit Up Straight* (1965), *Cheapness Means Forgiveness* (1970), *Mecanorgane* (1971), *Shop/Posh* (1973), (trans. with Chris Tysh) *Julie or the Rose* by Guillaume Apollinaire (1978), *Tea* (1979), *Ovals* (1985), *Echolalia* (1992)

Anne Waldman (1945-): *One the Wing* (1968), *O My Life!* (1969), (ed.) *The World Anthology* (1969), *Giant Night* (1970), *Baby Breakdown* (1970), (with Ted Berrigan) *Memorial Day* (1971), *No Hassles* (1971), (ed.) *Another World* (1972), *West Indies Poems* (1972), *Life Notes* (1973), *Fast Speaking Woman* (1975) *Journals & Dreams* (1976), *Sun the Blond Out* (1976), (ed. with Marilyn Webb) *Talking Poetics* (1978), *Shaman* (1978), (with Eileen Myles) *Polar Ode* (1978), *Sphinxeries* (1979), *Countries* (1981), *Cabin* (1981), *First Baby Poems* (1982), *Makeup on Empty Space* (1984), (with Susan Hall) *Invention* (1985), *Skin Meat Bones* (1985), *The Romance Thing* (1987), *Den Monde in Farbe Sehen* (1988), *Blue Mosque* (1988), *Tell Me About It: Poems for Painters* (1989), *Helping the Dreamer: New & Selected Poems, 1966-1988* (1988), *Not a Male Pseudonym* (1990), *Shaman/Shamane* (1990), *Lokapala* (1991), (ed.) *Nice to See You: Homage to Ted Berrigan* (1991), *Fate Accompli* (1992), *IOVIS* (1993), *Troubairitz* (1993), *Kill or Cure* (1994), (with Andrew Schelling) *The Quenching of the Lamp* (1994), (ed. with Andrew Schelling) *Disembodied Poetics: Annals of the Jack Kerouac School* (1994)

Lewis Warsh (1944-): *The Suicide Rates* (1967), *Highjacking* (1968), *Moving Through Air* (1968), (with Tom Clark) *Chicago* (1969), *Dreaming as One* (1971), *Long Distance* (1971), *Part of My History* (1972), *Immediate Surrounding* (1974), *Today* (1974), *The Maharaja's Son* (1977), *Blue Heaven* (1978), *Hives* (1979), *Methods of Birth Control* (1983), *Agnes & Sally* (1984), *The Corset* (1986), *Information from the Surface of Venus* (1987), *A Free Man* (1991), *Avenue of Escape* (1995), *Private Agenda* (1996), *Touch of The Whip* (1996)

John Yau (1950-): *Crossing Canal Street* (1976), *The Reading of an Ever-Changing Tale* (1977), *Sometimes* (1979), *The Sleepless Night of Eugene Delacroix* (1980), *Notarikon* (1981), *Broken Off by the Music* (1981), *Corpse and Mirror* (1983), (with Malcolm Morley) *Fallacies of Enoch* (1984), (ed.) *The Collected Poems of Fairfield Porter* (1985), (with Malcolm Morley) *Odysseys of Enoch* (1986), (with Norman Bluhm) *Poem Prints* (1987), *Forrest Bess* (1988), *Brice Marden: A Vision of the Unsayable* (1988), (with Toni Grand) *Dragon's Blood* (1989), *Radiant Silhouette: New & Selected Work: 1974-1988* (1989), (with Bill Barrette) *Big City Primer: Reading New York at the End of the Twentieth Century* (1991), *Don Van Vliet* (1991), (with Jürgen Partenheimer) *Giant Wall* (1991), (with Suzanne McClelland) *Flee Advice* (1991), *Edificia Sayanora* (1992), (with Bill Jensen) *Postcards from Trakl* (1992), *A. R. Penck* (1993), *In the Realm of the Unsayable* (1993), (with Clark Coolidge and Michael Gizzi) *Lowell Connector* (1993), *Hawaiian Cowboys* (1995), (with Ed Paschke) *Genghis Chan: Private Eye* (1996)

Designed by
Samuel Retsov

~

Text: Palatino

~

acid-free paper

~

printed by
McNaughton & Gunn, Inc.